‖‖ ‖ ‖‖‖‖‖‖‖ ‖ ‖‖‖‖ ‖‖‖‖‖‖‖‖‖‖‖ ‖ ‖‖
W9-AUX-888

Black-Latino Relations in U.S. National Politics

Social science research has frequently found conflict between Latinos and African Americans in urban politics and governance, as well as in the groups' attitudes toward one another. Rodney E. Hero and Robert R. Preuhs analyze whether conflict between these two groups is also found in national politics. Based on extensive evidence on the activities of minority advocacy groups in national politics and the behavior of minority members of Congress, the authors find the relationship between the groups is characterized mainly by nonconflict and a considerable degree of independence. The question of why there appears to be little minority intergroup conflict at the national level of government is also addressed. This is the first systematic study of black-Latino intergroup relations at the national level of United States politics.

Rodney E. Hero is professor of political science and the Haas Chair in Diversity and Democracy at the University of California, Berkeley. He is the author of *Racial Diversity and Social Capital: Equality and Community in America* (Cambridge, 2007), *Faces of Inequality: Social Diversity in American Politics* (2000), and *Latinos and the U.S. Political System: Two-Tiered Pluralism* (1992), winner of the American Political Science Association's 1993 Ralph J. Bunche award. He is coauthor of *Latinos in the New Millennium: An Almanac of Opinion, Behavior, and Policy Preferences* (Cambridge, 2012).

Robert R. Preuhs is assistant professor of political science at Metropolitan State University of Denver. His research focuses on representation, state politics, policy, and racial/ethnic politics. His research has been published in leading scholarly outlets, including the *American Journal of Political Science* and the *Journal of Politics*.

Black-Latino Relations in U.S. National Politics

Beyond Conflict or Cooperation

RODNEY E. HERO
University of California, Berkeley

ROBERT R. PREUHS
Metropolitan State University of Denver

CAMBRIDGE
UNIVERSITY PRESS

CAMBRIDGE UNIVERSITY PRESS
Cambridge, New York, Melbourne, Madrid, Cape Town,
Singapore, São Paulo, Delhi, Mexico City

Cambridge University Press
32 Avenue of the Americas, New York, NY 10013-2473, USA

www.cambridge.org
Information on this title: www.cambridge.org/9781107625440

© Rodney E. Hero and Robert R. Preuhs 2013

This publication is in copyright. Subject to statutory exception
and to the provisions of relevant collective licensing agreements,
no reproduction of any part may take place without the written
permission of Cambridge University Press.

First published 2013

Printed in the United States of America

A catalog record for this publication is available from the British Library.

Library of Congress Cataloging in Publication data
Hero, Rodney E., 1953–
  Black-Latino relations in U.S. national politics : beyond conflict or
  cooperation / Rodney E. Hero, Robert R. Preuhs.
     p. cm.
  Includes bibliographical references and index.
  ISBN 978-1-107-03045-9 (hardback) – ISBN 978-1-107-62544-0 (paperback)
    1. African Americans–Relations with Hispanic Americans.   2. African Americans–
  Politics and government.   3. Hispanic Americans–Politics and government.
    4. United States–Ethnic relations–Political aspects.   I. Preuhs, Robert R.,
  1970– II. Title.
  E185.615.H39   2012
  305.800973–dc23   2012023654

ISBN 978-1-107-03045-9 Hardback
ISBN 978-1-107-62544-0 Paperback

Cambridge University Press has no responsibility for the persistence or accuracy of URLs
for external or third-party Internet Web sites referred to in this publication and does not
guarantee that any content on such Web sites is, or will remain, accurate or appropriate.

To My Family – Kathy, Lindsay, Chris, Jennifer, and my mother and father and sister.

REH

To My Family – Jennifer, Alex, and Mara.

RRP

Contents

Tables and Figures

Tables

Figures

Preface

We began thinking about and initially working on the ideas and evidence in our analysis of black-Latino relations in the United States some time around 2001 (which is more than a decade before it is being published), to the best of our recollection. Our personal lives and situations changed in a host of complex ways. And countless professional responsibilities, developments, commitments (including other research projects) intervened, affecting, and often disrupting and delaying, our ability to focus on this project and give the concentrated periods of time required to move ahead with analysis, writing, and revision, and all their associated complications. In short, "life happens." At the same time, various political events in American society arose during the decade of 2000–10 that were and are directly relevant to our concerns. To name but a very few of the many that could be noted, the growth and visibility of the Latino population, perhaps punctuated in 2003 with the statement (from the U.S. Census Bureau) that the Latino population had surpassed the black population in size; the clamor and controversies over (illegal) immigration; and the emergence and election of Barack Obama. These and other events underscore and have heightened the salience of the issues we address in this book.

The increased significance of the topic is also reflected in the rather vast and varied body of research on black-Latino relations that proliferated over this time (some part of that research is summarized and reviewed in Chapter 2). We acknowledge here, and emphasize several times later, our appreciation of the previous work on the topic; it is informative and consequential, and we take it most seriously.

We have both long been interested in and have studied various aspects of race/ethnicity in American politics because of what we believe is its critical importance as an enduring feature of this political system. To a large extent, our research on these issues had been primarily approached with urban and state politics as the unit of analysis; we had also focused mostly on racial/ethnic groups separately and less on their interrelationships. As we thought more about broader political developments, coupled with emerging scholarly research, it occurred to us that there were other related yet distinct political processes and phenomena that were being overlooked and that also deserved consideration as part of the changing racial (including minority intergroup) landscape of American politics. As we began to articulate to ourselves what we thought was missing and/or ambiguous in the research on evolving racial/ethnic conditions, it occurred to us, first implicitly and later more explicitly, that certain intergroup relations and different, distinct institutional settings were worthy of attention. This led us to conclude that black-Latino relations at the national level warranted examination for several reasons: one, it had scarcely been looked at. Second, we felt that a fuller understanding of American politics, including black-Latino relations, required some attention to all levels of the governmental system. Accordingly, we sought and identified several databases we thought would permit an extensive and systematic analysis.

Our analysis is thus distinct from others in several ways. We focus on the *national* (rather than local or state) level, on *governance* (rather than attitudes and opinions), and on *elites* (rather than the masses). Taken together, these distinct and novel characteristics help to advance and expand the study of black-Latino relations, and by extension racial/ethnic politics, in America. At the same time, our approach has its own limits, certainly in contrast with or compared to other analytical foci and approaches. We certainly hope, however, that the distinctiveness and novelty of our study bring new evidence and insights to bear and that these far outweigh its limitations. In any case, we believe our core findings of nonconflict between and independence in black-Latino relations in national politics is certainly notable. And we trust that our attempts to explain the findings – focused on the institution of federalism and its implications for the geography/scope of politics, the types of policies, and the differences in the "essential character" of governments across the levels of the political system – will be seriously considered, even if one does not agree with it entirely.

We are pretty confident that the temporal span of our analysis is longer than about any other study of this sort. Some of our data cover a period of roughly thirty years, and even the shorter periods in our study are still longer than in most other studies. Indeed, a considerable amount of our data encompasses a substantial portion of the post–civil rights era, about 1970 into the early 2000s. As such, ours is also partly a story of American political development regarding a specific dimension of U.S. politics. An obvious path for future research is to extend the period of analysis up to the recent past, which has been characterized by some as a post-racial era. We are pursuing such longer-term analysis and expect to expand several substantive aspects of this research as well.

In a broad sense, this inquiry into unstudied or under-studied aspects of minority intergroup relations and thus our telling of an untold story – of "nonconflict" – provide a more complete, wider, richer, and more nuanced perspective on America's evolving multiethnic/racial democracy. Our hope is that readers will find the central questions, the unique focus and other attributes of our analytical approach, and our major findings to be substantively informative and intellectually engaging.

Acknowledgments

As with any project of the expanse reflected in this book, there are many people to acknowledge, indeed, to whom we owe and now wish to warmly express tremendous gratitude.

Al Tillery (then a colleague at the University of Notre Dame, now of Rutgers University, and a dear friend [to Rodney] for years) was important and particularly helpful in our thinking and formulation of ideas in the project's early days. Andrew Thangasamy – at that time a graduate student at the University of Colorado, Boulder – and Monika Klimek played a major role in the collection and coding of data, particularly for Chapters 3 and 4.

Patrick Flavin and Michael Keane, who were graduate students at Notre Dame at the time, did excellent work bringing together and developing materials for the discussion presented in Chapter 7. Three undergraduate students at Notre Dame – Justina Tong, Anna Porto, and Daniella Rosa – served as very able "research apprentices," conscientiously and skillfully examining, coding, and summarizing congressional testimony and amicus briefs that were essential supplements to our other evidence in Chapters 3 and 4. And as implied in the preceding sentences, but which deserves specific recognition, I [Rodney] benefited tremendously from the generous support of the department, departmental colleagues, the College of Arts and Letters, and other help that I received during my ten years at the University of Notre Dame. I am most grateful.

Our thinking and revisions of the ideas and evidence in the book were also informed and improved by the comments and observations we received at a number of presentations we made (individually or together) on parts of the book. These include the University of Washington's WISER

Center Second Annual Conference, which Gary Segura and Matt Barreto organized and were generous in inviting us to (in April 2008); paper presentation at the American Political Science Association annual meeting (August 2008); a presentation at Princeton's Wilson School Center for the Study of Democratic Politics (2007) directed (at the time) by Larry Bartels; Rutgers University, New Brunswick, at the invitation of Jane Junn (April 2009); Columbia University, invited by Rodolfo de la Garza (March 2009); Duke University, at the invitation of Paula McClain and Kerry Haynie (Spring 2009). More recently, there have been presentations at the UC-Berkeley Department of Sociology, requested by Cybelle Fox and Irene Bloemraad (September 2010), and at Purdue University (March 2011).

We are grateful to all of those who invited us and shared their time and observations with us.

We also had conversations with numerous friends and colleagues over a long period who listened patiently to our ideas and offered observations on the project. These include Larry Dodd, Michael Jones-Correa, and Paul Frymer, among many others.

Rodney also thanks the University of California, Berkeley, particularly the Department of Political Science and the Haas Diversity Research Initiative for their generous support and for providing an exciting intellectual environment. Rob is grateful for the general support of the political science departments at the University of Colorado at Boulder and Metropolitan State University of Denver for providing the opportunity to pursue his interests.

We also thank Eric Crahan of Cambridge University Press for his help, guidance, and encouragement; and we thank the anonymous reviewers for the Press for their thoughtful and helpful comments and suggestions.

Finally, and most important, we thank our families.

Abbreviations

ALP	Alternate Language Program
CAFTA	Central America Free Trade Agreement
CBC	Congressional Black Caucus
CHC	Congressional Hispanic Caucus
CUL	National Urban Coalition
ESL	English as Second Language
LCCR	Leadership Conference on Civil Rights
LULAC	League of United Latin American Citizens
MALDEF	Mexican American Legal Defense Fund
NAACP	National Association for the Advancement of Colored People
NADBank.	North American Development Bank
NAFTA	North American Free Trade Agreement
NALEO	National Association of Latino Elected and Appointed Officials
NCLB	No Child Left Behind Act
NCLR	National Council of La Raza
NHLA	National Hispanic Leadership Agenda
PUSH	People United to Serve Humanity
TANF	Temporary Assistance for Needy Families
UL	National Urban League
USCCR	U.S. Commission on Civil Rights
VRA	Voting Rights Act

I

Introduction

Relations between blacks and Latinos in American politics and society have become an increasingly relevant concern, arguably growing more important and complex over time. Though these matters have been studied extensively, virtually absent in the research is a systematic assessment of minority intergroup relations *at the national level*. Nearly all the research on such relations in governmental decision-making institutions has focused on urban/local politics, while another body of research has focused on mass attitudes (cf., for example, Browning, Marshall, and Tabb 1984; Telles et al. 2011; Nelson and Lavariega Monforti 2005, along with many other studies, a number of which are examined in Chapter 2). This book examines black-Latino relations in national politics with the central goal of describing and assessing them, and seeking to better understand their nature – specifically, whether those relations are most often characterized by conflict, independence, cooperation, or something else. To study this question, we examine an array of evidence that provides a firm basis for assessing black-Latino relations at the national level, which is essential if we are also to consider what might explain those relations. But, again, as things stand, because the existing research generally focuses on local politics or other dimensions of black-Latino relations, there has been little to no adequate evidence on which to base either empirical assessments or the theoretical understanding of black-Latino relations in national politics.

In later chapters we develop a great deal of evidence on Latino-black relations. In doing so, we keep in mind that most if not all politics, policy, and political issues are significantly different at the national level from those at other levels in U.S. politics – because of the differences in the "essential character" of the various levels, that is, unique "geography" of authority and particular types of policy responsibilities. Additionally, the role of ideology and of political parties tends to be substantially different at the national level and in local politics (cf. Trounstine 2010). Different geography leads to different constellations and configurations of interests at various levels; social relations may be affected by formal governmental or institutional settings. Highlighting such points, James Madison referred to the notion of the geography of politics as "sphere," while E. E. Schattschneider later (1960) spoke of similar ideas as "scope" (of conflict). When that different geography or scope is formally coupled with the different types of policy responsibility of the national government (versus state and local governments) – as it *always* is in some way(s), and to some degree, as broadly delineated in the U.S. Constitution (and in state constitutions) – the distinctiveness of the national government is further evident, as is that of local and state governments. Because of these fundamental differences between the levels of government in the political system (Miller 2007; Peterson 1981), it is plausible to think that *interminority group relations* might *also* be different at the national level – but this possibility has not been examined much if at all in the American politics research literature.

To learn the actual nature of black-Latino relations at the national level is an empirical matter, of course, but very little empirical evidence exists that would allow systematic assessment of those relationships. Addressing this empirical void is a principal concern of this study. We further articulate the core questions and more fully elaborate the analytical approach and the explanatory perspective that animate our exploration later in the present and in subsequent chapters. First, however, we provide an example regarding a rather different aspect and process, though it is a familiar one, of American politics which (also) illustrates the differences in black-Latino political relations, and we suggest these relations seem to vary with the levels of government, the issues at stake, and other factors, such as the role of political parties.

The election of Barack Obama as president of the United States in 2008 is universally recognized as a major event in American political and social history. Not only was Obama the first candidate of African American background to be elected president, but he was also the first African American to be nominated by one of the major political parties. The stages of the selection process that culminated in his ascendance to the presidency suggest several points, including some especially germane to central concerns of this book – delineating and examining political relations between blacks and Latinos in U.S. national-level politics. In the nomination stage of the presidential selection process, which is a series of state (or "subnational")-level primaries and caucuses, Obama received considerably less support from Latino voters in the Democratic primaries than did his major opponents, including Hillary Clinton, a U.S. senator from New York state (and wife of former U.S. president Bill Clinton, 1993–2000). Some observers claimed that the modest levels of Latino support for Obama were attributable to dislike between blacks and Latinos, some going so far as to claim that Latinos wouldn't vote for a black candidate because of racial bias and/or intergroup antipathy: intergroup tension was the alleged reason for weak support for Obama. However, in the later national election – where the issues and choices are different and the popular vote is aggregated through the electoral college – about two-thirds of Latinos voted for Obama, a percentage a bit higher than for most previous Democratic nominees in recent presidential elections, and substantially higher than white voters. Thus, the earlier allegations that Latinos would be reluctant to support a black presidential candidate turned out to be unfounded or at least overstated.

An interpretation emerged that Latinos did not harbor animosity toward Obama, based on race or similar considerations, but they simply liked the other candidate for the Democrat nomination more. Also, the candidacy of a black candidate may not have had the same symbolic attachment for Latinos as for blacks. Hence, the different voting preferences during the nomination stage were not necessarily a sign of conflict but of different choices and policy emphasis. There is another, very plausible, and not mutually exclusive, reason for this. In the general election (as compared to the nomination stage) the greater commonality of policy preferences and general ideology – particularly issues of economic and social equality of blacks, which was also significantly abetted by the *inter*party rather than intraparty nature of the contest – might be expected to override black-Latino differences that otherwise exist. And as it turned out, the Latino vote for Obama (of about two-thirds) was substantially higher than among whites, though not as high as among blacks. Interestingly, then, the ultimate outcome of this election, which has often been characterized as indicative of a "post-racial" society in the subnational primary arena, was interpreted by some as indicating inter-minority group tension. However, assessments of black-Latino relations in the (more) national arena of the presidential selection process led to a different assessment.

So, what might this outcome suggest to us about black-Latino relations in American politics? Is a strong general "comity" between blacks and Latinos the prevailing pattern – as the high Latino support for Obama in the 2008 general election seemed to indicate, and as has often been assumed to have been the case historically? Or is conflict common between blacks and Latinos in recent years, as echoed with some frequency in numerous research findings (cf. Telles et al. 2011, 13)? A considerable amount of scholarship finds that relations between blacks and Latinos are often competitive, even conflictual, especially in the urban/local spheres and are similarly manifested in groups' attitudes toward one another, as some survey research indicates. Are these findings of intergroup tension representative of the overall situation? However accurate they may be, it is very unlikely they tell the whole story, given that they assess just one level of and/or one set of actors in the complex system of American government.

Group relations, and indeed virtually all aspects of American politics, are influenced by the larger institutional structure of the U.S. political system (see Madison, *Federalist* #10). One such feature is "federalism" which has various manifestations and implications (see Madison, *Federalist* #39 and #10). The nomination and election process for choosing the president suggests this. But because governmental authority is allocated or "divided" and/or "shared" geographically or territorially among the national, state, and local "levels" of government, politics is different in these levels. Indeed, the geographic and the policy authority *within* levels of government "go together" and are essentially two sides of one coin; that also pertains to differences in the geographic, and the types of policy, authority *between* levels of government. That basic reality suggests an inadequacy of drawing general conclusions about many aspects of American politics if the national level is not considered. But to this point black-Latino relations have essentially only been studied at one level of the governmental system, the urban/local level. Though clearly important, that specific focus overlooks another major arena of American politics.

Here, we explore black-Latino relations at the national level through the extensive data we have collected and examine. It may be that forms of intergroup relations other than conflict and cooperation exist, and these may likewise vary across levels of the governmental system (cf. Rocha 2007a; Telles et al., 2011, chapter 1). Carefully assessing the evidence on black-Latino relations in national politics – what forms these relations may take, among other things – is the major focus of this book. And if that analysis reveals patterns of black-Latino relations that are different from those frequently shown in research at other levels of government – and our findings are clearly different from those at the local level – possible explanations can be considered.

Our brief account of relations between blacks and Latinos at two junctures in the 2008 presidential process implies that the political context – the arena, institutions, the prominence of different policy issues – matters for politics, group relations, and policy decision making. The apparent impact on intergroup relations in the different arenas, venues, and stages and the choices presented as suggested in the presidential electoral processes seem to also be manifest in institutions of governance – national, state, and local governments – in the American system. Indeed, this has long been argued by such luminaries as Madison (*Federalist #10*; also see Schattschneider 1960; Peterson 1981), and has been broadly understood and generally accepted in American politics scholarship. Yet the potential or actual implications of such ideas are often overlooked and as a result their possible ramifications and utility for analytical purposes are not always fully appreciated. The ostensible absence of appropriate data with which to assess the nature of black-Latino relations in national politics poses an obstacle to studying the questions, and we grapple with and at least partly remedy these limitations in this book

National and state (and local) governments are, importantly, interconnected and also have some concurrent powers and together constitute the American "compound republic" (Madison, *Federalist #39*). At the same time, the several levels of government are very different in a number of ways that have consequences for many issues in American politics. Along with a number of other important claims in *Federalist 10* (and elsewhere), Madison asserted that under the federal Constitution, "the great and aggregate interests" (or policy issues and concerns) would be "referred to the national legislature" (or government) while "local and particular" issues would be referred "to the State legislatures." Notably, Madison referred to the national government as the "general" government, implying that other state and local governments had more particular or narrower domains of policy responsibility. The importance of the greater geographic breadth of national policy responsibilities is amplified when we consider that different types of policy often lead to different types of politics, which could well include political relations between groups supporting and opposing policies (Lowi 1964). If these arguments are accurate in general (again see Madison; Schattschneider 1960; Peterson 1981), by extension they also could pertain to policies of interest and relevance to black-Latino relations. And this remains so even when we acknowledge the considerable fluidity and complexity in American federalism over time and into the present.

In this study, in examining black-Latino relations in several venues and processes within national politics, we ask if there is evidence of conflict or of other types of intergroup relations. Does the nature of relations (conflict, and so on) vary in the several dimensions of the behaviors of the major actors in national politics we examine: in advocacy groups' testimony at congressional hearings and in amicus brief filings; in the issues identified as most important by minority advocacy/interest groups *and* in the positions these groups take on those issues considered by Congress; in the votes of (minority) representatives in Congress; and in other indicators of behavior and types of analysis? The national government is a unique and crucial access point in the American system and there are, further, institutions and processes that are unique to and within this level of government. It is important to analyze this arena, and we do so by examining numerous activities of minority advocacy organizations seeking to influence policy and of elected officials (minority members of Congress), and the interplay within and between these actors in the national policy-making process.

The particular questions we ask have not previously been posed and the research approach we take has not previously been pursued, though there have been studies of related matters. On the one hand, a large number of studies have examined black-Latino relations at the urban government level, in school district politics, and occasionally at the state level, as well as of mass attitudes (we discuss these in Chapter 2). On the other hand, a number of studies have examined various aspects of the behavior of black and of Latino members of Congress (MCs); but those studies have focused on these representatives separately and have given scant attention to *inter-minority* group relations and politics. Our study is novel in addressing black-Latino intergroup relations at the national level as well as in the extent and variety of evidence we bring to bear, which includes the activities of several sets of political actors across several aspects of the policy process. We believe our study is also novel in the theoretical insights we draw upon and develop to assess black-Latino relations at this level of government. Together these provide basic, essential, and varied knowledge along with a distinct analytical approach on black-Latino relations; in so doing, the study advances research on black-Latino relations. Whether we look and where we look for evidence (the levels of government, the range and types of data) has implications for what we find, and the conclusions we draw. Examining this particular set of previously unstudied and certainly under-studied questions, and in the way we do, furthers the understanding of black-Latino relations in U.S. national politics.

But what makes these issues important in the first place? Black-Latino relations are an important component of America's social structure and social change. It is especially significant because of the evolving demographic diversity in American society and the way intergroup relations manifest, affect, and are affected by politics. Given the general importance of (interest) groups in American politics, especially emphasized by the highly influential "pluralist" interpretation, the situation of and the relationships between the two largest minority groups – who will be the major elements of the country's likely "majority-minority" composition at some not-too-distant date – seems patently worthy of extended attention. The rather large body of research that has emerged on the topic affirms this (see, e.g., Telles et al. 2011; Nelson and Lavariega Monforti 2005; and other studies considered in Chapter 2). And black-Latino relations will surely have implications for other groups in the society and for the political system as a whole. Both groups are socioeconomically disadvantaged and their efforts to influence the political system and public policy – whether independently or in combination, or if there is conflict – are important issues of empirical democratic theory generally and (in) equality and representation in the political process more specifically (cf. Griffin and Newman 2008).

Under what circumstances, in what jurisdictional settings, and by what types of policies do the two groups advance similar or divergent policy concerns and preferences are all important issues. Furthermore, and beyond strictly group characteristics and policy preferences, exploring whether the governmental structure of the American political system affects intergroup relations is an interesting, if largely neglected, question. If group and intergroup goals, resources, and associated group attributes were the only or overriding explanations of intergroup relations, we would expect black-Latino relations to be basically similar at the national level and the local/state level; that is, there would primarily be scaled-up or scaled-down versions of essentially similar intergroup relations. However, as we will see, this does *not* seem to be the case, which suggests something else is going on, that other factors merit scrutiny. Our major findings – of "nonconflict," and "independence" between blacks and Latinos in national-level politics – suggest that perhaps the institutions of the governmental system, factors "hidden in plain sight," may condition or mediate intergroup relations and thus influence the degree of contentiousness; these factors seem to help explain the proverbial "dog that didn't bark." Our research endeavor and analyses thus offer a different vantage point for understanding racial/ethnic diversity and intergroup relations in American politics. And the different vantage point leads to a different view of such relations.

The questions we analyze both emerge from and inform several bodies of scholarship. Our work is clearly imbedded within research on race/ethnicity in American politics and should shed light on understudied aspects of this area. When we consider the activities of black and Latino political "elites," specifically, interest or advocacy groups and members of Congress, we delve into the interest group, the Congress, and "representation," and judicial research literatures, among others. Distinctive attributes of the national government, which differ from those of local and state government, are, we suspect, important. The unique geographic breadth and the particular nature of policy authority of the national government are most directly significant, but the differences of the U.S. Congress and the Supreme Court set it/them apart within the structure and levels of government. Local government legislative bodies, city councils, are vastly different from the U.S. Congress in the types of authority they wield and the capacity they have; and there is, of course, nothing comparable to the U.S. Supreme Court in local governments. (The types of policy responsibilities and activities at the national level, and their differences from other levels are apparent in the data presented throughout the empirical analyses, in Chapters 3–7). These points should be remembered as we now turn to delineating and placing our analysis in broader perspective by discussing several background issues. We summarize recent social developments, discuss earlier expectations and subsequent findings about black-Latino relations, and further elaborate upon several substantive and theoretical arguments that guide our analysis.

Background

The importance of understanding contemporary and evolving black-Latino relations is underscored by thinking about it in broader historical terms. By the middle of the twenty-first century, the American racial and ethnic landscape will reach a new milestone; white non-Hispanics will no longer make up the majority of the country's population. Instead, what are commonly considered racial and ethnic minority groups are expected to jointly comprise about 50 percent of the population, up from 34 percent in 2008, according to U.S. Census estimates (U.S. Census 2008a);

in other words, the United States will be a majority-minority country. The Hispanic/Latino and Asian populations have been growing rapidly while the black and the white populations are increasing modestly by comparison. Latinos in 2009 comprise about 16 percent of the nation's population, surpassing blacks (who currently make up about 13 percent) in 2003. And in some U.S. states – including the nation's two largest, California and Texas – majority-minority populations have already been realized, with Latinos as the plurality minority group in both these states. By 2050, the Census Bureau estimates that black and Latino populations will remain the two largest racial/ethnic minority groups, but with Latinos comprising 30 percent and blacks accounting for 15 percent of the population. Combined, blacks and Latinos will roughly equal non-Hispanic Whites.

This basic information is relatively familiar to many scholars and those interested in public affairs; less clear, however, is what these developments might mean for relations between blacks and Latinos and more generally for American politics and society. The historical condition of blacks/African Americans has been viewed as the core of the "American dilemma" of race; yet at the same time, America has an image of itself as "a nation of immigrants." Concurrently, the Latino experience in the United States has been interpreted as having "racialized" as well as "ethnic" and "immigrant" dimensions (see, e.g., Schmidt et al. 2010; Hero 1992; Skrentny 2002). What do these varying characterizations of these groups suggest, and what do changes toward an increasingly multiethnic society imply, for American politics generally and for minority intergroup relations, particularly those between blacks and Latinos? Despite much popular discussion, references to, and considerable speculation about multiethnic politics and about "moving beyond a 'black/white' paradigm," few studies of American national politics have considered such questions directly (see, e.g., Clarke et al. 2006; McClain 1993; McClain and Karnig 1990; Meier and Stewart 1991; Browning, Marshall, and Tabb 1984; Kim 1999). The present study is an effort to engage these issues.

The Promise of the Multiracial Coalition

In a 1990 Martin Luther King Jr. Day speech, Cesar Chavez, the leader of the United Farm Workers (UFW) and an important figure in Latino/ Chicano civil rights history, underscored the similarities in the struggles for equal rights shared by blacks and Latinos in the United States. Chavez recalled King's 1968 letter of support for Chavez's first fast in which King wrote, "Our separate struggles are really one. A struggle for freedom, for dignity, and for humanity" (Chavez 1990). The notion that blacks and Latinos share a similar struggle for civil, economic, and political rights is neither new nor objectively naïve. While the black struggle is the basis for most of the civil rights era legislation in the 1960s and 1970s, Latino rights became a part of a range of laws and other policies adopted during this era (Skrentny 2002). Affirmative action programs aimed at boosting economic and, importantly, educational equality have been applied to both groups, and the current animosity toward groups that benefit from affirmative action programs seems to vary by region, based on the size of the black or Latino population. Where the black population is large, blacks are perceived as the "undeserving" beneficiaries, while similar animosity is applied toward Latinos in regions with larger Latino populations (cf. Fox 2004).

By almost all measures of objective data, blacks and Latinos share a subordinate status to whites. Both blacks and Latinos have substantially higher unemployment rates than do whites (U.S. Census Bureau 2008b); they are almost two to three times as likely to live in poverty as whites, and they have median family incomes of around two-thirds the income of white families (U.S. Census Bureau 2008c). Blacks and Latino students are more likely to drop out of high school and less likely to score well on standardized college entrance exams than white non-Hispanic students, and both are also more likely than whites to face suspension and other disciplinary actions in school (National Center for Education Statistics [NCES] 2008). Blacks and Latinos have higher case rates of AIDS (acquired immunodeficiency syndrome) than whites, yet are also more likely than whites to lack health insurance (Kaiser Family Foundation 2008). The list goes on, and the gaps between whites and blacks or Latinos – while reduced in some instances and over a very long time frame – persist. The ratio between black and white unemployment rates, for instance, is about the same in 2008 as it was in 1972 and roughly comparable patterns emerge for Latinos. In short, there are ample grounds to assume that politically, economically, and socially, black and Latino struggles are similar; indeed, they have important commonalities and are "one" in some important ways. Shared subordinate status provided a basis for multiracial coalitions that emerged in the national and some localized governmental contexts.

One of the more visible manifestations of this coalitional impulse was led by Jesse Jackson, the well-known black civil rights leader and 1988 Democratic presidential primary candidate who formed PUSH (People United to Serve Humanity) in 1971 with the goals of "economic empowerment and expanding educational, business and employment opportunities for the disadvantaged and people of color." The term "people of color" become synonymous with groups of various minority racial/ethnic backgrounds. Jackson's Rainbow Coalition, founded in 1984, mirrored the ideals of the unitary struggle of blacks and other minority groups (including Latinos) and was devoted to political empowerment of minority groups as well as broader policy objectives aimed at changing the inequitable conditions experienced by both blacks and Latinos. "Rainbow coalition" subsequently became a common term for multiracial coalitions in American politics. In many ways, and with some high-profile leadership, blacks and Latinos appeared to present a unified front advocating health, social, political, and economic policy benefits to alleviate the disadvantages shared by both groups.

Political realities and prominent scholarly theoretical interpretations suggest there is "strength in numbers." If shared ideals alone were not sufficient, awareness that a coalition of two large racial/ethnic minority groups would presumably facilitate their political influence should encourage such black-Latino coalitions. According to leading interpretations of American politics such as pluralism, coalition formation is a necessary part of gaining influence for groups when their numbers, while substantial, are not a majority, and it is particularly important when coupled with groups' disadvantaged socioeconomic status (Schneider and Ingram 1993). Both Latinos and blacks would presumably benefit from merging their political power in a unified front (Kaufmann 2007). With common ideals and goals of formal and social equality and inclusion, further abetted by common interests and practical political considerations, coalition might be expected as the norm in black-Latino relations. Contemporary headlines from the popular media as well as scholarly studies tell a different story, however. They suggest that commonality does not necessarily lead to cooperation; in fact, it may often lead to contentious intergroup relations (cf. Jones-Correa 2011, 90; Nelson and Lavariega Monforti 2005; Telles et al. 2011).

The Apparent Reality

Instead of stable black-Latino coalitions, political scientists have found "cracks in the rainbow" (Kaufmann 2003a) and others call into question the "presumed alliance," describing in some detail a seeming "unspoken conflict between Latinos and blacks" (Vaca 2004; cf. Telles et al. 2011). Moreover, the breadth of evidence emerging from academic studies suggests a tenuous relationship between the two groups, one that in some instances may even border on hostility (see Chapter 2). One interpretation is that when two groups have little in the way of economic resources, competition over resources triggers racial prejudice and conflict, as indicated in studies of urban politics and of black attitudes toward Latinos revealed in surveys in cities and metropolitan areas. For instance, Gay (2006, 983) suggests the general tenor of the literature and common perceptions of animosity:

> Idealized notions of "natural" intergroup comity and mutual support collapse when confronted by a finite number of public and (low-skilled) private sector jobs; by the lack of educational resources to meet the needs of black children and Spanish-speaking Latino children; by a shortage of adequate and affordable housing; and by the desire among both groups for descriptive political representation on neighborhood councils, on school boards, and in municipal government."

This description of competitive black-Latino relations in local situations linked to finite economic and education resources and constrained opportunities for election to office is echoed in other studies (see Chapter 2; cf. Telles et al. 2011, various chapters). Thus, reinforcing the headlines in popular accounts that present examples of conflict between blacks and Latinos, a body of scholarly research provides numerous examples where there is simply little evidence of a "rainbow coalition" unified by a "common struggle." (We discuss studies of local politics and mass attitudes in greater detail in Chapter 2.)

Certain assumptions have been made about the early promise of a black-Latino coalition; on the other hand, there is considerable evidence indicating conflict in local politics, and in black-Latino public opinion, that has emerged from research on the actual nature of black-Latino relations (again, cf. Telles et al. 2011). Yet remarkably few studies have considered issues of black-Latino relations in national-level institutions (for some partial exceptions, see Pinderhughes 1995; Skrentny 2002). The paucity of studies of black-Latino relations in national politics occurred despite its relevance for some of the most important and contentious issues faced by racial and ethnic minorities. The list of major policies enacted at the national level affecting blacks and Latinos is long indeed. These policies paved the way for the initial formal inclusion of minorities in the political process and were fundamental to changes felt strongly in state and local government (Browning, Marshall, and Tabb 1984). These changes were also taken as affirming the theoretical accuracy and normative virtues of American political pluralism (though various analyses have questioned pluralism's reassuring assertions; e.g., Pinderhughes 1987; Hero 1992).

A few obvious examples of landmark policies emanating from the national level and in which Congress played a central role include the Civil Rights Act of 1964 and its amendments), the Voting Rights Act of 1965, the Fair Housing Act of 1968, and the Immigration and Nationality Act of 1965 (and the Immigration Reform and Control Act of 1986); in the realm of social welfare policy, the Personal Responsibility and Work Opportunity Reconciliation Act of 1996 was the most significant change in social welfare programs in sixty years. Add to this very basic list certain elements of the 2001 education reform, "No Child Left Behind," Motor Voter legislation in 1993, changes to food stamps, work programs, job corps, health care, HIV/AIDS prevention, and many more; these are national policies that deal directly or indirectly with issues important to blacks and Latinos. The impact of these is striking and generally very different from those of local and state legislative bodies.

It is not only in the congressional realm, however, but also in the federal courts (examined in Chapter 3) that policy changes important to both groups have emerged. Among these were the *Brown v. Board of Education* decision in 1954, issues of affirmative action in the 1978 *Bakke* case and recently the *Bollinger* decisions in 2003, and numerous decisions before, between, and after. The federal courts play a prominent role in the lives of blacks and Latinos and in most cases a role that is consequential. In *Thornburgh v. Gingles* (1986), the court's decision on race-based districting fostered large increases in black and Hispanic representation in state legislatures and Congress after the 1990 round of redistricting. Yet, in 1993 the court essentially reversed this decision in *Reno v. Shaw* (Canon 1999, chapter 2). And, in the myriad of additional issues from voting rights (e.g., *Harper v. Virginia Board of Elections 1966)*, racial discrimination in the workplace (*Wards Cove Packing, Inc. v. Antonio 1989)* to school financing (i.e., *San Antonio v. Rodriguez 1973*), the courts have played a prominent role in policy issues and concerns shared by both blacks and Latinos. (In contrast, local courts and even state courts have generally played much lesser roles; and the geographic breadth of impact is less if and when they do play a role.) Despite this extensive list of impressive policy consequences that could presumably be bases for either conflict, or cooperation, few studies address the nature and extent of black and Latino intergroup relations at the national level or across national institutions.

Pluralism and Black-Latino Relations

The policy issues discussed regarding intergroup relations notwith-standing, there is somewhat limited theoretical guidance or substantive research to draw upon in addressing the specific questions of primary interest in our study. Virtually the entire study of minority intergroup political relationships has focused on the local/urban level of politics. Cities have historically often been perceived as *the* arena where "new" or minority/ethnic groups and immigrants have first been incorporated into American politics. And city politics research provided important theoreti-cal grounding and empirical evidence for the profoundly influential "plu-ralist" interpretation of politics (see Dahl 1961). Pluralism's analytical influence pervades virtually all of the research on minorities in American politics of the last several decades, even into the present.

Pluralism interprets American politics as grounded in groups acting as advocates for their members in a system where there is essentially proce-dural "fairness," equal footing for each advocacy group, multiple access points through which influence can be pursued, and occasional but not sustained coalitions of groups as they advance and/or compete over pol-icies, resources, and benefits in the political system. The political system is thus alleged to be responsive to various groups at various times and responsiveness to citizen preferences is based on the ability of individuals with shared concerns to form effective advocacy groups. And the breadth of influence by any one group or set of groups is expected to be greatest in policy areas of most direct concern to them but rather modest beyond those areas. This very short rendering suggests that while group competi-tion is central to pluralist analysis, racial and ethnic minority groups may especially need to form coalitions to compete with nonminority groups. Such coalitions don't guarantee success, but they might be able to influ-ence government decisions within certain realms with roughly similar results achieved by other groups. Interminority group relations would seem to be largely a matter of cooperating when policy preferences are shared across their constituencies and competing when (certain) prefer-ences are not shared.

Not always acknowledged in portrayals of pluralism applied to minority group relations are two points that existing studies of inter-group relations sometimes understate. One is that racial and ethnic minorities commonly face socioeconomic impediments and resource constraints to an extent that casts doubt on the basic assumption of an "equal playing field" for each of the groups individually and perhaps in their interrelations as well. Another is that commonality does not necessarily lead to group coalitions (see Lavariega Monforti 2005, 252; Gay 2006).

Yet another largely overlooked point is that the geography of governmental authority and the allocation of responsibility for different types of policies salient to minority groups differs across levels of the governmental system (cf. Peterson 1981). Pluralism highlights multiple access points where policies are made and through which groups may seek to affect policy. But what seems not to be emphasized sufficiently is that those access points are hardly one and the same and are not just larger or smaller versions of each other; they differ in several, often fundamental ways, with various consequences – possibly including consequences for intergroup relations. Thus, as critical as they are, it is not only group size, socioeconomic resources, and circumstances and the like that intergroup politics is about. There are variations in the governmental level, the specific types of policy authority therein, and the extent of a group's access to and influence over decisions in these venues. And this may change the way minority groups behave – including, perhaps, how they *relate to one another*. A rethinking of pluralism's explanations is necessary as those apply to blacks and Latinos as groups individually and, more directly for present purposes, in the groups' interrelations.

Group-based politics for racial and ethnic minority groups may in general be better understood as a two-tiered system (Hero 1992), rather than standard pluralism, with minority groups facing a different set of political realities as they engage in politics from the second tier. Two-tiered pluralism emphasizes the unequal positions of racial and ethnic minority groups relative to the majority group within the general pluralist American system (cf. Bartels 2008), and the consequences of these different positions for group influence. An implication of two-tiered pluralism applied specifically to minority intergroup relations is that black-Latino relations is different from the common "black-white paradigm" that has long shaped the thinking about intergroup politics. Not only are different groups analyzed (that is, blacks-Latinos rather than black-white, or group competition in general) but *both* blacks and Latinos are largely in the "second tier" of politics due to their similar socioeconomic status, combined with a "racialized" status to a greater or lesser degree. This injects a "horizontal" dimension to the black-Latino situation not present in the black-white (or Latino-white) situation, likely making the possibilities for conflict or cooperation, or other forms of relationships, more complicated or at least different.

Two-tiered pluralism grants the importance of multiple access points in the political system. The types of policy responsibilities and the simultaneous geography of policy authority are, thus, distinct in important ways (Peterson 1981). While the impact of the "double" subordinate status (that is, socioeconomic *and* political) of blacks and Latinos is significant in general, its implications might also be conditioned by the different nature of the various levels of government as "access points."

Basic overlapping of ideas and/or (material) interests ought to lead blacks and Latinos to form coalitions and cooperate; shared interests and shared ideals, primarily based on calls for equality, are the basis of the historic pursuit of, and theoretical expectations for, minority coalition. Furthermore, unlike groups in the "first tier" of politics, these two minority groups often face a common perception that they seek redistributive or, according to critics, "special treatment" vis-à-vis whites – in a "minority versus non-minority" split – as they seek policy responsiveness. Yet the apparent reality of black-Latino relations is not infrequently one of conflict, at least at suggested by research on the local level. Is this because redistributive policies at the local level are more likely to have a *between*-minority (black "versus" Latino), zero-sum quality than the minority versus non-minority split that may occur more frequently at the national level? Are interests or ideology different and do they play out and affect black-Latino relations differently at alternate levels of the governmental system? As authority for different types of policy and the geographic arenas of policy-making change at the same time, the nature of black-Latino relations could also be affected.

The nature of the policies themselves at the national level more often emphasize general issues of equality and more equitably distributed benefits (for example, civil rights, affirmative action, welfare, Medicaid) and other dimensions (immigration, macro-economics, banking, finance, agriculture, foreign policy, among others – see our empirical analyses in subsequent chapters) in ways that are fundamentally unlike local policy conflicts such as competition over jobs or the election of minority candidates from one group or another. Our analyses of a range policy issues at the national level is presented in Chapters 3 to 7. Readily apparent in the discussion and in many tables in those chapters is a unique set of policy responsibilities that is especially evident when juxtaposed to the types of issues that cities and school districts address (as shown clearly in the literature discussed in Chapter 2). And these differences appear to us to be substantive and qualitative, not merely ones of degree.

Questions often examined in studies on minority intergroup relations at the urban level involve police and fire departments, and local school districts in the educational arena, regarding whether blacks versus Latinos (or whites) get jobs as police officers, firefighters, and teachers, or which racial group is more or less successful in gaining positions on city councils or as mayors, on school boards and as school superintendents. These are unquestionably important issues and warrant all the research attention they have received because cities have often been "crossroads of equality" regarding race/ethnicity in American democracy (Hero 2005). But they are different in their geography or scope and types of policies when contrasted with national and state responsibilities. If "policy (frequently) shapes politics" as much as the reverse (see Lowi 1964; Eshbaugh-Soha and Meier 2008), then the *factors that shape policy in the first place* are also manifestly important for intergroup relations; institutions certainly shape policy, through the allocation of governmental authority and related means.

While the variation of conflict across levels in the federal system is important in itself, its possible intersection with the premises of two-tiered pluralism leads to additional reasons to anticipate different intergroup relations between blacks and Latinos. Second-tier status means that minority groups are quite often apt to seek similar policy goals that differ from those of other racial/ethnic groups. But when blacks and Latinos differ they are less likely at the national level to be put in situations where their interests collide directly to the point that their ideological similarities are undermined substantially. The consequences of a policy advocated by one minority group may not be perceived to have the same effect on the other as it does when compared with largely white, first tier interests. Policy advocacy at the national level by one second tier group can simultaneously be perceived as competition by groups in the first tier but is less likely to be viewed as competition among groups that share a second tier status. Therefore, two-tiered pluralism and the geography of politics and policy authority may interact and affect the likelihood of different black-Latino relations at different levels of government.

Beyond Conflict and Cooperation

Our main goal is to describe and delineate minority group relations at the national level as well as begin to offer explanations of those relations. Along with the possibility that conflict will not necessarily be the predominant mode of black-Latino relations at the national level and that the degree of conflict could vary according to geography and related policy type, we also suggest that the nature of black-Latino relations should not be considered only in the common conflict versus cooperation dichotomy; black-Latino relations are more complicated than suggested by the concepts of "competition" or "cooperation" (as Rocha 2007a well describes; also see Telles et al. 2011). We might see less conflict than seems to be found in urban-level studies because there will be less direct overlap in competing, material interests, and hence less contentiousness. And policies that do overlap will also be less conflictual. Minority groups and their (interest group) advocates are probably more able to pursue their own group's goals while relatively seldom reacting strongly (negatively or positively) to the other group's policy positions where the policy "space" is broader.

It has been argued that factors affecting minority group coalitions are "interests" and "ideology." Accordingly, group policy orientations and interrelations may be more or less similar based on their divergence or convergence on interests and ideology, or more concrete versus abstract (see, e.g., Sonenshein 1993; Carmichael and Hamilton 1967). Here we emphasize that interests are often understood based on whether policies are viewed as more or less "zero-sum" by groups affected by the issues. Following the implications of the two dimensions of ideology and interests, some broad relational possibilities can be identified. We label these types of relations cooperation, conflict, independence, and negotiation. This simply suggests that something other than an either/or perspective exists, presenting additional possibilities associated with the complexities of black-Latino politics (Rocha 2007a; Telles et al. 2011).

When there is a convergence or agreement between groups on *both* ideology and interests, "cooperation" would be expected. Conversely, "conflict" would be highest when there are differences or disagreements in terms of both ideology and interest (more zero-sum policies). We would expect that interest divergence is more common than ideological divergence between blacks and Latinos because to some extent there is a broad consensus around concerns and particular support for civil rights, racial/ethnic and economic equality, and related values. How those values are actually applied or allocated across groups in particular policies and circumstances – that is, where interests come in – can be a source of tension. But the ideological agreement can temper the tension and may help channel it away from overtly conflicting outcomes, and this may be more likely in some levels of government or institutional contexts than others.

Apart from the circumstances we posit regarding conflict and cooperation, the nature of other relations is murkier. However, where there is basic agreement of ideology but difference of interests, "independence" may be possible (McClain 1993; Rocha 2007a; Telles et al. 2011). Thus, groups may not be in direct conflict and simply go their own way under such conditions. Ongoing discussion seeking to establish mutually acceptable policies is likely. This may lead to distributive politics where the substantive differences are not fully resolved, and to policy positions where there's a little something for everyone. Symbolic or recognition politics may also take place. Finally, negotiation possibly occurs where there is ideological disagreement and interest concerns are not clearly at stake or diverge. Again, the assumption is that there are relatively few instances of ideological divergence because minority advocacy groups most often (though not always) share broader "purposive" goals. Latinos and blacks have been seen as parts of "liberal" coalitions in urban politics and, similarly, part of Democratic and liberal coalitions in state politics. (For urban level coalitions, see Browning, Marshall, and Tabb 1984. The inclusion in state-level party coalitions has been shown by Preuhs 2006, 2007.)

Furthermore, both these minority groups (with a few notable exceptions) strongly support Democratic candidates in congressional and presidential elections and both groups are also liberal on economic policy. We expect these partisan tendencies would be clearer and stronger in national politics than in local politics (Trounstine 2010; also see Chapters 5 and 6). Thus, closer attention is given here to independence than cases of ideological divergence.

Table 1.1 provides a summary of this argument, diagramming the various combinations of ideas and interests, the anticipated types of black-Latino relations, and expected incidence of each – conflict, cooperation, or independence/negotiation – in national contrasted to local politics. That is, the impact of ideological and interest relations varies as the level of government (or geography) changes and the types of policies under consideration also change. At the national level, the competition over material benefits between minority groups tends to be less of a factor, though it may be seen as high between minorities and nonminorities (whites). When ideas and interests are shared and salient, no conflict and maybe even concurrence emerge at this level (and we hypothesize it is more common than at the local level). At local levels, while the ideals and general ideology may be shared, the policies are more interest-based, they more often tend toward zero-sum, and material interests more often conflict

TABLE 1.1. *Summary of Likely Empirical Findings with Respect to the Analytical Framework*

Ideology and Interests*		Expected Intergroup Relations	Relative frequency of Conditions (Low to High) in Local and National Institutions
Shared Ideology High	Shared Interests High (less often zero-sum)	Least Conflict (Cooperation or Comity)	LOCAL Low NATIONAL Moderate
Shared Ideology Modest to High	Shared Interests Low to Modest	Little/No Conflict (Independence or Possibly Negotiation)**	LOCAL Moderate NATIONAL High
Shared Ideology Low	Shared Interests Low (more often zero-sum)	Most Conflict	LOCAL High NATIONAL Low

* Interests are (also) very much affected by the authority for different policy and types of policy – that authority is and policy types are fundamentally different at the national and local levels.
** It is possible for independence and negotiation to lead to similar empirical observations, and thus we include both types of relations and observations in the same cells.

when the allocation of resources to one minority group may diminish allocation to the other minority group (Lavariega Monforti 2005). Additionally, however, even if ideas or interests are shared, they may not have the same degree of salience for each group. Thus, one group's important issue may simply not be high on the agenda of the other. This is more likely to happen, we think, in the institutions of the national government since the range of potential issues is broader here if contrasted relative to what it is in local politics, and the probability of a salient policy for one group being directly at odds with the other is lessened. (Again, Table 1.1 highlights these arguments.)

Examining these propositions requires appropriate and at least a reasonably broad range of evidence. Accordingly, we provide evidence on national-level politics that speaks to the larger questions and, furthermore, our data encompass an extended period, not a single year. What issues are most important to blacks and Latinos, as suggested by advocacy group activities? How similar and/or different are the groups in this respect? To what extent are similarities and differences apparent in the congressional and legal arenas? To the extent the issue concerns overlap, do they engender cooperation, conflict, or something else at the national level? What are the groups' positions on those issues? Additionally, do the voting records of African American and Latino members of Congress suggest conflict over or support for the concerns of the counterpart group? To assess these, we examine data on minority advocacy groups as well as members of Congress and their actions and interactions in different venues and arenas of national institutions. This analysis of elites from both groups, at the national level, offers distinct evidence on the questions, focused on important elements of the national policy-making process. We systematically examine interelite behaviors of two sets of minority advocacy groups and two sets of members of Congress (blacks and Latinos) at the national level to determine the nature of the *interminority* group relations there; and we contrast that evidence with what is suggested in the urban politics research. Attention is also given, if indirectly, to another iteration of intergroup relations – that is, the role of whites is part of the story as well.

In the pages that follow, various intriguing and, we think, significant findings emerge. Most important, we find little to no evidence of conflict between blacks and Latinos at the national level, contrary to the findings of conflict identified in research on local politics. Also, we suggest that thinking in terms of whether there is conflict *or* cooperation overlooks other possibilities; and we find considerable evidence of groups' "independence" (cf. Telles et al. 2011). We show that at the national level there is essentially a complete absence of conflictual relations between (a) black and Latino advocacy groups and (b) black and Latino members of Congress, on various policy issues. We think the geography of policy authority and interests and the associated policy responsibilities of the national governments, as these stand in contrast to local government, have something and perhaps much to do with what we find, or don't find. The different role and impact of political parties and of ideology at the national level (contrasted with the local level) also seem important (Trounstine 2010, 416–17).

Analytic Approach

Our focus is on black-Latino relations at the national level, and we examine, for the first time, whether there are general patterns of black-Latino relationships by analyzing various aspects of policy and politics at this level. However, to provide a reference point and present the most similar and relevant research, in Chapter 2 we survey and assess a number of studies of urban/local politics showing that conflict has emerged. Moreover, we suggest that while conflict is found, it may not be as complete and all encompassing as sometimes portrayed (cf. Telles et al. 2011, chapter 1 and passim; Nelson and Lavariega Monforti 2005). We also discuss the explanations in several studies suggesting that the nature of the policies, particularly the extent of their zero-sum quality, along with other factors, such as context and groups' relative socioeconomic status, lead to variations in the type of relationship between blacks and Latinos. The implications of that research are also considered. Our review in Chapter 2 provides a basis for us to contrast and juxtapose the general urban/local level and other findings with our findings in several venues within the national level. The findings are noticeably different.

Most of our analysis in the remaining chapters is based on a variety of original data on national-level minority advocacy groups' activities and minority elected officials' behaviors in the congressional arena and the Supreme Court, and we have longitudinal evidence for some of this. We look at black-Latino relations in both "mediating institutions," through the activities of minority advocacy groups (most directly in Chapters 3 and 4), and in the "formal" institutions of government, through the roll call voting of black and Latino members of Congress (MCs) (in Chapters 5 and 6). We also present several policy illustrations that consider a combination of interest groups' and elected officials' activities (in Chapter 7). The evidence consistently indicates no conflict, showing a high degree of "independence," where groups emphasize particular policy areas and advocate specific outcomes on their own, that is, apart from one another. There is also some evidence of "cooperation." Where the two groups have overlapping interests and/or ideology, and even at times when they seem not to, we find virtually no evidence that commonality leads to conflict at the national level, while commonality sometimes leads to conflict at the local level. Before we present our findings in further detail, it is worthwhile to indicate the central questions and types of data we bring to bear in the empirical chapters (Chapters 3–6).

Chapter 3 focuses on the efforts of black and Latino minority advocacy (interest) groups and their activities in attempting to influence national-level policy makers. It assesses the similarities and/or differences of these actors in their policy concerns and policy positions as demonstrated through their participation in offering testimony at congressional hearings and in the legal arena, specifically the filing of amicus briefs. Drawing on data from over a thirty-year period, we find a considerable degree of "independence" between Latino and black advocacy groups in congressional testimony yet much similarity in the views expressed by group spokespersons. With regard to advocacy in the legal arena, analysis of friend of the court (amicus) briefs from a thirty-year period further affirms the general finding of relative specialization or independence regarding group activities and that there is little if any outright competition between black and Latino advocacy groups. We supplement the evidence on hearings and amicus data with examples illustrating the similarities and the (modest) differences in the views expressed on an array of policy items. There is considerable independence and, arguably, substantial concurrence, though it varies somewhat by policy-type and by institution (the congressional versus legal arena). However, we see no evidence of conflict between black and Latino advocacy groups in these endeavors.

In Chapter 4 we examine the advocacy groups' similarities and differences regarding what are deemed the most important policy issues, and the overlap thereof, which we refer to as "salience," and whether the preferences about those issues are the same, or "congruent." We draw on data developed by advocacy groups in their efforts to influence voting decisions in the 104th to 108th Congresses, providing an analysis of the congressional "scorecards" of groups that represent blacks and Latinos, specifically, the National Association for the Advancement of Colored People (NAACP) and the National Hispanic Leadership Agenda (NHLA) to determine the degree to which the same issues are identified as among the most salient, and whether positions on those issues differ. The evidence indicates only modest overlap in the issues identified as the most salient by Latino and black advocacy groups; that is, the issues identified are seldom one and the same. On the other hand, on the issues which *are* identified by both groups, there is complete congruence or agreement. The chapter also notes the policy areas where there is more or less overlap and more or less congruence between black and Latino advocacy groups' proclaimed preferences. And, finally, we also show that there is indeed a benefit to being on the same side; preferred positions are most likely realized when both the NAACP and NHLA identify the vote as important. Again, we see no evidence of conflict in the several sources of evidence considered in this chapter.

In Chapter 5 we examine relations within the major formal representative institution of the national government. We focus on roll call votes of black and Latino members of the U.S. House of Representatives on issues identified as among the most important by the advocacy groups and we assess the degree to which minority lawmakers' voting does or does not indicate conflict; we also consider whether the voting of these MCs appears to suggest support for the concerns of the "other" group. Are our earlier findings of an absence of conflict in interminority advocacy group behavior (in Chapters 3 and 4) echoed in the behavior of elected officials within Congress? The "bottom line" is that there is no evidence of conflict. There are indications of compatibility (or cooperation, though certainly not conflict) but these are not consistently (statistically) significant and may thus be indicative of "independence." In short, there is solid evidence suggesting that black members of Congress (MCs) have voting records consistent with concerns salient to Latinos beyond what would be predicted based on other major factors (such as political party, district socioeconomic traits, and so on). And Latino MCs have voting records modestly supportive of the most salient concerns of blacks (after accounting for other factors). At minimum, then, black and Latino representatives' voting indicates an absence of conflict and some support for the other group's concerns at the same level that, and even higher than, party affiliation alone would suggest; this implies considerable compatibility if not outright "cooperation."

Chapter 6 extends our understanding of minority substantive representation in Congress by examining the way black and Latino Members of Congress are oriented toward policy decisions that are distinct from the dominant liberal-conservative ideology when advocating their own group's interests, yet rely on ideological cues that foster cross-group support. Here, we begin to flesh out how descriptive representation matters as an important element of black-Latino relations. Are both groups' representatives influenced by the same ideological "cues" in making voting decisions concerning their own, and the "other," group's concerns? Most scholarship on this topic has focused on whether minority legislators are "more" supportive of minority concerns or general liberal leanings than are white legislators. Yet substantial theoretical discussion has suggested there are other significant dimensions of descriptive representation worthy of consideration, specifically, whether minority representatives think about and behave in ways that differ from white legislators on policy issues. This chapter also addresses the important issue of how ideology fosters support (or mitigates conflict) in the national legislative arena. Comparing Latino and black representatives with each other as well as with their white counterparts (with data from four Congresses, 104th to 108th), we show that an effect of descriptive representation is that racial/ethnic minority representatives seem influenced in their advocacy of minority concerns by cues that stand apart from the conventional liberal/conservative political ideological framework. Black and Latino representatives' policy orientations differ in a qualitative sense (as well as to a quantitative degree) from nonminority representatives; but these differences are most clearly applied when black or Latino representatives are considering their own group's policy issues. When considering other groups' policy issues, *ideology* plays a fundamental role in ameliorating potential conflict and, in the case of black representatives, strong liberalism leads to increased support for Latino issues. Broad "ideas" appear to decrease black-Latino conflict in the national legislative arena.

Chapters 3–6 examine dimensions of black-Latino relations at the national level using descriptive data and quantitative analysis. In Chapter 7, we consider intergroup relations by focusing on several specific public policies to further examine the idea that policy attributes might generate various types of group relationships, given the ideological and interest factors entailed. These examples are simply meant to illustrate or highlight evidence not readily apparent in other types and dimensions of data in our study. We examine five policies that reflect some of the major topics included in the advocacy group scorecards; indeed, several of these are issues where there is shared salience or overlap in the NAACP and NHLA scorecards. We take these policies to be broadly reflective of black-Latino advocacy group and elite officeholders' preferences. The policy areas are welfare (particularly the 1996 welfare reform legislation); education (the "No Child Left Behind" legislation); Voting Rights (renewal in 2006); Immigration; and the North American and Colombian Free Trade Agreements (NAFTA and CAFTA). Extensive evidence drawing on information from advocacy group proclamations (on websites) and several other sources further suggest an absence of conflict between black and Latino advocacy groups and minority members of Congress as well.

The final chapter (Chapter 8) summarizes the empirical findings and places our questions, evidence, and conclusions in broader theoretical perspective. We seek to emphasize what we have learned about our central dependent variable, the nature of black-Latino relations at the national level, along with the lessons and broader substantive and theoretical implications for thinking about both previous and future research which we think emerge from our study.

Elites and "the Masses": Brief Caveats

Our empirical analyses focus on the behavior of national-level advocacy groups and elected representatives. These advocacy groups and elected representatives are political "elites" and professional political groups and individuals. They are situated at the forefront of national politics and policy and are clearly relevant political actors to examine in terms of intergroup relations. While the importance of mass attitudes is widely, and correctly, recognized and studied, there is broad acknowledgment that elites and "leadership" are also central elements of politics (including American politics), both implicitly and explicitly and including race/ ethnicity scholarship. Furthermore, the importance of elites regarding black-Latino relations has been underscored in recent research (Wallsten and Nteta 2011); however, on the whole, there has been much more study of masses than of elites. Some analysts might question our focus on minority advocacy groups, including this particular set of minority advocacy groups, and the policy issues they emphasize.

An observation, and criticism made by some observers is that groups such as the National Council of La Raza (NCLR), League of United Latin American Citizens (LULAC), NAACP, and others (from which we draw some of our data) are not really "membership" groups; instead, they are said to be organized and run by professionals and a professional elite and, furthermore, have a middle-class bias. Thus, they do not – and cannot, due to their limitations and biases, it is implied – speak for the broader groups and mass populations they allege to represent. That criticism should not to be taken lightly. It should also be kept in perspective, however.

Some of the groups, such as NCLR, have a large number of local chapter affiliates; others, such as the NAACP, have local chapters as well. Aside from that point, leading scholars, including Skocpol (2003), have argued that the decline of mass membership groups and the emergence of professionalized interest groups has been a significant trend, in general, in the United States dating back several decades (cf. Putnam 2000). Skocpol contends and demonstrates, if bemoans, a widespread move from "membership to management in American civic life." Marquez's (1993) depiction of the evolution of LULAC as a political organization (from the 1920s to late 1980s) is broadly consistent with Skocpol's analysis. Yet despite reservations about LULAC's continued relevance, Marquez suggests that the group remains an important part of "the face" of Latino politics (for better or worse). If, for the sake of argument, one concedes that some minority advocacy groups are, indeed, relatively professionalized (and not "membership-based" organizations), they are hardly unique but reflect a national pattern. It thus seems inappropriate to dismiss these minority advocacy groups if they have some of the allegedly problematic attributes. In any case, it is hardly new or unusual that the most activist elements of interest groups come from its more educated, professional strata.

Others have questioned whether the policy preferences asserted by minority advocacy groups match those of the masses they purport to represent. Assessing the consistency of advocacy group positions with mass opinions is not as simple or direct as implied by critics, however. Yet there is solid evidence that minority members of Congress represent their minority constituents better than do white MCs who represent districts with large minority populations (Griffin and Newman 2008; Minta 2011). We maintain that national advocacy groups and elected representatives are important elements of minority politics on the national stage. These elite individuals and organizations extend influence over policies that are of interest to minority citizens, albeit the mass preferences are not unanimous; but the preferences of other "mass" groups "represented" by interest groups are not unanimous, either. The black and Latino elites we examine are at the forefront of policy debates and major sources for advocacy, influence, and representation. Moreover, these elites are directly involved with the policy-making process and attuned to policy implementation and "oversight" (Minta 2011); thus they are arguably the most proximate and appropriate actors to analyze to engage the varied questions we pose. A focus on the national level and on elites (rather than masses, which have received a great deal of research attention) in no way implies that studying the minority group masses and the local level of politics is unimportant or even "less" important. Ours are simply additional, different analytical lenses focused on national politics meant to examine an important set of issues – which have not been studied previously as we do here – from an alternative and complementary approach that moves us toward fuller, more complete understanding.

We begin our investigation by summarizing and assessing the "conventional wisdom" on black-Latino relations, as suggested by previous research, in the next chapter (Chapter 2).

2

What Previous Research Tells Us about Black-Latino Relations

A central question in this book is the nature of black-Latino relations in American national politics. In the evidence we present in later chapters, black-Latino conflict is found to be essentially nonexistent in the arena of national institutions and policy authority; additionally, the evidence regarding national-level elite behavior indicates that intergroup relations are generally marked by "independence" and there is also some indication of comity or cooperation. These findings are more notable when contrasted with the results of several research efforts over the last few decades at the local level, where findings of conflict are not unusual, and signs of tension are also evident (cf. Telles et al. 2011; Nelson and Lavariega Monforti 2005). The purpose of this chapter is to summarize evidence and related theorizing from previous analyses which is relevant, but also stands in contrast to our subsequent detailed examination of national politics. Serving as a "preface" to our later analysis, we describe specific questions that have been studied, show how these studies examine the issue, and identify the forms and variations of intergroup relations. We also consider the causes for the relationships that are claimed since those occur in the urban, local education, and state politics (that is, "subnational") levels, and in mass attitudes research.

The literature discussed in this chapter is comparative *within* particular levels and types of governments. That is, in that research, cities are studied individually (in case studies) but are also frequently compared to other cities, school districts are compared to school districts, and states to states. But analyses attempting to make other comparisons – say, cities to states – are not done here because the different jurisdictional spheres and varied policy and geographic/territorial authority of the two types make such comparisons theoretically and practically inappropriate. The governments at the local and state (and national) levels have different, albeit sometimes overlapping, policy responsibilities and draw primarily on different tax bases; furthermore, cities are technically "creatures of the state." Hence, the absence of research directly comparing these different levels of government is based on a clear recognition that their geographic scope and/or related policy authority makes them incommensurable for many analytical purposes. As strongly emphasized by Peterson (1981) and others, they differ in their essential character, and this has numerous implications. Hence, in our analysis we will *contrast and/or juxtapose,* but we cannot really *compare* across the levels of government on various policy and other dimensions; and we think this may also pertain to black-Latino relations. Nonetheless, we can potentially learn much from the studies, findings, and theoretical claims of the black-Latino relations research at the local and state levels; there are some broad similarities that are relevant for and can be juxtaposed to our inquiry at the national level. Again, however, the differences in the "essential character" of different governments must be recognized. Several themes from the past research are especially noteworthy for present purposes.

Assessments of Latino-black relations in urban government often indicated competition or conflict; that has also been the case regarding research on black-Latino relations in school district politics (cf. Rocha 2007b; Telles et al. 2011; Nelson and Lavariega Monforti 2005). The general pattern is particularly evident where issues or policies have "zero sum" qualities, that is, where the gains of one group come at or are at least perceived to come at a direct cost to the other group (Lavariega Monforti 2005, 252). On the other hand, where policies are seen as less zero sum – where the goals or outcomes of one group may have less negative impact for the other and/or where both groups can benefit simultaneously – less competition is found. Some examples of the latter include minimum wage laws in cities, and student performance on standardized tests in the education arena. However, such instances seem to occur rather infrequently in urban politics, or so the published research implies. These findings are germane to our study because types of policies, themselves associated with the particular level of government involved and (primarily) responsible for them, inform our thinking; also, research on mass attitudes has in some instances found negative feelings between blacks and Latinos, some associated with similar factors.

Patterns vary somewhat depending on several factors that prominently include the specific policy questions probed, and, again whether the policies have either/or consequences for the minority groups. In some instances, when both blacks and Latinos face socioeconomic disadvantage, policy competition occurs; in other cases such shared disadvantage leads to compatibility or cooperation. The somewhat stronger tendency toward competition in local politics (versus national politics) seems at least partly attributable to public policies and/or the particular dimensions of policies faced by minority groups at the local level; these often present constrained, either/or (zero sum) choices when contrasted with the national level, where both/and (or less zero sum) possibilities are more common. Either/or situations seem more likely to lead to conflict. Both/and circumstances are less likely to generate conflict but do not necessarily mean that actual cooperation occurs, though such circumstances may facilitate "independence" and hence mitigate conflict. Another point should be considered, however.

The frequency with which competition or conflict is found in urban politics might be overstated in the urban politics research because that research may (somewhat unconsciously) focus disproportionately on issues where black-Latino conflict is visible, more easy to detect, and/or more likely to begin with. On the other hand, there may well be a significant degree of interminority group cooperation or independence at the local level, but research may not have emphasized, identified, or focused on it adequately, or maybe has not done so "in the right way" analytically (cf. Telles et al. 2011, 13, on both these points). We think more frequent conflict at the local than national level is probably the case. However, we also acknowledge the urban-level findings of conflict may be at least slightly exaggerated, or cooperation and/or independence are understated. This could stem from possible, if inadvertent, selection bias associated with the particular (sets of) cities, the specific questions posed, and the policies examined in the urban politics studies, tilting the research toward considering more visible phenomena and contentious issues rather than others.

Though we summarize a considerable volume of major works in local (and other subnational) politics in this chapter, we do not pretend this review is comprehensive. For example, there have been (at least) two edited volumes that focus directly on black-Latino relations (Telles et al. 2011 and Nelson and Lavariega Monforti 2005); combined, these volumes contain some thirty-plus chapters. Notably, for all their richness and insights, not one of the thirty or so chapters in those two edited volumes address black-Latino relations in national government politics and institutions; this is also largely the case for essentially all the research on the topic of which we are aware. (Furthermore, a substantial portion, arguably the clear majority or more of the chapters in the two volumes, suggest some evidence of conflict or competition). Occasionally we discuss these volumes as a whole and discuss some specific chapters within those volumes. In general, rather than a comprehensive review of the urban, state, and mass attitude research, in this chapter we aim to give a flavor of the questions and major findings of previous studies, highlighting what this evidence tells us about the nature of minority group relations at these levels and policy arenas in the political system. At the same time, we acknowledge that there is additional, extensive scholarship in sociology, psychology, and other disciplines on the topic of black-Latino relations. But our discussion does not address that other literature because our emphasis is on governance, and we wish to avoid straying from those concerns and the evidence most directly relevant to it.

The research approaches and questions in the literature on black-Latino relations at the local (and state) level differ in several ways. One strand focuses on politics and policy in decision-making institutions. Typically, these examine the impact of the size or proportion of blacks and Latinos within a given population (for example, in a city or school district), and/or the impact of black and Latino "descriptive representation" – the presence of elected representatives of black or Latino background – on policy processes and outcomes. Commonly, such studies assess whether larger minority (black or Latino, or sometimes both) populations and their socioeconomic resources are associated with a greater number or percentage of Latinos or blacks holding elected or appointed positions in government. Studies in the genre also examine whether larger minority (black or Latino, or sometimes both) populations, and their socioeconomic resources are associated with not only a greater number or percentage of Latino or black elected officials but further with different public policy outputs or outcomes. The specific policies examined across studies vary somewhat but usually focus on issues thought to be particularly salient to minority group concerns or are generally oriented toward social indicators presumed to be especially important to minority groups, such as government employment. Commonly, a small number and range of policies, for which specific governments – local or school districts or states – have particular aspects of policy authority, are assessed, most often over a limited period of time. Seldom in this research are there specific and/ or detailed references to or analysis of such matters as Latino or black interest group efforts to influence city policies through various means or governmental institutions, or systematic analyses of actual voting or other behaviors of local elected officials are. Links between attributes of the minority population and/or of the composition of city councils (or school boards) and policy outputs or outcomes are most often inferred, but seldom examined or demonstrated directly.

Another body of research has considered the perceptions, attitudes, or opinions of Latinos toward blacks, and vice versa. Questions typically boil down to how favorable or supportive the attitudes of the groups are toward one another, and what explains the attitudes. This research catalogues the attitudinal profiles of blacks and Latinos (regarding each other) and assesses a number of factors (independent variables) that might account for the dispositions identified. An implicit, and probably reasonable, assumption is that the aggregations of individual-level attitudes will have (substantial) implications for intergroup interactions, including the likelihood of group cooperation and/or competition in the political process. And knowing the reasons for and implications of the attitudes presumably helps us understand the particular forces shaping those relations and likely social and political consequences. A related strand of research uses survey data to inquire directly into the (perceived) levels of "competition" or "commonality" of one group toward the other, such as Latinos' perceptions regarding competition or commonality with blacks (see Jones-Correa 2011).

Related, yet distinct research examines the similarities and differences of black and Latino public opinion on various policy *issues*. Here, the assumption is that issue or policy similarity is at least as important as the extent of groups' attitudes toward each other. In short, both of these lines of research place greatest importance on essentially individual-level opinion and perceptions but seldom if ever address actual governmental decision making per se. There is also research on state politics that is relevant and which we consider as part of our discussion of the previous literature aiming to understand it on its own substantive and theoretical terms and ascertain its insights and implications. In any case, carefully understanding the issues engaged in studies of black-Latino relations, and their most prominent findings and theoretical explanations provides an important backdrop to our own analyses. A review of the previous research on local and state governments also shows that the particular sets of questions studied and how they are studied are quite different from what we examine in the empirical Chapters (3–7) that follow. This is in large part because of the differences in the "essential character" of the different levels of government.

Urban Government and Politics

Urban Case Studies

Much of the research on black-Latino relationships and politics/policy has focused on the city or urban level, while other studies address the school district level. The research has employed two major approaches: case studies and quantitative analyses. Browning, Marshall, and Tabb's (1984, hereafter, BMT) studies are the leading examples of the case study research and spawned a number of similar research efforts. These authors came to various important conclusions through their pioneering and influential analysis of the political situation of blacks and of Hispanics and their "struggles for equality" in ten northern California cities as this evolved from the 1960s to the 1980s and beyond. While the two minority groups were generally examined separately, BMT also spoke about coalitional politics. Their discussion noted several cases where blacks and Latinos were not mutually supportive; for instance BMT say that

it would not be accurate to conclude that blacks generally supported the political aspirations of Hispanics. Some black activists regarded Hispanics as whites who were achieving political influence ... on the coattails of the black mobilization movement (1984: 124).

And even when blacks and Latinos supported similar policies and coalitions "relationships between the groups sometimes remained highly competitive." It appears that similar policy preferences did not obviate competition and that the implementation of policies had distributive consequences such that differences remained. Browning, Marshall, and Tabb extended their research over time and fostered and facilitated a number of related studies. Several examples of these related studies can be briefly summarized.

In an assessment of New York City politics, Mollenkopf (2003, 127) claimed "it cannot be taken for granted that blacks and Latinos will find common cause as 'people of color.' When they are after the same turf, as sometimes happens, black and Latino leaders compete directly with each other." Moreover, he further contends that the political cultures, racial identities, and class positions of these groups' electoral constituencies differ significantly. Additionally, Mollenkopf (2005) argued that the situation blacks face in Los Angeles as well as New York is complicated; blacks are in "an ambiguous position" because they are "outside the circle of powerful whites, yet enough of a political establishment to worry about challenges from newer, faster-growing immigrant minority groups"

(Mollenkopf 2005, 3). Latinos are the primary immigrant group to which Mollenkopf referred.

Sonenshein showed that in the 2001 Los Angeles mayoral election minorities "bifurcated into African Americans seeking to hold onto their gains from before, and Latinos playing the role of insurgents shaking up the system" (2003, 72). For other minorities, "tensions with blacks are built around day to day economic and political competition" (Sonenshein 2003a, 345). Both the Mollenkopf and Sonenshein studies underscore that local, "interest-based" politics in zero sum type circumstances engender conflict. As something of a counterpoint to Sonenshein's assertions, in the 2005 mayoral election the level of black support for the winning candidate, a Latino (Antonio Villaraigosa), was considerable. Thus, particular circumstances and dimensions of policies may alter general tendencies but this research implies that local politics frequently presents either/or choices for minority groups (cf. Telles et al. 2011).

In the concluding chapter of an edited volume, Browning, Marshall, and Tabb (2003, 372) suggest that a lesson to be learned from the analyses of a handful of cities is that "forming multiracial coalitions is difficult.... The groups are different in many ways and their entry into political participation inevitably carries a strong commitment to the defense and benefit of the group and an unformed sense of the possibilities of collaboration with other groups." Further, Sonenshein emphasizes that multiracial coalition issues are *not* simply "numerical extensions of the same black-white dynamics that underlie bi-racial coalitions" and which have been the focus of a number of the case study and other research endeavors. Sonenshein (2003a, 353–4) continues: "Latinos and Asian Americans have their own ideologies, interests and internal divisions [and] these groups ... may not have the same goals and objectives as blacks and whites." In somewhat similar fashion, some observers have characterized the instances in which blacks heavily supported Latino candidates, and vice versa, in urban electoral coalitions as unusual, or "outliers" (Kaufmann 2007, 89). All these studies focus on the urban level, of course, and they do not engage the question of whether any of their findings and theoretical explanations also apply in whole or in part at the national level.

Despite the predominance of findings of tensions between blacks and Latinos, there is also evidence indicating instances of mutually supportive behavior. For instance, Browning, Marshall, and Tabb assert, "It is not proving difficult for African-American and Latino [city] council members and for white and Asian members with progressive or lower-income constituencies to pass a living-wage ordinance, which 79 cities have done" (2003, 384). Additionally, there is evidence of similar candidate preferences of blacks and Latinos in some Los Angeles elections (Browning, Marshall, and Tabb 2003, 55), in Denver in elections and public policies over an extended period of time (Hero and Clarke 2003; cf., Barreto 2007; Kaufmann 2003b), and in Chicago in the 1980s in the electoral coalition of Harold Washington (BMT 2003; Pinderhughes 2003). And in voting in San Francisco on referenda issues having to do with such things as the general provision of "jobs, housing, education, and local government services" (de Leon 2003, 181; also see Segura and Fraga 2008), blacks and Latinos have roughly similar preferences. However, whether these similarities remain between the groups when actual policy decisions, implementation, and allocation occur is not clear.

Some substantial portion of the cities and issues examined in the urban politics literature finds conflict, especially in zero sum conditions. But where there are similarities between blacks and Latinos at this level of government regarding certain types of policies, conflict does not seem to occur – as where the gains of one do not come at the cost of the other, for example, support of minimum wage legislation and referenda voting on jobs, housing, and government services. In a general abstract sense this is probably not surprising because of the broad benefits likely to accrue mostly to socioeconomically disadvantaged groups. Whether such agreement is as common in the allocation or implementation stages of policy is, however, not so apparent (cf. BMT 1984, 124). Moreover, the (relative) frequency of one or the other types of policy issues in urban government becomes an important question; this is the case even more so when contrasting urban to national government.

In sum, there are numerous examples of competition, even conflict in the interactions of blacks and Latinos in urban politics, at least as indicated in much of the case study evidence; likewise, there are instances of competition in levels of support for mayors in elections as well as on some issues of day-to-day governance. On the other hand, there are also examples of cooperative relations. Regarding black-Latino relations generally in urban politics, it has been said that "no consensus has been reached on the pattern of relationships," that is, whether they are competitive, cooperative or otherwise (McClain 2006, 757; cf. Jones-Correa 2011). That said, it appears to us that the preponderance of evidence from the case studies – at least on the cities and on the issues studied – is perhaps more suggestive of competition than of independence or cooperation in black-white relations (cf. Kaufmann 2007; Telles et al. 2011;

Nelson and Lavariega Monforti 2005). And other evidence supports this assessment, as we see in other, quantitative, research.

Quantitative Studies of Socioeconomic and Political Cooperation and Competition in Urban Politics

Another approach to assessing black-Latino relations has been analyzing minority groups' relative electoral successes, and some policy outcomes, focusing on socioeconomic data and examining connections to the size of minority populations in a number of cities (rather than single-city case studies). The measures used in these studies consider objective evidence (not survey data based on perceptions) and have included such dependent variables as relative municipal employment rates for minority groups, officeholding in positions such as mayor and representation on city councils, and data on groups' relative socioeconomic status. McClain and Karnig (1990) and McClain (1993) examined municipal employment outcomes for blacks and Hispanics in forty-nine cities with at least 25,000 population and 10 percent black and 10 percent Hispanic populations. One finding was that as black and Hispanic [general] political success increases, political competition may be triggered (McClain and Karnig 1990, 542). In a later study, McClain (1993) found that black and Hispanic municipal employment outcomes are not correlated much. Still, evidence also indicates that competition in municipal employment appears as the size of the black work force increases. Additionally, in cities with black majorities or pluralities, Hispanics seem to fare less well in municipal employment outcomes, while in cities in which Hispanics are a majority or plurality, "the consequences for blacks are more diffuse" (McClain 1993, 399).

In another iteration of this research, McClain (2006) compared the group of cities in the year 2000 from the earlier rounds first examined in 1980 (McClain and Karnig 1990) regarding the political and socioeconomic conditions for blacks and Latinos. We take these findings as broadly illustrative of overall patterns, in part because this is one of the few studies specifically examining black-Latino relations across a number of cities and using directly comparable indicators to assess them. According to McClain, the data "present a very mixed picture" concerning the evidence on socioeconomic and/or political competition or cooperation over the twenty-year period. To place these findings in a context that allows us to discern patterns, we developed a simplified summary of McClain's findings (drawn from data in Tables 2, 3, 4, and 5 in McClain 2006), and we present these in Table 2.1 here. Of the eight data results that involve black-Latino relations in the table, five are negative and

TABLE 2.1. *Simplified Summary Adaptation of McClain (2006) Findings on Intergroup Relations in 49 Cities (2000 Data Only)*

	Black City Council Representation	Latino City Council Representation	Black Mayors	Latino Mayors
% Black population	–	Neg & signfct	–	Not signfct
% Latino population	Neg & signfct	–	Not signfct	–
% White population	Neg & signfct	Neg & signfct	Neg & signfct	Not signfct
% Asian population	Neg & signfct	Neg & signfct	Neg & signfct	Not signfct
% Blacks w/ College degree	–	Not signfct	–	Neg & signfct
% Latinos w/ College degree	Neg & signfct	–	Neg & signfct	–
% Whites w/ College degree	Pos & signfct	Pos & signfct	Pos & signfct	Pos & signfct
% Asian w/ College degree	Not signfct	Neg & signfct	Neg & signfct	Not signfct

Notes: Neg means negative, Pos means Positive, and signfct means relationship was found to be (statistically) significant.

statistically significant (cf. Trounstine and Valdini 2008, 560); the others are not statistically significant negatively or positively (cf. Nelson and Lavariega Monforti 2005). Hence, though the data do not present an entirely clear or consistent picture, there is substantial evidence of competition (or conflict) in these findings and no positive relationships.

School Districts

A large literature examines the education arena of American politics in local school districts. Education is commonly referred to as "a state responsibility, locally administered," meaning that state governments have the primary formal authority for education, though in general they delegate some measure of that authority to local school districts and those districts thus can have much influence over actual policies and implementation. The vast majority of school districts in the United States are single-purpose governments; that is, they have authority only for elementary and secondary education and do not have legal jurisdiction in other policy areas – unlike city and state governments (and, of course, the national government) which are general purpose governments. (The general purposes for which local and state, and the national government have responsibility vary considerably as well, as we emphasize throughout this study.) Among the central issues explored in the school district research are the impacts that smaller versus larger black and Latino populations, the minority groups' socioeconomic resources, and fewer or more Latinos and blacks as school administrators or as teachers have on political and policy outcomes. (The numbers/proportions of Latinos and blacks as school administrators or as teachers have been used as both independent and as dependent variables in these analyses.)

A sizable portion of this research on black and Latino outcomes has examined "second-generation discrimination," which refers to disproportionately poor or unequal treatment or underrepresentation of minority students in schools that had been formally desegregated; that is, there was minority re-segregation *within* schools in various negative ways (Meier and Stewart 1991). One of the earlier studies on this found considerable discrimination toward blacks but higher proportions of black students in schools were associated with less second-generation discrimination against Hispanics. That is, it appears that various actions of school officials (who were largely of white racial background) led to second-generation discrimination that focused more heavily on black students and was lessened for Latino students. It was speculated or inferred (but not examined directly) that this may occur because Hispanics are/ were seen as more similar socially to Anglos than are blacks; Anglos are thus more willing to be supportive of Hispanics than of blacks and to discriminate against the latter (Meier and Stewart 1991, 134–5, 156–7). In short, there was evidence of negative implications for blacks in education relative to Latinos, though the extent of any Latino direct agency, efforts, or responsibility for those consequences was not examined, and is thus not clear. There have been a number of subsequent studies of similar issues.

Meier et al. (2004) examined relations between Latinos and African Americans in 194 multiracial school districts in Texas, assessing several questions: what explains the greater or lesser presence of Latino and black education administrators, the percentage of Latino and black teachers, and, finally, the Latino and black students' pass rates on a particular standardized test (used in Texas schools)? They found that "more African-American administrators are associated with fewer Latino administrators," and "Latino administrators are negatively associated with the percentage of African-American administrators." Additionally, African American school board members are positively associated with more African American administrators, and Latino board members are similarly associated with more Latino administrators. Furthermore, there is evidence of group competition regarding teachers: higher numbers of African American teachers are associated with lower percentages of Latino teachers, and vice versa. Thus, a number of indicators suggest competition (or conflict). On the other hand, when student *performance* – based on pass rates on the standardized test – was examined, there is no evidence of competition. Instead, outcomes are found to be complementary; black students do better on the tests as Latino students do better, and the reverse is also the case.

Reflecting on the different findings on different policy dimensions, Meier et al. distinguished between zero sum outcomes, such as employment and electoral success, and common outcomes as public goods, such as favorable public policy. Competition emerges, they contend, when there is scarcity, and when the focus is on zero sum types of issues, since sharing or log-rolling can not readily accommodate two groups with claims on specific, finite resources, such as seats on the school board, positions as school principal, and government jobs. The likelihood of cooperation increases, however, when political efforts are focused more broadly. Certain policy issues, and outcomes, can conceivably be favorable to both groups and thus lend themselves to complementarity, as with the students' pass rates, in a way that individual employment opportunities, administrative positions, and officeholding outcomes do not, particularly within the relatively narrow policy and geographic arena of local (school district) politics (cf. Rocha 2007a; Segura and Rodrigues 2005).

Though the Meier et al. argument is based on local, specifically school district, politics, the general logic of their argument seems applicable and portable to different levels of government; it may be especially important as policy types vary in some generally consistent pattern. We might therefore anticipate less conflict or competition where the issues at hand are commonly broader, facilitating "sharing or log-rolling" among blacks and Latinos, and less zero sum; this conclusion echoes other studies discussed later in this chapter. Furthermore, if there is a higher proportion or frequency of certain types of policies at one level of government versus another, say, the local versus the national, different politics and (minority) intergroup relations might be expected to emerge.

Urban Education Reform

Yet another vantage point on black-Latino relations is provided in research in multiethnic settings that examined educational policy and governance. In their study of urban education reform – illustrated with evidence from Denver, Los Angeles, San Francisco, and Boston – Clarke et al. (2006) argued that contemporaneous educational problems and proposed reforms that were especially relevant for black-Latino relations had been shaped by political and policy legacies. When court-ordered desegregation ended in the 1990s, opening up some possibility for major reform, new school constituencies of Latino parents often defined "the problem with schools" differently from many African American and Anglo parents; that is, there were different problem definitions though not necessarily ideological differences, per se. Parents from different minority groups had different preferences for policy solutions. The growth and impact of Latinos in urban school districts alone was not sufficient to change local education policies, which highlights the ways existing practices and the policy inclination they privilege are important to understanding black-Latino relations, because standing practices shape preferences and filter ideas. Latinos, as a new school constituency, tended to emphasize achievement goals and also sought to protect cultural heritage through bilingual education and culturally sensitive curricula. It was not that black parents necessarily opposed such reforms; rather, they remained unconvinced that these redesigns served *their* interests (Clarke et al. 2006, especially 10–11).

This study of urban education reform suggests that black-Latino relations were strongly shaped by the lasting effects of past public policies created to address the concerns of one minority group (blacks) at an earlier point in time, and the ideas and understandings those policies imbed, as well as the policy implications that resulted. That is, the legacy made it more difficult, if only indirectly, for the other, new group – in these cases, Latinos – to bring changes they preferred. Under such circumstances, it is hard to characterize black-Latino relation as conflict/cooperation and/or cooperation or even as independence; there may be some of all three at once (cf. Telles et al. 2011). This underscores both the variety and complexity of black-Latino relations, even regarding a very particular type of policy – education, and education *reform*, more specifically.

State Politics and Policy and Black-Latino Relations

Beyond the research in cities and school districts, considering the research on black-Latino relations in American state governments' decision making is an appropriate additional step. The states are, after all, fundamentally important domestic public policy-making institutions, directly and through their significant authority over local governments in a variety of ways. Furthermore, blacks and Latinos tend to be concentrated in roughly a dozen or so states in the South, Southwest, and Northeast, which increases the utility of examining their relations in states. However, there has been very little research on black-Latino relations in the states. Although relevant research is limited in quantity, the states' roles along with our broader analytic strategy indicate that considering black-Latino relations across all governmental levels of the American system makes sense and is essential to our goal of fuller analysis of those relations.

A sizable body of research attests to the ongoing significance of race on welfare policy in the American states, though only one or two studies consider black-Latino relations very directly. One study examined whether states exercised new discretion given by the welfare reform legislation of 1996 to include or exclude immigrants for welfare eligibility (Hero and Preuhs 2007). Specifically investigated were state policy choices regarding (a) whether states decided to make immigrants eligible for welfare benefits (in the first place) and (b), the extent to which the decision to be more or less inclusive of immigrants for welfare eligibility in the first instance may have subsequently affected overall benefit levels offered by states under TANF (Temporary Assistance for Needy Families). It found that states' decisions regarding inclusion are best explained by the extent of urbanization, education, and need, and to a lesser degree, state political ideology – but, interestingly, not the size of black or Latino populations. It also found that welfare benefit levels are reduced in states that adopted more broadly inclusive policies, which presumably benefit a large immigrant population. That is, more extensive inclusion of immigrants for welfare eligibility was associated with lower benefit levels for recipients in general – which would affect *non*-immigrant blacks and Latinos and others, as well as the immigrants who receive welfare. This arguably indicates negative perhaps even conflictual or competitive impacts of immigrant inclusion for blacks and other welfare recipients. As immigrants become potential recipients of aid, blacks – who are disproportionate beneficiaries of welfare assistance since as a group they are disproportionately poor – might face reduced levels of benefits. In short, racial composition did not affect states' decisions on immigrants' eligibility or inclusion but it did affect decisions about actual allocation in ways that could be interpreted as intergroup conflict.

State policy referenda voting data provide another lens on intergroup relations. Hajnal et al. (2002, 170) examined ballot proposition voting in California from the 1970s to 2000 that suggests probably as much difference as similarity between Latinos and blacks on minority focused initiatives, and the variation across the votes again suggests that the nature of the policies at issue matter. Of the six initiatives analyzed, three especially and another one to a lesser degree showed substantial differences in black and Latino preferences. Proposition 187, which concerned the denial of public services to illegal immigrants (in 1994), was supported by 47 percent of blacks but only 23 percent of Hispanics (a twenty-four point difference); Proposition 63, on Official English (or English only, 1986), was supported by 60 percent of blacks and 38 percent of Latinos (twenty-two point difference); and on Proposition 38, which called for English-only ballots, there was a seventeen-point difference. There was an eleven-point spread between blacks and Latinos on a measure limiting bilingual education (Proposition 227, in 1998; 48 to 37 percent, respectively). On the other hand, there was only a seven-point difference on an initiative concerning busing to end segregation (Proposition 21, in 1972), 46 to 39 percent, respectively; and blacks and Latinos were essentially the same on an anti-affirmative action initiative (Proposition 209 in 1996).

The level of disagreement between Latinos and blacks varies fairly dramatically on some issues and it appears to depend on the type of issue, specifically, whether the ostensible consequences of the measures have more of a zero sum, an either/or, or a both/and nature. Policies that seem especially targeted at Latinos are opposed more by Latinos (limiting bilingual education, English only, denial of public services to illegal immigrants) but to a lesser degree by blacks. However, where black and Latino interests are aligned due to the broader implication of the policy to both minorities (for example, affirmative action), the difference in support is modest. Convergence or divergence is influenced by policy content, even as the governmental arena (state-level) is constant for these initiative votes.

State politics research has also looked into whether representation by minority politicians can provide a greater degree of representation for minority interests. Much of the literature on descriptive representation – or black lawmakers representing black constituents or Latino lawmakers representing Latino constituents – suggests that states with more diverse legislatures, those with more descriptive representation of minorities, reflect different policy preferences (Bratton and Haynie 1999; Hicklin and Meier 2008; Owens 2005; Preuhs 2005, 2006; Preuhs and

Juenke 2011; Juenke and Preuhs 2012). The overwhelming affiliation of black and Latino state legislators with the Democratic Party should also be noted because similar party affiliation provides a broader ideological and interest coalition base for advancing policy positions held in common. (This is clearly relevant at the national level though rather more ambiguous and varied in local politics.) What these studies have not addressed, however, is the main concern of the present study, intergroup relations. The evidence that currently exists is insufficient to say much about black-Latino *intergroup* relations in state legislatures, though we can note an analysis that is suggestive in this regard.

One way to assess black and Latino legislators' levels of agreement is to examine the similarity of the two groups' preferences with each other within legislatures. If blacks and Latinos both hold the same general ideological orientations relative to other (white) members of their legislative chambers, then we may be able to infer there is a greater likelihood of legislative agreement; but if the two groups diverge very much, we take this as evidence of a lack of cooperation. Juenke and Preuhs (2009, 2012) created scores for individual state legislators that represent each individual's ideology on a single, liberal-conservative, dimension for the 1999–2000 legislative session. These scores are state legislative equivalents of the well-known NOMINATE scores developed for the study of the U.S. Congress (Poole and Rosenthal 1997). Moreover, because the data used in the study identify black and Latino Democrats, how much these two groups of legislators' ideologies match in a number of state contexts could be examined. Since there is typically a very strong effect of legislators' party affiliation, combined with the fact that there were only a handful of Latino and/or black Republicans in the legislatures included in the dataset, Latino and black Democrats in six states (California, Florida, Illinois, New Jersey, New York, and Texas) were compared. Each of these states has at least a few black *and* Latino legislators and they are also some of the most diverse states in terms of relative largely black and Latino populations; additionally, they are among the largest in overall population and/or percentage of Latinos.

The measure of comparison is the average distance members of each group fall from the median (or mid-point) member of the particular legislative chamber, which allows for meaningful comparison across states. Negative values mean the average black or Latino legislator is more liberal than the median of their respective chambers' members' ideologies. Commonality in ideological positions would be indicated by a positive relationship between the two groups' averages. Figure 2.1, a scatter plot

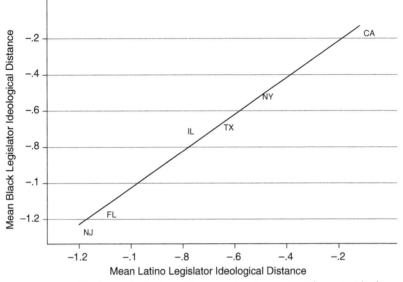

FIGURE 2.1. Black and Latino Democratic State Legislators' Ideological Orientations

of the two groups' ideological distances from their chamber – with black legislative averages (means) in each state placed on the horizontal axis and the Latino legislative averages on the vertical axis – reveals a striking relationship. The six states fall almost directly on the bivariate regression line, demonstrating a very strong correlation between black and Latino voting patterns, and, thus, ideology. In short, Latino and black (Democratic) state legislators have very similar ideological orientations, suggesting at least common inclinations and general policy preferences among these elected officials in state legislatures. Finding this with regard to a broad indicator of ideological similarity among elites (elected representatives) also in state government institutions may not be surprising. Yet it supports our general thesis about the influence of the governmental level examined and of policy issues on intergroup relations, and does so even more when contrasted to differences in black versus Latino voters' inclinations on various California policy referenda, and the conflict identified in urban-level studies.

The foregoing summary of black-Latino relations in urban, school district, and state politics points to frequent instances of intergroup competition, identifies some exceptions to this, and suggests explanations for the various findings that have been advanced by the scholars who undertook the research. Itself informative, this literature also provides guidance and serves as a touchstone for assessing intergroup relations as possibly influenced by the level of government and types of policies. The findings of conflict seem to occur most when the issues involve finite resources and zero sum type situations. On the other hand, where the success or well-being of one group does not necessarily imply detrimental consequences for the other group, conflict is less likely to be manifested, as suggested by findings on local minimum wage legislation and education outcomes, such as test scores. In a similar vein, evidence from the states suggests something roughly similar; blacks' and Latinos' convergence or divergence in voting in California on specific referenda varied with the particular nature of the policy. At the same time, findings based on a broad indicator – black and Latino, compared to nonminority, legislators on state NOMINATE scores (Juenke and Preuhs 2009, 2012) – showed strong general ideological affinity, suggesting how the policies, the actors examined (elite versus masses), and the evidence considered lead to different conclusions.

Mass Attitudes Research

There is another body of research, focused on the individual or micro-level, on mass attitudes or public opinion, which has also often found black-Latino competition or conflict. That research does not examine black-Latino relations within (national) *governing institutions,* as in our subsequent chapters, and as is the case for the urban politics research just discussed; nor does it examine elite behavior, as we do in our own analyses. Nonetheless, the mass attitudes research deserves attention because it is almost certainly the most voluminous (see, for example, Telles et al. 2011; Nelson and Lavariega Monforti 2005) and has played a prominent role in scholarly and popular perceptions of black-Latino relations; it also provides several relevant insights useful for our larger analysis.

Blacks and Latinos' Attitudes toward Each Other
Numerous studies that have appeared in prominent scholarly journals address the attitudes of blacks toward Latinos, and vice versa. (And many other studies have appeared in edited volumes; see Telles et al. 2011; Nelson and Lavariega Monforti 2005). Oliver and Wong (2003) analyzed "inter-group prejudice in multi-ethnic settings," drawing on

1992–94 survey data on whites, blacks, Latinos, and Asians in Atlanta, Boston, and Los Angeles; for present purposes, it should be noted that of these three cities only Los Angeles had particularly large Latino *and* black populations. The core questions examined concerned (a) groups' stereotyping of each other on several dimensions (regarding perceptions of the outgroup's intelligence, self-sufficiency versus welfare dependence, being easy to get along with, and treating other groups equally); (b) perceived competition (whether [i] more good jobs for other groups mean fewer for one's own group, and [ii] whether more influence in local politics for other groups means one's own group will have less influence in local politics); and (c) immigrant threat (asking how much political influence and economic opportunity people of the respondents race would have "if immigration continues at its current rate" (Oliver and Wong 2003, 573, 576). Their general finding was this:

> In multiethnic contexts, the relationship between racial environments and attitudes defy simple formulations. Hostility toward another group is based not simply on the group's size, but on its relative economic position, the historical period, and the contextual unit being measured. (Oliver and Wong 2003, 579)

While in general, racial environment clearly matters (Oliver and Wong 2003, 580), the relationship between the size of the racial outgroup and racial animosity depends on the unit of analysis. Specifically, at the *neighborhood* level more racial diversity is associated with less racial dislike, while at the *metropolitan* area level "diversity corresponds with more racial stereotyping and feelings of competition." And the situation is yet more complex when *economic* context is taken into account. "Blacks in low status neighborhoods have more negative attitudes and perceive more competition with minorities than those in high status neighborhoods." In contrast, Latinos residing in high status neighborhoods have "greater animosity toward minority out-groups (although not toward whites)" (Oliver and Wong 2003, 580; cf. Gay 2006). Their findings also "suggest that proximity to out-groups increases racial conflict [but] only when that proximity is defined relative to a larger geographic area" (Oliver and Wong 2003, 577).

Gay's (2006) study of blacks' attitudes toward Latinos in Los Angeles drew on data similar to that used by Oliver and Wong. One major finding was that the relative economic status of racial groups is an important influence on black attitudes. Gay asserts the importance of socioeconomic conditions and also emphasizes there are two aspects of economic environments, "the material condition of *neighborhoods* and the material conditions of *group life*" (Gay 2006, 984, emphasis added). In contexts where Latinos' group material conditions makes them economically advantaged relative to blacks, blacks are more likely (a) to have negative perceptions of Latinos (regarding intelligence, self-sufficiency, sociability, involvement in drugs and gangs, tendency to be poor, and treatment of outgroups); (b) to be reluctant to extend to Latinos the same policy benefits they themselves have (such as "special job training and educational assistance," and "guarantee special preferences in hiring and promotion"); and (c) to view black and Latino economic and political interests as *in*compatible (regarding whether [i] more good jobs for other groups mean fewer for one's own group and [ii] whether more influence in local politics means one's own group will have less influence in local politics). And, where there are larger economic disadvantages of blacks compared to Latinos, the size of the Latino population may further heighten negative attitudes. Gay concludes that what emerges from her analysis is

> an image of two groups locked in competitive social relations, where tangible signs of greater outgroup advancement are sufficient to amplify fears and activate hostility. Yet just as it is true that Latinos and blacks compete for jobs, educational resources and political power, it is also true that the two groups share similar objective circumstances relative to whites. Competition and commonality may work at cross-purposes in shaping black attitudes toward Latinos: competition may predispose blacks toward negative attitudes; recognition of shared disadvantage relative to whites might encourage a more positive orientation. Perhaps social environments influence black attitudes by privileging one fact of black-Latino relations over the other. (Gay 2006: 995)

Both Gay, and Oliver and Wong point to the importance of social and geographic (i.e., spatial or urban versus metropolitan) context for group-based perceptions between minority groups, and Gay's findings specifically highlight the role of material interests and how competition over jobs and political power can be magnified when socioeconomic gains for one group are viewed as losses for another. Gay's claim, that social environments influence black attitudes by "privileging one fact of black-Latino relations over the other," seem particularly important. We suspect that the social context of intergroup (elite) relations in the broader, national governmental arena, including its distinct role and authority in policies addressing socioeconomic inequality, facilitate "recognition of shared disadvantage" among blacks and Latinos, particularly "relative to whites," at this level. And this might, in turn, encourage "a more positive orientation" to a greater extent than at the narrower, more constrained local level where "competition" is more likely to engender negative attitudes.

Gay is saying that competition leads to negative attitudes and cooperation engenders positive attitudes, and these may (also) vary across context. It's possible the causal arrow between positive/negative attitudes and perceptions of competition/commonality go in the other direction than Gay suggests. More relevant here is that it is also possible that level of government and the associated types of policy at issue are an important aspect of context that affects black-Latino attitudes toward each other.

McClain's survey in the Durham, North Carolina, area (conducted in mid-2003) found that Latinos' stereotypes of blacks are more strongly negative than whites' views of blacks. Specifically, "58.9% of the Latino immigrants ... reported that few or almost no blacks are 'hard working'; approximately one-third (32.5%) of the Latino immigrant respondents reported feeling that few or no blacks 'are easy to get along with'; and slightly more than a majority (57%) of the Latino immigrant respondents reported feeling that few or almost no blacks could be 'trusted'" (2006, 582). And when the survey asked about the groups with which Latinos have the "most" and the "least in common," the overwhelming majority of the "Latino immigrant respondents (78.3%) feel that they have the most in common with whites and the least in common with blacks (52.8%)." More educated Latinos have significantly less negative stereotypes. To the extent Latinos have a stronger sense of group identity with other Latinos (*intra*-Latino linked fate), their negative views of blacks are significantly tempered. In general, McClain et al.'s (2006) results suggest that cooperation between blacks and Latinos may be limited by negative stereotypes of blacks held by Latino immigrants – a group that, in objective socioeconomic terms, may have the most to gain from coalitional behavior.

Kaufmann argues that though both blacks and Latinos are economically disadvantaged relative to whites by certain objective standards, these shared objective conditions are not sufficient to sustain Latino-black coalitions. "Beyond the rational incentives of shared political interest, a sense of shared fate or commonality between members of different groups is essential to building successful coalitions" (Kaufmann 2003a, 200). Kaufmann finds that 75 percent of blacks perceive a "fair amount" or a "lot in common" with Latinos, which is somewhat higher than blacks' sense of commonality with whites (61 percent). On the other hand, among Latinos only 33 percent perceived a "fair amount" or a "lot in common" with blacks, the same percentage of Latinos who said they had a fair amount or a lot in common with whites (Kaufmann 2003a; also see Rodrigues and Segura 2007, 154–5).

Kaufmann explored various factors that might explain Latinos' levels of perceived commonality with blacks and the one that stood out is pan-Latino affinity. As Latinos (of the various nationality backgrounds) indicated a stronger pan-ethnic orientation – saying they have a greater sense of commonality with other Latinos – the more likely they were to *also* perceive commonality with blacks. Kaufmann's findings suggest a more nuanced picture of the potential for black-Latino coalitions, with what may be called a feeling of commonality within a group as a main indicator of the sense of affinity across groups. We suspect sense of commonality would also in general vary between elites and by the level of government. For example, Latinos in Congress years ago created the Hispanic Caucus, and Hispanic is a pan-ethnic term which also implies sense of intragroup commonality; according to Kaufmann's argument, this would also suggest stronger interblack-Latino links at the elite level compared to black-Latino masses emphasized in Kaufmann's and similar studies. Further, the policies or issues at stake, as shaped by the broader geography of politics, would also matter in affecting a sense of shared fate or commonality.

A great deal of other research on black-Latino relations is found in edited book volumes (leading examples include Telles et al. 2011; Nelson and Lavariega Monforti 2005). The studies in those books have on the whole been very thoughtful, well done, and intellectually insightful in a variety of ways and have thus made important contributions to the research. However, those studies draw almost exclusively on survey and/ or ethnographic data and do not examine actual governance and formal decision-making institutions and processes; nor do any of the analyses in those volumes examine the *national* level and its decision-making institutions and processes. For all the value these studies provide, then, they have limits with respect to the major questions of the present analysis.

Over all, the research on mass attitudes clearly has something important to offer for better understanding intergroup relations between blacks and Latinos. Some analysis (Kaufmann 2003a, Gay 2006) suggests that shared low socioeconomic status might be a source of coalition or cooperation between blacks and Latinos; others argue, however, that low socioeconomic conditions, especially when one group is somewhat disadvantaged relative to the other (though still less well-off compared to whites), is likely a source of competition (Gay 2006; McClain et al. 2006; cf. Kaufmann 2007). Perceived competition is most pronounced when the immediate material interests, such as jobs, are at odds and when one group is (or is seen as) disadvantaged relative to the other – in short, more zero sum. These findings are suggested by Gay's (2006) study of Los Angeles blacks and McClain et al.'s (2006) findings regarding Latino immigrants. However, the specific understanding of perceived common-ality, Gay (2006) suggests, is (also) affected by context. If those research perspectives also allow for notions of geographic breadth of authority and associated types of policies as part of the conceptualization of con-text, our speculation about the impact of those actors influencing black-Latino relations at the national level (and contrasted with the local level) dovetails with it quite well.

Voting Patterns and Partisanship

In addition to examining groups' attitudes, other evidence, specifically, the partisan affiliation and the voting patterns of blacks and Latinos in elections, especially city elections involving black and Latino candidates, has been taken as a barometer of cooperation or conflict at the mass level. Nationally, there is a strong tendency of blacks and Latinos (with some exceptions, such as Latinos [Cubans] in Florida for much of the recent past) to disproportionately affiliate with the Democrat Party and vote for candidates of that party. The Democratic affiliation and voting of blacks, though, is stronger than that of Latinos. Because partisan predilections are often interpreted as prima facie evidence of black-Latino similarity or commonality, significant departures from expected patterns are often interpreted to imply conflict.

While there is evidence that black voters have supported Latino can-didates at high levels, and vice versa in urban elections (Hero 1989), there is also ample evidence of black-Latino competition and nonsup-port. For instance, Kaufmann notes city elections in the early 2000s in Miami, New York City, Los Angeles, and Houston in which blacks and Latinos supported different candidates. In two cases, blacks in Miami and Latinos in Houston, each group "abandon[ed] otherwise longstanding Democrat party affiliation patterns to support Republican candidates" (Kaufmann 2003, 200). Barreto's (2007) analysis of mayoral elections with Latino candidates in five major cities reveals mixed results regard-ing the claim that conflict emerges when blacks and Latinos are asked to vote for Latino mayoral candidates. In each of the cities (Los Angeles,

Houston, New York, San Francisco, and Denver), Latinos were more likely to vote for Latino mayoral candidates. In Los Angeles, Houston, and San Francisco, analysis showed that blacks were less likely to support the Latino candidate (after a variety of other factors were controlled), thus showing some evidence of black-Latino conflict. However, analysis showed that in New York, blacks were more likely than others to support the Latino candidate – again, with other factors controlled. This leads Barreto to conclude that while there are instances of both conflict and cooperation on behalf of blacks toward Latino candidates, it is not clear there is a universal intergroup propensity for this in cities' electoral politics. In notable contrast to such views concerning black and Latino support for candidates of the other racial/ethnic group in urban elections, both groups have a history over the last several decades of disproportionately high and consistent support for Democrats in (national) presidential elections.

A study of the voting behavior patterns of Latinos, blacks, Asians, and whites in the 2003 California recall election of the sitting governor and voting for a new governor, with a prominent Latino candidate (Lieutenant Governor Cruz Bustamante) on the ballot, found that Latinos and blacks voted rather similarly to each other, and distinctively different from whites and Asians on the recall and in the gubernatorial election (Segura and Fraga 2008). This pattern was essentially duplicated in voting on a proposition on the ballot at the same time, which sought to make illegal the use of racial and ethnic identifiers and categories by all state agencies and all of California's counties, cities, and school districts. Particularly notable to present purposes is the similar positions of blacks and Latinos on these several issues, and their distinctiveness relative to white and Asian voters.

Similarity/Differences in Group Attitudes about Issues and Policies

Another basis on which black and Latino attitudes are assessed involves each group's attitudes about policy issues. Some research indicates that blacks and Latinos hold similar views on issues such as affirmative action, government health programs, military spending, and the death penalty; moreover, blacks and Latinos are more similar to each other than they are to whites on these and other issues (such as assisted suicide and school vouchers; see Rodrigues and Segura 2007, 157). Along the same lines, a 1999 study notes that Latinos and blacks are similar in their support for the size of government, and differ considerably from whites in that regard (discussed in Kaufmann 2003, 200; also see Bowler and Segura 2012; Hochschild and Rogers 2000). Presumably, greater policy agreement would be associated with greater possibilities for coalition-like behavior, above and beyond what common economic/social circumstances and/or favorable groups' views of one another would predict. These policy issues addressed in such studies are also rather broad and provide a strong basis for interest (and ideological) convergence. Affirmative action, for instance, can help both groups much of the time, often depending on context.

In this research on policy opinions, the salience of the particular policy issues posed to those being surveyed is assumed, and though much of the time the issues selected are indeed plausible in this respect, the assumption is often not examined. It is not clear that these policies hold the same weight in broader political orientations or electoral decisions that may require trade-offs affecting where and when coalitions or conflict will emerge. It could be that though blacks and Latinos have similar opinions on issues of various sorts, if one or the other do not see it as an especially important issue, the implications for disagreement are presumably lessened.

Conclusion

This chapter has reviewed a considerable body of political science literature on black-Latino relations in local (and state) governmental arenas as well as mass attitudes. In our view, the evidence indicates several important points particularly relevant to the present study. First, there is, overall, some amount of evidence suggesting competition or conflict (cf. Telles et al. 2011; Nelson and Lavariega Monforti 2005). And while this seems generally accurate to us, it may be that the degree of competition is overstated and/or the extent of cooperation is understated based on the issues and policies chosen for examination by scholars. Second, the types of issues matters considerably concerning blacks and Latinos in relation to one another, especially regarding whether issues are more zero sum, either/or, or less so; evidence for this is suggested by several urban politics studies (using various methods, case study or quantitative), school district studies, mass attitude, and some state-level studies research (e.g., Hajnal, et al. 2002).

Meier et al. (2004), for example, emphasized differences in intergroup relations when zero sum situations, such as elections to school boards, positions as administrators, and teaching positions – each of which is constrained in the number of positions available – versus broader policy issues, such as students' passage rates on standardized tests, are in question. Furthermore, Gay (2006) notes more positive black attitudes toward issues of equal access for Latinos, such as special job training and education assistance, which are more procedural, versus more negative attitudes on issues that are directly substantive, such as Latinos' inclusion in preferences for affirmative action programs (cf. Canon 1999). The quantitative research by McClain (2006) on black-Latino relations in a number of cities and over a period of time regarding aggregate socioeconomic and political conditions indicates competitive black-Latino relations. The findings of differences between black and Latino voters (masses) on California referenda measures, depending on the specific type of issue, indicates this as well. Yet those findings stand in interesting contrast to the high similarity among black and Latino state legislators (political elites) on broad, ideological indicators (state-level NOMINATE scores; see Juenke and Preuhs 2012).

The analytical focus of our book is on various actions of minority advocacy groups as well as members of Congress (who can be defined as political elites) as major actors in and barometers of the nature of black-Latino relations at the national level. It may be that competition/conflict is less frequent at the national level because of differences in the geographic breadth and the related policy authority and other factors that are different at each level. Yet because of those very differences, differences in the essential character of levels of government (Peterson 1981), we cannot directly assess our claims. It is virtually impossible to find something approaching exactly equivalent policies at the local level and compare them directly with sufficiently similar policies of the national government – precisely *because* of the differences in their geography (scope or sphere), *and* types and range of policy authority, along with institutional and other attributes (such as the role of political parties), make the levels of government incommensurable; we would be comparing apples and oranges at best. Instead, the central thrust of our analysis is to carefully and extensively consider black-Latino intergroup relations at the national level, a novel undertaking, and we do so with a variety of evidence (evidence that would not be applicable or appropriate and does not really exist for local governments because of their differences contrasted with the national level). As we have done in this chapter, we can carefully and extensively summarize the various findings on intergroup relations at the local level, and we can in turn *juxtapose* and/or *contrast* those to what we find at the national level in later chapters, but we cannot directly compare them (Peterson 1981).

While the survey-based studies we examined in this chapter (such as Oliver and Wong 2003; Gay 2006; Kaufmann 2003; McClain et al. 2006) have an individual (micro)-level/attitudinal focus, thus differing considerably from urban government or national *government* analyses, they ultimately give substantial attention to the importance of social context or social structure in shaping attitudes (see especially Oliver and Wong 2003; Gay 2006; cf. Meier et al. 2004). Gay, in particular, attributes an important part of intergroup attitudes to the types of issues at stake. The relative economic situation of one's own group, particularly compared to other (minority) groups, is found to matter considerably in explaining attitudes, particularly black attitudes toward Latinos. Oliver and Wong (2003) suggest that minority groups' attitudes vary by geography, by neighborhood or metro area, and by socioeconomic circumstances; they also differ for blacks and whites versus Latinos and Asians. The size of the other minority group also matters (Gay 2006; McClain 2006) as part of the context.

We believe we contribute to and advance the substantive knowledge of black-Latino relations by providing evidence in our following chapters from within the institutional context of the national government – concerning two major institutions (Congress and the Court), regarding different sets of elite actors (advocacy groups, which are mediating institutions, and members of Congress), and various types of political activity, including participating in congressional hearings, filing amicus briefs, creating legislative scorecards, voting on legislation, and more. In several instances, the data cover an extended period of time (about thirty years). Additionally, we posit theoretical arguments about the importance of distinct geography of interests that concomitantly imply differences in the types of policy authority at the national (versus local/state) level; these differences are, in turn, outgrowths of the institution of American federalism. We suggest the widely recognized importance of the nature of policy issues for the nature of politics (Lowi 1964; Eshbaugh-Soha and Meier 2008) as a possible explanation for the typically nonconflictual relations between Latinos and blacks that we identify at the national level. Institutional context may shape the social contexts and social structures that Gay and others find to be important.

3

Black-Latino Relations in
Congressional Testimony and the Legal Arena

As with American politics in general, black-Latino intergroup relations take place in various arenas in the political system and the groups' interactions might well be affected by, and thus vary, across the different governmental, political, and policy contexts. In Chapter 2, we saw considerable evidence of "conflict" at the urban/local level and in mass attitudes regarding blacks and Latinos. In this chapter, we begin to examine black-Latino relations in a different governmental context – the national level – assessing the relations of black-Latino advocacy groups regarding two major policy-making institutions and certain access points for potential influence. Specifically, we focus on the efforts of black and Latino minority advocacy or interest groups seeking to influence policy in the U.S. Congress and the U.S. Supreme Court. We present evidence that allows us to assess similarities and/or differences in the groups' policy concerns and positions as demonstrated in Congress, specifically, congressional testimony, and in the legal arena, the filing of amicus briefs. These data represent important additional evidence that is valuable for studying and advancing understanding of black and Latino interest group activity and intergroup relations. These questions have not been previously posed, or certainly not posed in quite this way, and this type of evidence has not previously been considered. As will be seen, we do not come across any signs of conflict in the extensive and varied evidence we consider, unlike what is often found in the urban-level data reviewed in the previous chapter. Instead, we see indications of "independence" and of some "cooperation."

Groups advocating for minorities play a role in defining, redefining, and pursuing interests and policies. Organized advocacy groups are presumably important because they are critical actors in conveying or transmitting the concerns and interests of the groups for whom they speak; this is emphasized in pluralist interpretations of American politics. They are thought of as pivotal mediating institutions seeking to affect the agenda and decisions of the formal institutions of governments such as Congress and the Supreme Court. Efforts of this nature include seeking to influence legislation through the presentation of congressional testimony. In another institutional venue, the courts, the filing of amicus curiae (friend of the court) briefs is a common activity used to influence decisions. And in Chapter 4, other advocacy groups' activities such as their ratings of members of Congress are examined. To be sure, groups pursue other methods and venues but the ones noted are the activities addressed in this chapter as part of our broader inquiry into minority intergroup relations.

Despite an upsurge in relevant political science research, many issues concerning black-Latino politics and minority groups generally remain understudied, including the nature and extent of advocacy and/or interest groups' activities. However, these are the groups that take the lead in advocating for minority groups, play a more direct role in shaping policy and policy decisions in national institutions, and presumably provide a pivotal link in the pluralist/interest group model of politics. The nature and the breadth of policy concerns represented by these groups' activities have manifest implications for understanding groups and group interrelations, as developed later in the chapter. The minority advocacy groups that are the focus here include the National Council of La Raza (NCLR), League of United Latin American Citizens (LULAC), the Mexican American Legal Defense Fund (MALDEF), NAACP, and the National Urban League (UL). (Other evidence on the activities of subsets of these groups and others is the basis for analysis in later chapters). These groups have generally been viewed as the most visible, influential, and historically significant organizations advocating for black and Latino interests (as discussed in Chapter 2).

Congressional Testimony

Testifying at congressional hearings is a way for advocacy groups to provide information on specific policy issues as well as broader legislative agendas. It is one of the few venues where advocacy groups are able to engage in a public and direct interaction with lawmakers. While the actual impact of testifying in a congressional hearing is admittedly difficult to assess, for our purposes, the types of issues that advocacy groups address in hearings, as well as the messages regarding cross-group issues in their testimony, offer evidence on black-Latino relations in the legislative decision-making process. By identifying the issues considered in the hearings in which minority advocacy groups participate we gain knowledge about the issues salient to particular minority advocacy groups, and have evidence on which issues are more or less important to black and Latino groups. Analyzing the content of congressional hearing testimony also allows us to ascertain whether the groups have similar positions and to determine the degree to which competition or compatibility or something else is indicated in this part of the national legislative process. This early stage of policy formation is a first element we employ to assess the degree of cooperation, conflict, or independence.

We bring together a wide set of available data on the congressional hearing activities of five advocacy groups (the NAACP, the Urban League, the NCLR, MALDEF, and LULAC). Our initial focus is on the hearings in which each group testified and the topics covered in those hearings. We want to know whether groups testified at the same hearings and which topics were most likely to include black and Latino testimony versus only one group presenting testimony independently. To identify hearings at which these groups testified, we made a search of the Lexis-Nexus' Congressional Universe for hearing testifiers based on the full name or acronym of each group from 1970 to 2000. The hearings identified by this process were then merged through Congressional Information Service hearing identification numbers to the Baumgartner and Jones's *Policy Agendas* congressional hearings database to code topics and subtopics for each hearing. Overall, we were able to identify 781 unique hearings that could be placed in the mutually exclusive categories of (only) *black advocacy groups testified,* (only) *Latino advocacy groups testified,* or *both groups testified.* We thus have a fairly complete set of hearings (over 50,000) spanning thirty years and have been able to identify both the topic of those hearings and whether one of the minority advocacy groups testified at any particular hearing. These data provide an unprecedented look into minority group participation at the early stages of national legislative activity.

There are some limitations of these data for examining black-Latino relations, however. First, hearing testimony is not coded for direction or position. It is difficult to determine whether a group supports or opposes a piece of legislation. It is particularly difficult to code direction of the testimony when a hearing does not address a specific piece of proposed legislation but is instead aimed at fact-finding or the gathering of broad opinions from stakeholders. Thus, we initially present only evidence regarding the types of issues for which minority advocacy groups provide testimony and the types of issues over which they tend to testify at the same hearing. We cannot make inferences about the extent of congruence with this larger set of data but we can identify issues where black or Latino groups alone testify on certain issues, implying they neither compete nor cooperate directly. We attempt to compensate for the limitations of these data by subsequently taking a closer look at a random sample of hearings in which the groups testified. A second caveat regarding this evidence is that participation in congressional hearings is not entirely indicative of minority advocacy groups being proactive on these issues, nor necessarily which ones they find most salient. Congressional actors invite those who testify, often doing so to have inclusion of relevant stakeholders rather than responding to all requests to testify. Thus, there is the possibility of selection bias in gauging the issues that groups find salient through their propensity to testify. (At the same time, however, if congressional actors indeed see the groups as stakeholders, and invite their testimony, it suggests the relevance and/or legitimacy of the group regarding the policies discussed.) These qualifications about the data notwithstanding, the evidence provides useful and at least suggestive information as a first step in and one part of our overall analysis.

To begin, what are the topics considered in the hearings at which minority advocacy groups testify? The frequency distributions of hearings by major topic for each of the six advocacy groups compared to the distribution of all hearings, presented in Table 3.1, are instructive. Several points should be noted. First, each group's testimony departs substantially from the overall distribution of congressional hearings, as confirmed by statistically significant relationships (in chi-square tests for each column, p <.000). The pattern that emerges is not surprising. With the exception of the Urban League, each group tended to testify at hearings on the topics of (1) civil rights, minority rights, and civil liberties; and (2) government operations, which includes appointments and nominations. Special attention is given to basic rights, and on who will hold important government positions. Latino groups also tended to testify at hearings that addressed topics of labor, employment, and immigration to a greater extent than the NAACP and the Urban League. Which of these minority advocacy groups were involved in hearings is also notable in light of the overall distribution of hearings. Of all hearings from 1970 to 2000, only 2.2 percent were on the topic of civil rights, minority rights, and civil liberties.

TABLE 3.1. *Minority Advocacy Participation in Congressional Hearings, 1970–2000, by Topic*

Topic	All Hearings	Black Advocacy Groups		Latino Advocacy Groups		
		NAACP	Urban League	LULAC	MALDEF	NCLR
Macroeconomics	4.4% (2210)	4.0% (16)	9.7% (19)	3.2% (4)	2.2% (3)	5.6% (6)
Civil Rights, Minority Rights, and Civil Liberties	2.2% (1125)	29.0% (115)	8.2% (16)	18.1% (23)	31.9% (44)	17.6% (19)
Health	5.2% (2610)	3.0% (12)	5.1% (10)	1.6% (2)	2.2% (3)	.93% (1)
Agriculture	3.6% (1801)	.25% (1)				
Labor, Employment and Immigration	4.0% (2006)	5.8% (23)	12.8% (25)	25.2% (32)	18.1% (25)	32.4% (35)
Education	2.8% (1403)	7.6% (30)	5.1% (10)	7.9% (10)	10.1% (14)	7.4% (8)
Environment	5.3% (2679)	3.3% (13)	1.5% (3)			
Energy	5.5% (2781)	.76% (3)	2.0% (4)	.79% (1)		.93% (1)
Transportation	4.72% (2372)	.50% (2)	1.53% (3)			
Law, Crime and Family Issues	5.2% (2616)	9.6% (38)	4.6% (9)	3.9% (5)	4.3% (6)	1.9% (2)
Social Welfare	2.9% (1465)	1.8% (7)	15.3% (30)	2.4% (3)	.72% (1)	11.1% (12)
Community Development and Housing Issues	2.3% (1172)	2.8% (11)	7.7% (15)	3.2% (4)		5.6% (6)

(continued)

TABLE 3.1. (*cont.*)

Topic	All Hearings	Black Advocacy Groups		Latino Advocacy Groups		
		NAACP	Urban League	LULAC	MALDEF	NCLR
Banking, Finance, and Domestic Commerce	8.0% (3995)	2.5% (10)	4.6% (9)	1.6% (2)		
Defense	8.1% (4071)	1.3% (5)	2.6% (5)			
Space, Science, Technology and Communications	3.8% (1899)	1.8% (7)	1.0% (2)	.80% (1)		
Foreign Trade	3.2% (1585)	.25% (1)				.93% (1)
International Affairs and Foreign Aid	7.7% (3882)	2.0% (8)	1.5% (3)	4.7% (6)		
Government Operations	13.6% (6813)	22.7% (90)	14.8% (29)	25.2% (32)	29.7% (41)	14.8% (16)
Public Lands and Water Management	7.6% (3796)	1.3% (5)	2.0% (4)	1.6% (2)	.72% (1)	.93% (1)
Total	100% (50281)	100% (397)	100% (196)	100% (127)	100% (138)	100% (108)
χ^2 (p- value)*		1500 (0.000)	272 (0.000)	370 (0.000)	753 (0.000)	434 (0.000)

Note: Column percentages and (cell total) are reported. * Chi-square test and probability levels refer to differences in the distribution for each groups' hearing topics and the overall distribution of hearing topics. Abbreviations: NAACP (National Association for the Advancement of Colored People), LULAC (League of United Latin American Citizens), MALDEF (Mexican American Legal Defense Fund), NCLR (National Council of La Raza).

60

Yet the percentage of these hearings in which the minority groups were involved is considerable. Of hearings devoted to civil and minority rights and civil liberties, the NAACP testified in 29%; the Urban League in 8.2%; LULAC in 18.1%; MALDEF in 31.9 %; and the NCLR in 17.6 %. These minority advocacy groups are clearly much more likely than other groups to focus on these issues, often concerned with procedural equality, than on congressional hearings as a whole.

Offering a broader look at the data, Table 3.2 presents the distribution of hearings in which black, Latino, and black and Latino groups testified by combining the individual groups into three categories. These categories are not mutually exclusive, and thus Table 3.2 provides a sense of what types of issues seem most salient to each of the racial/ethnic groups, as well as the distribution of topics for which both types of groups testified. Overall, the pattern is similar to that found for each individual group, and the statistical significance tests for each column indicate that the patterns indeed diverge from the overall congressional hearing pattern (p <.000 for each column). Civil rights and government operations are the most frequent topics in hearings where black and/or Latino groups both testified. This suggests that, at the very least, those who hold congressional hearings tend to ask at least one advocacy group from each racial group to testify with approximately similar frequency on these specific topics.

To examine how issues influence the propensity of each type of group to testify, and whether they testify at the same hearings, Table 3.3 presents the percentage of cases within each major topic for only black groups testifying, only Latino groups testifying, and when both groups testify. In this way, the impact of issue type on bilateral or individual advocacy can be examined. If interests and issues are shared across all groups, then the distribution of individual advocacy and interracial/ethnic group joint testimony would be expected to remain fairly constant across issues and topics. But that is hardly the case as indicated in Table 3.3 and the statistically significant differences in hearings topics across individual group testimony and joint testimony (chi-square significance p <.000). The rate of joint presentation of testimony is much higher in civil rights, minority rights, and civil liberties than the remaining categories. Government operations and law, crime, and family issues also proved to be topics where there was some, albeit limited, representation from black *and* Latino groups at congressional hearings. Other topics revealed differences between black and Latino groups in the topics of the hearings at which they testified. On the whole, this evidence seems to

TABLE 3.2. *Distribution of Testimony by Black Groups, Latino Groups, and Both, 1970–2000*

Topic	Black Groups	Latino Groups Testified	Black and Latino Groups
Macroeconomics	5.7% (32)	3.9% (12)	1.2% (1)
Civil Rights, Minority Rights, and Civil Liberties	21.7 % (121)	23.5% (72)	43.4% (36)
Health	3.4% (19)	1.6% (5)	1.2% (1)
Agriculture	.18% (1)	0.0 (0)	0.0 (0)
Labor, Employment and Immigration	8.2% (46)	21.9% (67)	12.1% (10)
Education	6.6% (37)	9.2% (28)	3.6% (3)
Environment	2.7% (15)	0.0 (0)	0.0 (0)
Energy	1.3% (7)	.65% (2)	0.0 (0)
Transportation	.90% (5)	0.0 (0)	0.0 (0)
Law, Crime and Family Issues	8.1% (45)	3.3% (10)	7.2% (6)
Social Welfare	6.3% (35)	4.9% (15)	4.8% (4)
Community Development and Housing Issues	4.7% (26)	2.9% (9)	2.4% (2)
Banking, Finance, and Domestic Commerce	3.1% (17)	.65% (2)	0.0 (0)
Defense	1.6% (9)	0.0 (0)	0.0 (0)
Space, Science, Technology and Communications	1.6% (9)	.33% (1)	0.0 (0)
Foreign Trade	.18% (1)	.33% (1)	0.0 (0)
International Affairs and Foreign Aid	1.8% (10)	2.0% (6)	0.0 (0)
Government Operations	20.6% (115)	23.5% (72)	24.1 (10)
Public Lands and Water Management	1.4% (8)	1.3% (4)	0.0 (0)
Total	100% (558)	100% (306)	100% (83)
χ^2(p- value)*	1300 (0.000)	1300 (0.000)	703 (0.000)

* Chi-square test and probability levels refer to differences in the distribution for each group's hearing topics and the overall distribution of hearing topics (see Table 3.1).

suggest relations where there is some commonality on a few topics but considerably more difference or "independence" regarding most others.

Blacks tended to testify on health care issues more than their overall rates would suggest. This is also the case for macroeconomics; law, crime and family; and community development and domestic commerce. Latino groups' testimony tended to be more frequent for hearings on education

TABLE 3.3. *Distribution of Congressional Hearings Testimony WITHIN Major Topics by Black, Latino, and Black and Latino Groups Testifying, 1970–2000*

Topic	Only Black Groups Testified	Only Latino Groups Testified	Black and Latino Groups Testified at Same Hearing	Total
Macroeconomics	72.1% (31)	25.6% (11)	2.3% (1)	100% (43)
Civil Rights, Minority Rights, and Civil Liberties	54.1% (85)	22.9% (36)	22.9% (36)	100% (157)
Health	78.3% (18)	17.4% (4)	4.4% (1)	100% (23)
Agriculture	100% (1)	0.0% (0)	0.0% (0)	100% (1)
Labor, Employment and Immigration	35.0% (36)	55.3% (57)	9.7% (10)	100% (103)
Education	54.8% (34)	40.3% (25)	4.8% (3)	100% (62)
Environment	100% (15)	22.2% (2)	0.00 (0)	100% (15)
Energy	77.8% (7)	0.0% (0)	0.0% (0)	100% (9)
Transportation	100% (5)	8.2% (4)	0.0% (0)	100% (5)
Law, Crime and Family Issues	79.6% (39)	23.9% (11)	12.2% (6)	100% (49)
Social Welfare	67.4% (31)	21.2% (7)	8.7% (4)	100% (46)
Community Development and Housing Issues	72.7% (24)	10.5% (2)	6.1% (2)	100% (33)
Banking, Finance, and Domestic Commerce	89.5% (17)	0.0% (0)	0.0% (0)	100% (19)
Defense	100% (9)	0.0% (0)	0.0% (0)	100% (9)
Space, Science, Technology and Communications	90.0 (9)	10.0 (1)	0.0% (0)	100% (10)
Foreign Trade	50.0% (1)	50.0% (1)	0.0% (0)	100% (2)
International Affairs and Foreign Aid	62.5% (10)	37.5% (6)	0.0% (0)	100% (16)
Government Operations	56.9% (95)	31.1% (52)	12.0% (20)	100% (167)
Public Lands and Water Management	66.7% (8)	33.3% (4)	0.00 (0)	100% (12)
All Topics	60.8% (475)	28.6% (223)	10.6% (83)	100% (781)

$\chi^2 = 124$, p < 0.000

and labor, employment, and immigration. Other categories had such few cases where either a black or Latino group testified that trying to draw even tentative conclusions is ill-advised. There is, then, a good deal of variation across issues in terms of the propensity of black and Latino groups to testify at specific hearings, suggesting that the particular interests and/ or expertise of these groups may be as or more important a factor than an underlying ideological orientation toward civil and minority rights.

To further examine whether variation in minority group advocacy is to some extent driven by the ostensibly distinct interests of the respective constituencies of black and Latino advocacy groups, a purposive sample of more specific illustrative subtopics is presented in Table 3.4. Since a general orientation toward congressional testimony on topics of civil rights could be explained by either interests or cooperative ideological motivations, examining the subtopics provides more detailed evidence about patterns of black and Latino groups' testimony. The table presents the within-subtopic variation in the frequency of testimony alone or with the other racial/ethnic groups for seven subtopics. The cell entries in bold indicate that the within-subtopic percentage of cases is higher than the overall percentage of cases falling in one of the three mutually exclusive categories, which gives a rough indication of whether the subtopic tended to be one of black interest, of Latino interest, or of shared interest (i.e., both testified at the same hearing). Statistically, the cross-tabulation is significant (chi-square significance p <.000) and the lambda coefficient suggests that the categories explain about 23 percent of the variation in patterns of testimony. Also note that while the small number of hearings in some topics precludes a longitudinal perspective for all hearings in the sample, we can examine the propensity for black, Latino, or both advocacy groups to testify on each illustrative subtopic across three decades (1970s, 1980s, and 1990s). There is no statistically significant difference in the pattern within each subtopic across decades (chi-square p <.05). At least within this set of issues, the minority advocacy groups tended to testify in the same way across the time periods of the dataset, suggesting temporal continuity.

The relationships in Table 3.4 between issues and the frequency of black and Latino groups to testify alone or at the same hearing suggest that the specific interests of groups tend to lead to different priorities or areas of salience. Two subtopics, ethnic minority and racial group discrimination and nominations and appointments, tended to have a high degree of individual and combined group testimony, indicating that both groups are broadly interested in these topics. But at the same time, the

TABLE 3.4. *Distribution of Hearings WITHIN Selected Subtopics by Black, Latino, and Black and Latino Groups Testifying, 1970–2000*

Topic	Only Black Groups Testified	Only Latino Groups Testified	Black and Latino Groups Testified at Same Hearing	Total
Ethnic Minority and Racial Group Discrimination	55.1% (43)	28.2% (22)	16.7% (13)	100% (78)
General Civil Rights	48.9% (22)	15.6% (7)	**35.6% (16)**	100% (45)
Voting Rights and Issues	45.0 (9)	20.0 (4)	**35.0% (7)**	100% (20)
Census	38.2% (13)	**42.1% (15)**	17.7% (6)	100% (34)
Nominations and Appointments	**56.4% (31)**	29.1% (16)	14.6% (8)	100% (55)
Immigration and Refugee Issues	4.2% (2)	**79.2% (38)**	16.7% (8)	100% (48)
District of Columbia	**77.8% (7)**	22.2% (2)	0.0% (0)	100% (9)
All Above Topics	43.94% (127)	35.99% (104)	20.07% (58)	100% (289)

$\chi^2 = 70$ (p < 0.000); Cramer's V =.35; Lambda =.23

Note: **Bold** indicates within percentage for the subtopic is notably above within of all topics.

groups' participation via testimony does not consistently suggest independence or cooperation. General civil rights and voting rights issues tend to elicit testimony by both black and Latino groups at the same hearings, with over 35 percent of hearings on these issues having both black and Latino groups testify, compared to the overall average of 20 percent of these subtopic hearings where both groups testified. A few subtopics are notable in that they are more likely to have either a black or Latino advocacy group testify, but not both. Latino groups are more likely to testify by themselves at hearings on census issues and immigration and refugee issues, which is not surprising. But the lack of black advocacy group participation, particularly on immigration issues, does suggest that broad black-Latino relations are nonconflictual rather than broadly cooperative. A similar type of pattern of minority group-specific testimony is found in District of Columbia issues for black groups. While only nine hearings on District of Columbia issues were held between 1970 and 2000 where one or both types of groups testified, seven of those hearings (about 78 percent) had only black advocacy groups testify. Hearings on the District of Columbia are dominated by black advocacy group testimony, which is not surprising given the large concentration of black residents and thus black advocacy group constituents in that area. But the high incidence of black testimony at these types of hearings underlines the point that not all issues are equal when it comes to group decisions to testify, or more likely, of congressional perceptions or recognition of who are seen as important stakeholders.

The analysis of congressional testimony thus far highlights some important aspects of intergroup minority advocacy (certain data limitations notwithstanding). The results suggest that there is a considerable degree of variation in the types of issues on which minority advocacy groups testify. If a reasonable measure of issue salience for these groups is the degree to which their testimony is distributed across issues, then we can say that these groups tend to find civil rights and minority rights, which are broader or more universal issues, the most salient relative to other topics. However, they also vary in the salience of other issues. Issues that are ostensibly more specific to black or to Latino concerns tend to in fact receive a higher degree of attention than the general civil rights issues. Nevertheless, it is important to note that when one group or the other is clearly more involved in testimony in particular areas, the groups are participating in policy discussions on their own, suggesting independence but – and probably most important to contrasting national and local intergroup relations – no indication of "conflict" (though without apparent direct "cooperation").

As acknowledged earlier, we cannot evaluate issue congruence, or the taking of the same position, simply from the fact that black and Latino groups testified at the same hearing. Nor can we conclude that the issues and interests are not shared if groups testified in separate hearings. To deal with these limitations and address the positions of the groups' testimony we drew a random sample of seventy-five hearings at which a black group, a Latino group, or both groups testified from the 781 total hearings within our larger sample. Of these randomly selected cases, we were then able to code seventy-three for the general nature of, and arguments presented in, the testimony and whether the groups mentioned each other, the other racial/ethnic group broadly, or minority issues generally. From this coding, we are able to develop a bit more information regarding the intergroup relations that occur in these hearings.

In the seventy-three hearings coded, only black groups testified in thirty-six hearings (49 percent of the sample), only Latino groups testified in twenty-eight hearings (38 percent of the sample), and advocacy organizations representing both groups testified in nine hearings (12 percent of the sample). In the random sample with data on which groups testified there is a slightly higher proportion of hearings with only Latino groups testifying and of hearings in which both groups testified than was found in the overall sample (reported earlier). In the overall sample, Latinos testified in about 29 percent of the hearings, and both groups testified in about 10.6 percent of the hearings. The distribution of issues was similar to the larger sample, but the low number of hearings in some issue areas means that variation from the larger sample is expected. For our purposes, however, the smaller sample provides a reasonable basis for investigating the substance of testimony regarding intergroup relations.

One way to assess the degree of cross-group support for issues is whether groups mentioned other advocacy groups or other minority groups in presenting their testimony. While general direction is still difficult to evaluate for this size sample, the mention of other minority groups as being affected by, or holding interests in, the issue discussed can be a measure of the degree to which narrow interests or broader interests are used as supporting arguments and the basis for the advocacy groups' positions. Table 3.5 shows the degree to which advocacy groups mentioned other groups in their congressional testimony. The rows represent the percentage (and number) of hearings in which black groups only, Latino groups only, and both groups mentioned the other minority groups' advocacy organizations specifically (for instance the NAACP mentioning NHLA), the other minority group (such as the NAACP mentioning Latinos, or the NCLR mentioning blacks), and the percentage of hearings in which general references were made to other minority groups in addition to blacks or Latinos. Since each of these may have occurred in the same hearings, the columns do not sum to 100 percent.

The table indicates that mentioning other groups or advocacy organizations is fairly consistent by both black and Latino organizations, but the mention of other groups is less frequent when testifying alone than when both groups testify. Mentioning other minority groups or groups other than blacks or Latinos was most pronounced when both groups testified. For instance, in two-thirds of the hearings in which both groups testified, other minority groups were mentioned. This compares to between one-third and one-tenth of hearings for black-only and for Latino-only participation, respectively. Nevertheless, black and Latino groups, whether testifying alone or together, did mention the other group in a fair amount of hearings, albeit less than half generally. It is thus reasonable to

TABLE 3.5. *Mention of "Other" Minority Groups by Minority Advocacy Groups in Congressional Hearings Testimony*

	Black Group(s) Testifying	Latino Group(s) Testifying	Both Black and Latino Groups Testifying
Testimony Mentioning Other Advocacy Group	13.9% (5)	21.4% (6)	22.2% (2)
Testimony Mentioning Other Minority Group Generally	13.9% (5)	17.9% (5)	22.2% (2)
Testimony Mentioning Other Minorities	36.1% (13)	10.7% (3)	66.7% (6)
Cases	36	28	9

Note: Cells contain the percentage and number in parentheses based on the total cases for type of hearing. Categories are not mutually exclusive, and thus row totals and percentages may not sum to 100%.

conclude that groups tended to focus on their own group's interests, but also referred to the situation of the other group to support their position in a consistent, but limited, manner. This pattern reflects a general pattern of independence with a limited degree of cross-group recognition.

A second issue is whether black and Latino groups share the same position on the issue when testifying in congressional hearings. As we noted, determining this is a somewhat difficult task as the hearings can span multiple dimensions and groups can pursue different lines of argumentation on a single topic. However, recognizing this limitation, the nine hearings in which both groups testified were examined for broad indicators of conflict or opposing viewpoints. In each case, the general positions of the advocacy groups were compatible. The testimony of black and Latino groups at the same hearing appear to signify a high degree of cooperation and mutual interests. For instance, both groups testified in favor of stricter enforcement of the Fair Housing Act's provisions. Black and Latino groups also shared opposition to a multiracial category in the U.S. census while supporting the use of statistical sampling techniques. This further supports the contention that these groups are recognized as important stakeholders in congressional hearings in the issue under consideration, and also that these groups have similar positions on those issues. Again, we see no indication of conflict here, and there are suggestions of independent and some cooperative dispositions between the two groups.

Minority Advocacy Group Activities in the Legal Process: Supreme Court Amicus Briefs

Participation in the legal arena through judicial advocacy is a long-standing method and access point that minority interest groups use to signal their policy positions and seek to influence public policy, particularly when other venues are adverse or nonresponsive to minority interests. The 1954 *Brown v. Board of Education* case is perhaps the most obvious example, yet numerous other cases at all levels of the judicial process hold broad implications for minority groups throughout the country. Here, we examine these potential points of influence by focusing on cases filed with the U.S. Supreme Court from 1974 to 2004 for which an amicus curiae, or friend of the court, brief was filed by black and Latino advocacy groups. Amicus briefs state the positions of the groups on the case in question, and attempt to both inform the court of pertinent legal (and political and social) aspects of the case and persuade the court to adopt the group's position. As such, they are essentially substantial policy statements and provide insight about the issues before the court that groups find salient and, at the same time, provide evidence that helps us assess whether groups hold similar positions on the issues. The finding that emerges in the following analysis – no evidence of conflict whatsoever – is striking and consistent with those indicated in our analysis of congressional testimony.

As with the analysis of congressional hearings, we focus on a set of prominent advocacy groups. Specifically, black advocacy groups include the NAACP and the Urban League; Latino advocacy groups included the NCLR, LULAC, and MALDEF. The first step is to examine the cases for which briefs were filed and the degree of overlap in salience, and then subsequently examine the congruence in general positions regarding the preferred direction of the decision. We also examine five cases more closely for which both black and Latino advocacy groups filed briefs to illustrate and shed some light on what drives their mutual positions.

Using the full names of the groups and their acronyms as the search terms, we began the analysis by identifying cases through a Lexis-Nexis search in which one or more of the groups filed amicus briefs. The search for amicus briefs from 1974 to 2004 yielded 270 instances where these five groups, individually or jointly, filed briefs, 147 cases where at least one black advocacy group (NAACP and the Urban League) signed on to a brief, eighty cases where at least one Latino group submitted a brief, and forty-three cases where both black and Latino groups filed briefs; note that these totals are not mutually exclusive. In all, 184 unique cases fell into the mutually exclusive categories of black advocacy group amicus cases, Latino advocacy group amicus cases, or black and Latino advocacy group amicus cases. The last category included any case for which at least one black and one Latino group filed a brief.

To identify the issues represented by these briefs, we drew on the widely used coding framework from Spaeth's Supreme Court Database (Spaeth 2005) in which one or more of the groups filed amicus briefs. (Our data-set extends beyond the 1998 end year of the Spaeth database available at the time of coding; we applied the same coding scheme as Spaeth to the post-1998 data to maintain consistency throughout the time period.) While the groups varied in the number of briefs filed overall, ranging from twelve for LULAC to 143 from the NAACP, there is actually a considerable degree of consistency in the types of cases for which the groups filed amicus briefs. The most frequent issue for each group fell in the category of civil rights. Even with the most cases, and not surprisingly the broadest set of issues addressed, the NAACP filed more than 57 percent of its amicus briefs for cases within the civil rights category. The remainder of the minority advocacy groups filed an even larger percentage of their briefs within this category. In terms of broad categories, then, this initial slice of evidence suggests that minority advocacy groups share a general orientation toward intervention in Supreme Court cases on issues of civil rights. This is hardly an unexpected finding, but it does confirm a general consistency in the types of issues in which minority advocacy groups engage in the judicial process. Only the Urban League's distribution was significantly different from the set of cases included in the sample (chi-square p <.012). In general, then, the groups tended to submit briefs on the same types of issues.

While minority advocacy groups are inclined to be involved in the judicial process on the same types of issues, suggesting general commonality of concerns, the core questions of our study regarding group competition or conflict, independence, and cooperation remain. If groups identify the same types of issues as important, do they tend to take the same or opposing positions, or simply pursue different cases independently on their own? Given the variation in the number of cases in which groups filed amicus briefs, we focus the remainder of the analysis of Supreme Court briefs on the black, Latino, and both Latino and black amicus categories as described earlier. Again, these unique categories are mutually exclusive and thus capture the tendency to engage in the same cases or pursue different cases across racial/ethnic minority advocacy groups.

Filing a brief for the same case is not necessarily evidence of cooper-ation. Our unit of analysis is the case, and thus black and Latino groups might be regularly filing briefs on opposing sides of the case. To evaluate whether black and Latino groups are on the same side in the same case, for each case and each group we coded whether the brief was filed on behalf of the respondent or on behalf of the petitioner. Our findings are striking in that *there were no instances of black and Latino groups sup-porting opposing sides.* Based on these data there is simply no evidence of conflict or competition. When black and Latino groups file amicus briefs for the same case, they are apparently always engaging in at least paral-lel or minimally cooperative activities. This key finding indicates that in the realm of Supreme Court advocacy, minority advocacy groups either cooperate by signing on to briefs for the same side, or engage cases on their own.

Given this notable absence of competition, the next question is how much do different issues elicit cooperative or independent activity? To find out, we return to the mutually exclusive categories of black, Latino, or both groups filing briefs and examine the within-topic variation in cooperation when at least one group filed a brief. Table 3.6 presents these results for all issue categories by showing the percentage of each group's filings that were devoted to the range of categories included in our sample of cases. There were 104 cases of black groups submitting amicus briefs without a Latino group also submitting a brief; Latino groups submitted briefs on their own for thirty-seven cases. There were forty-three cases in which at least one black and one Latino group submitted amicus briefs. Thus, about 23.4 percent of the cases for which at least one black or one Latino group submitted amicus briefs are points of cross-racial/ethnic cooperation. While we have no general basis for comparison to judge the magnitude of this level of cooperation, it is about double the rate of commonality for all the hearings in our congressional hearing dataset. Thus, this finding certainly undermines claims of some who suggest that multiracial/ethnic conflict is common.

Does the degree of interracial/ethnic minority advocacy group coop-eration vary by topic? Comparing the percentage of cooperative cases within each major issue category (see Table 3.6) shows clearly that some issues lend themselves to agreement more than do others. Civil rights, privacy, unions, and judicial power all have higher than average percent-ages of cases that suggest cooperation. However, given the low num-ber falling outside of civil rights cases, it is not feasible to infer any real degree of independent versus cooperative dispositions in these realms;

TABLE 3.6. *Distribution of Amicus Curiae Briefs, Percentage and Cases WITHIN Major Issues by Black, Latino, and Black and Latino Filings, 1974–2004*

Issue	Black Amicus	Latino Amicus	Black & Latino Cooperation	Row Total
Criminal Procedure	76.9% (20)	23.1% (6)	0.0% (0)	100% (26)
Civil Rights	50.5% (50)	16.2% (16)	33.3% (33)	100% (99)
1st Amendment	55.6% (5)	33.3% (3)	11.1% (1)	100% (9)
Due Process	33.3% (1)	66.7% (2)	0.0% (0)	100% (3)
Privacy	57.1% (4)	14.3% (1)	28.6% (2)	100% (7)
Attorneys	56.3% (9)	31.3% (5)	12.5% (2)	100% (16)
Unions	50.0% (1)	0.0% (0)	50.0% (1)	100% (2)
Economic Activity	100.0% (3)	0.0% (0)	0.0% (0)	100% (3)
Judicial Power	50.0% (8)	25.0% (4)	25.0% (4)	100% (16)
Federalism	100.0% (1)	0.0% (0)	0.0% (0)	100% (1)
Federal Taxation/ Misc.	100.0% (2)	0.0% (0)	0.0% (0)	100% (2)
All Topics	(56.5%) (104)	(20.1%) (37)	(23.4%) (43)	100% (184)

$$\chi^2 = 27.26 \ (p < 0.202)$$

indeed, the differences are not statistically significant. At the same time, it can be noted that among criminal procedure cases, there were no incidences of black and Latino cooperation, suggesting that on these types of cases advocacy groups tend toward independent rather than cooperative advocacy.

A theme of our study is understanding the degree to which general interests and/or more narrow interests affect minority advocacy group activities. Again, given the small number of cases outside the civil rights categories (see Table 3.6), we are not be able to glean much from simply asserting that civil rights are broad issues and that the rest are narrow interest-based activities. To try to examine the potential for interests to form the base for amicus filings, our analysis turns to the sub-issues within the civil rights categories. Our assumption is that if an underlying general orientation toward civil rights drives minority advocacy group activities, we would expect to see a relatively uniform distribution of involvement across the subcategories of civil rights cases since all civil rights issues ought to be of concern if ideological orientations to equality were presumably driving a group's behavior. However, if there are distinct differences in participation regarding black and Latino interests but few instances of cooperation otherwise, we might surmise that at least some of the activity is driven by group-specific interests and concerns. Each group essentially would be choosing to engage in Supreme Court cases that are important to them without effort exerted to promote "other" groups' interests. And again, because civil rights cases are really the only cases with significant participation, we focus on this subgroup for our analysis. It is, also, a strong test for the role of "interests" since this is an area where broader ideological goals ought to be shared in the first place.

Table 3.7 provides the "within civil rights" sub-issue percentages of black amicus, Latino amicus, and black and Latino cooperation cases showing how the groups' briefs were distributed across each sub-issue. We can compare the percentages across groups (within each sub-issue) to evaluate the relative emphasis each group placed on the issue. First, note that the variation across sub-issues is significant (chi-square p <.000), and thus there is a difference in the sub-issues in terms of the type of group and level of engagement. The sub-issues eliciting most cooperative activity are affirmative action (80 percent of cases had amicus curiae briefs filed by both black and Latino groups), reapportionment (57.1 percent filed by both black and Latino groups), and employment discrimination (47.4 percent filed by both black and Latino groups). It is also notable that a very small percentage of cases in each of these categories are characterized by individual behavior, where black or Latino groups filed briefs, but not both. In fact, in none of the reapportionment or affirmative action cases did Latino groups file amicus briefs without a black group. And in only 20 percent of cases regarding affirmative action did black advocacy groups file briefs without Latino groups. The points of cooperation, in many ways, seem to occur where ideology is prominent and overlaps with interests, consistent with our expectations. These results, however, need to be compared to the rate of cooperation on other sub-issues.

Overall, while the sheer incidence of cases in other sub-issues is fairly small, and thus caution is essential in drawing inferences about particular sub-issues, the rate of cooperation is relatively lower in all other sub-issues. In the fifty-eight civil rights cases falling outside the sub-issues of employment discrimination, affirmative action and reapportionment, only seven, or 12 percent, had amicus briefs filed on their behalf by both Latino and black advocacy groups, a rate much lower than the overall

TABLE 3.7. *Distribution of Amicus Curiae Briefs WITHIN Civil Rights Issues by Black, Latino, and Black and Latino Filings, 1974–2004*

Civil Rights Issue	Black Amicus	Latino Amicus	Black & Latino Cooperation	Row Total
Voting	100% (4)	0.0% (0)	0.0% (0)	100% (4)
Voting Rights Act of 1965	50.0% (4)	50.0% (4)	0.0% (0)	100% (8)
Desegregation: Excluding Schools	85.7% (6)	14.3% (1)	0.0% (0)	100% (7)
School Desegregation	66.7% (6)	11.1% (1)	22.2% (2)	100% (9)
Employment Discrimination	47.4% (9)	5.3% (1)	47.4% (9)	100% (19)
Affirmative Action	20.0% (3)	0.0% (0)	80.0% (12)	100% (15)
Reapportionment	42.9% (3)	0.0% (0)	57.1% (4)	100% (7)
Deportation	25.0% (1)	50.0% (2)	25.0% (1)	100% (4)
Employment of Aliens	0.0% (0)	100% (2)	0.0% (0)	100% (2)
Sex Discrimination: Excluding Employment	50.0% (3)	33.3% (2)	16.7% (1)	100% (6)
Sex Discrimination in Employment	50.0% (3)	16.7% (1)	33.3% (2)	100% (6)
Poverty Law	0.0% (0)	100% (1)	0.0% (0)	100% (1)
Handicapped	100% (1)	0.0% (0)	0.0% (0)	100% (1)
Indigents: Counsel Appt	100% (1)	0.0% (0)	0.0% (0)	100% (1)
Liability	75.0 % (6)	12.5% (1)	12.5% (1)	100% (8)
Misc	0.0% (0)	0.0% (0)	100.0% (1)	100.0% (2)
All Civil Rights Cases	(51.5%) (50)	(16.2%) (16)	(33.33%) (33)	100% (99)

$\chi^2 = 63.82$ (p < 0.000); Cramer's V =.57

rate of 33.3 percent for all civil rights cases. This suggests independence on these issues due to a lack of overlapping concern but lacking a zero sum quality. A few notable instances that point to group-specific, perhaps interest-oriented, behavior are that only Latino groups filed amicus briefs for employment of aliens cases; 85.7 percent of the desegregation (excluding schools) cases had amicus briefs filed only by black groups; and a majority of cases addressing school desegregation were filed by black groups.

Other factors besides a simple pursuit of interests may help explain variation in rates of cooperation. One may be the timing of the cases and the asymmetrical distribution of resources available to the groups during the time period that key sub-issues were decided by the court. For instance, Latino groups, other than MALDEF, were not as involved early in our sample period as was the NAACP, and thus cases of school deseg-regation, which were prominent in the 1970s and 1980s, may not have been addressed by Latino groups due to a lack of available resources. Nevertheless, MALDEF was very active during this period, and since desegregation orders generally dealt with black students, it is not unrea-sonable that black interests (and a lack of Latino interest group activity) led to rates that were somewhat lower in these cases relative to affirma-tive action cases (see, however, Clarke et al., 2006). Other evidence, such as the absence of any black groups filing an amicus brief on employment of aliens cases, also suggests that interests tend not to be overridden by broad ideological orientations or membership in civil rights coalitions (or that there may be group specialization and/or resource constraints). To assess the possibility of time dependence in cooperative activity, we examined the black, Latino, or both amicus brief filings categories in pre-1990 and post-1990 time periods to see whether there were dis-tinct changes in the level of cooperation over time. The pre-1990 period included eighty-seven of the cases and the post-1990 category included ninety-seven cases from our sample. There was no significant difference in the distribution across these time periods (chi-square p <.45). In short, while some differences in issues emerge over time, there seems to be little difference over time in the propensity of black and Latino racial/ethnic minority advocacy groups to cooperate in amicus filings for particular issue areas.

A Closer Look at Amicus Briefs: Six Illustrative Cases

The analysis presented so far provides fairly persuasive evidence that when black and Latino advocacy groups are involved in Supreme Court cases, the issues involve overlapping interests and ideologies. Cases involving affirmative action, employment discrimination, and legislative redistricting are prominent examples of both high rates of cooperation and a clear overlap of interests. While such an analysis provides important insights, particularly in terms of the complete lack of black and Latino groups taking opposing positions on cases heard by the Supreme Court, understanding how groups arrive at their positions cannot be detected by such an analysis. It may be, for instance, that similar positions arise from very different reasons. And if this is the case, then the congruence in positions found in the analysis may not reflect "cooperation" or overlap in a meaningful way. Rather, these groups may have essentially arrived at the same conclusion by advocating their own but different interests and goals. If this is the case, then we ought to characterize congruence as more in line with independence than with cooperation.

To delve more deeply into the reasoning behind the positions taken in amicus filings, we provide some more specific details about six relatively high profile cases in which both black and Latino groups filed an amicus brief either separately or jointly. These cases, while not intended as a comprehensive reflection of all the cases used in our quantitative analysis, do serve to illustrate that while there are some distinct group-specific bases for reaching similar positions, in most cases a broader ideological argument is present. And, to some degree, even the specific interest-based types of arguments are very similar.

We selected the six cases to reflect a possible range of issues – from those that are clearly specific to the interests of minority communities to broader ideological cases that have little direct and immediate impact on the constituents of minority advocacy groups. These six cases are *Gratz v. Bollinger* (2003), *Romer v. Evans* (1996), *Oklahoma City Schools v. Robert* (1991), *U.S. Department of Commerce v. U.S. House of Representatives* (1999), *Wards Cove Packing Co. v. Atonio* (1989), and *Wygant v. Jackson Board of Education* (1986). We use the cases as a way to compare and contrast the central arguments brought to the court by black and Latino advocacy groups and to illustrate how the central arguments fit within the context of ideational arguments about general equality and group-specific interests. A summary of major points of our analysis is presented in Table 3.8, which reports the groups that submitted each brief, whether they filed the briefs separately or jointly, and their major arguments in the order that they were presented in the brief. As the table indicates, there is a significant amount of overlap in the reasoning for each group's positions even outside of the case where black and Latino groups jointly filed the brief. The next section summarizes each case and the groups' positions.

TABLE 3.8. *Description of Arguments Presented in Amicus Briefs by Black and Latino Advocacy Groups for Six Illustrative Cases*

Case	Group	Specific Reference Made to Other Group	Which Group Listed First on Brief	Priority of Reasoning
Gratz v. Bollinger, 539 U.S. 244 (2003)	NAACP	None	Own Brief	State has compelling interest to eradicate remnants of racial discrimination, particularly with respect to educational opportunity because educational deprivations targeted toward a certain race are vestiges of our history of slavery.
				State has compelling interest to achieve complete racial diversity in institutions of higher education because it provides a beneficial learning environment for all students.
	NCLR and LULAC	None	NCLR LULAC	Given Latino students' unique historical and cultural backgrounds and influences, as well as the political, economic, and social obstacles that they have faced, they provide unique insights and contributions to the university environment that is essential for creating a more comprehensive educational experience.
				Public education bears a pressing responsibility to eradicate societal discrimination that has historically limited Latino students' educational experiences; therefore, affirmative action policies that halt the increasing educational gap between minorities and whites must be adopted.
	MALDEF	None	Own Brief	State has compelling interest to consider race as one factor among many to achieve complete racial diversity; therefore, affirmative action policies (as opposed to percentage plans which have not been shown to work in Texas) must be adopted.

(continued)

TABLE 3.8. (cont.)

Case	Group	Specific Reference Made to Other Group	Which Group Listed First on Brief	Priority of Reasoning
Romer v. Evans 517 U.S. 620 (1996)	NAACP	None	NAACP. NCLR	"No special rights" claim that forms basis of supporters of Amendment 2 arguments confuse the real issue at hand which is that such an amendment fundamentally violates the equal protections of gay citizens and is not an attempt to prevent a class of citizens (i.e., gay citizens) from access to "special rights" that other citizens do not have.
				Amendment 2 creates a suspect class by denying equal protection rights to a targeted group where no other group of Colorado citizens is denied such rights and thus should be subject to the strict scrutiny test.
	NCLR	None	Own Brief	It is an unconstitutional infringement on the fundamental right to participate equally in the political process by arranging the electoral system in a manner that will consistently diminish the influence of a group of voters on the political process as a whole.
				Amendment 2, which would close Colorado's courts to a minority group (i.e., homosexuals) is a specific instance of an abridgement of one's fundamental right to the judicial process.
				Amendment must be held under the strict scrutiny test because it has the effect of making the affected group a "suspect class."
	MALDEF	None	NAACP MALDEF	The effects of Amendment 2 render its provisions unconstitutional because it would prevent gay citizens from participating equally in the political process.
				Assertions that gay voters exercise too much power in Denver, Boulder, and Aspen (because these cities had enacted gay rights ordinances) are unfounded and question and devalue the political views of voters in those cities who voted for those ordinances.

Oklahoma City Schools v. Robert Dowell 498 U.S. 237 (1991)	NAACP	None	Own Brief	School segregation has substantially contributed to housing segregation and courts have established that residential segregation is a vestige of racially dual school systems.
				Mutually reinforcing nature of school and housing segregation needs to be remedied and efforts toward school desegregation need to be established and maintained to facilitate a long-term process of neighborhood integration.
				Before a court can permanently dissolve an injunction mandating efforts toward school desegregation, a school district must show that its desegregation efforts have also extended to correcting discriminatory practices in housing, thus fulfilling a school district's remedial obligation.
	NCLR	None	Own Brief	Oklahoma City Schools have not achieved "racial unitary" status and thus have not demonstrated that the original court-imposed injunction has sufficiently fulfilled its purpose to allow its termination
				School systems must pursue "aggressive desegregation efforts" to ensure that inner-city minority children have access to equal education opportunities because it improves minority student academic achievement.

(continued)

TABLE 3.8. (*cont.*)

Case	Group	Specific Reference Made to Other Group	Which Group Listed First on Brief	Priority of Reasoning
U.S. Department of Commerce v. U.S. House of Representatives 525 U.S. 326 (1999)	NCLR	None	Own Brief	The text of the U.S. Constitution and the Census Act, as well as past practices of gathering census data, contradict the House of Representatives' assertion that "the only permissible census is one in which all the data is derived from counting singly every individual who can be located." (Constitutional argument)
				Congress lacked standing to bring this suit because it will not suffer an injury from the use of statistical methods to determine congressional apportionment. (Legal argument)
				The secretary of commerce has discretion under the Census Act to use statistical sampling for the purpose of congressional apportionment. (Legal argument)
	NAACP	None	Own Brief	The Census Act includes plain terms that authorize the use of statistical sampling and gives discretion to the Secretary of Commerce in regards to using statistical sampling. (Legal argument)
				The Census Act must not be interpreted in isolation from its constitutional and statutory context. (Constitutional argument)
	Urban League	None	Own Brief	Protecting minority voice in the political process is vital and prohibiting the use of the secretary's new methods would be at the severe disadvantage of minority groups. (Racial argument)
				The Census Act authorizes and gives discretion to the secretary to use sampling methods in conducting the census. (Legal argument)
				The Constitution does not prohibit the use of statistical sampling in determining apportionment from the census and activities taken with regard to the Census should be focused toward the "Constitutional goal of equal representation" rather than focused on particular census-taking methods. (Constitutional argument)

Case				
Wards Cove Packing Co. v. Antonio 490 U.S. 642 (1989)	MALDEF	None	NAACP MALDEF	The legislative history of Title VII, its 1972 amendments, and past uniform administrative interpretations of the statute all demonstrate that the Griggs precedent is consistent with the intent of Congress. Three separate pieces of evidence all combine to reflect a "distinct nature of the discriminatory practices," including evidence for individual disparate treatment, direct evidence of intentional discrimination, and evidence of a pattern of practice of intentional discrimination (which is sufficient to establish a prima facie violation in the absence of direct evidence of intentional discrimination). If the Griggs ruling that established evidentiary standards for disparate impact cases were to be overruled, it "would be contrary to the remedial purpose of Title VII."
	NAACP	None	NAACP MALDEF	Same as above.
Wygant v. Jackson Board of Education 476 U.S. 267 (1986)	MALDEF	None	Own Brief	The 14th Amendment does not require employers and unions to adopt a seniority system for layoffs. (Constitutional argument) While Article XII (Jackson Board of Education lay-off policy) is race conscious, it does not create a preference for minority employees, does not immunize them from layoff, and does not require that minority employees be laid off at a slower rate than nonminority employees.
	NAACP	None	NAACP Own Brief	The petitioner does not state a claim on which relief can be granted because the district court's denial of petitioner's motion for summary judgment is not appealable. (Legal argument) The district court properly denied the petitioner's motion for summary judgment. (Legal argument)

Note: Abbreviations – NAACP (National Association for the Advancement of Colored People), NCLR (National Council of La Raza), LULAC (League of United Latin American Citizens), MALDEF (Mexican American Legal Defense Fund).

Gratz v Bollinger (539 U.S. 244, 2003)
In this case, two white residents of Michigan applied to the University of Michigan in the fall of 1995 and 1997. Both were denied admission to the university and took part in a class-action lawsuit, alleging racial discrimination and equal protection violations. In a 6–3 decision, the U.S. Supreme Court ruled that the University of Michigan's affirmative action policy, which gave an automatic twenty points for an applicant who is a member of three select racial minority groups (African Americans, Latinos, and Native Americans), violates the Equal Protection Clause of the Fourteenth Amendment and Title VI of the Civil Rights Act of 1964 because its point system was not a proper way to further the compelling state interest of providing educational diversity on campus. Thus, this decision abolished the university's admissions policy of using a point system; however, affirmative action was not deemed unconstitutional in and of itself. The Court struck down a specific application of affirmative action but reaffirmed that universities could consider race when making admissions decisions because maintaining campus diversity is a compelling state interest. The case ultimately established that affirmative action policies to remedy effects of past discriminatory practices are consistent with the Equal Protection Clause of the Fourteenth Amendment and Title VI of the Civil Rights Act of 1964; but in striking down the explicit point system, the Court left a mixed-bag for minority advocacy groups. Four black and Latino groups filed three separate amicus briefs in support of the University of Michigan's admissions policy (see Table 3.8). The NAACP and MALDEF filed separate briefs while the NCLR and LULAC filed a joint brief.

The NAACP's position was based on both the specific experiences of African Americans in the United States regarding limited access to educational opportunities and the argument that diversifying the student body in general is a compelling state interest. First, the NAACP emphasized the state's compelling interest in eradicating historical remnants of racial discrimination, particularly with respect to educational opportunity. In supporting this position, the NAACP referenced *Regents of University of California v. Bakke*. In this case, the Supreme Court ruled in favor of Bakke and argued that college admission could use race only as one of numerous factors, and not the single most important one, in deciding whether an applicant should be admitted. However, the Court still recognized that "the attainment of a diverse student body" is "clearly a constitutionally permissible goal for an institution of higher education," thereby ruling that affirmative action policies are constitutional (although the one used in this case was not). Second, the NAACP addressed the issue of achieving complete racial diversity in institutions of higher education and argued that the state also has a compelling interest in obtaining this goal. "The Thirteenth Amendment and the 1866 Civil Rights Act both inform the university's compelling interest in identifying and admitting a racially diverse student body." Thus, while the NAACP's basic arguments stem from establishing the necessary "compelling state interest" needed to allow racially based admissions policies, the underlying theme was based on both the specific experiences of African Americans and the larger ideological goal of diversifying educational institutions. In the first argument, group specific interests were emphasized; in the second, benefits to other groups as well as the state were cited.

The NCLR and LULAC filed a joint brief in which they focused on the experiences of Latino students as those who have been historically excluded from educational opportunities and noted the benefits of diversifying educational institutions. First, the NCLR and LULAC emphasized that Latino students possess unique and personal insights on a variety of issues. "Latino students are in a unique position to enhance the diversity of ideas on college campuses in furtherance of the university's educational mission." Second, the NCLR and LULAC emphasized that Latinos have traditionally been discriminated against and thus public education bears a pressing responsibility to eradicate societal discrimination, and thus "the University of Michigan has a compelling interest in remedying the continuing effects of discrimination against Latinos." With these arguments, the NCLR/LULAC brief closely reflects the NAACP arguments for the existence of a compelling state interest. However, the groups diverged in the basis for such a conclusion by relying on their own racial/ethnic groups' experiences as the primary example. And while the NAACP argued for the benefits of broadly diversified student populations, the NHLA/LULAC brief focused primarily on the benefits of the diversity of ideas Latino students are said to bring to higher education.

Finally, MALDEF submitted a brief that focused almost exclusively on the failure of alternative plans, such as Texas's "10 percent" plan, which guaranteed admissions to higher education to students in the top 10 percent of their high school class. The failure of such alternative plans in turn meant that there was indeed a compelling state interest. MALDEF's brief distinguishes itself from the other briefs in essentially avoiding a group-specific argument based on the historic discrimination against a particular minority group.

In general, both black and Latino groups had similar positions on the role affirmative action policies should have in public education while citing slightly different reasons and evidence for their position. However, the order in which they presented these two points, as well as the minorities whom they addressed in their briefs, varied slightly. The NAACP first addressed the institution of slavery and how the practice of separate but equal has led to discriminatory practices against blacks. As a second point, they highlighted the state's compelling interest in achieving complete racial diversity (without specifically mentioning which races/ethnicities) in institutions of higher learning for the benefit of all students.

The NCLR and LULAC first emphasized that due to Latino immigrants' historical and cultural uniqueness in the United States they are in a special position to enhance the diversity of ideas on college campuses in furtherance of universities' educational mission. Latinos' Spanish language and culture, personal immigration stories, and experiences with racial discrimination provide a distinct vantage point from which Latino students can shed light on current issues in America. A second point emphasized how Latino immigrants' historical and cultural uniqueness has unfortunately spurred racial prejudice toward Latinos as a group and has similarly bred and perpetuated discriminatory practices against Latinos over time, particularly in housing, employment, immigration, citizenship, voting, criminal justice, and education, and that universities have a compelling interest in remedying such continuing effects of racial discrimination.

Both black and Latino groups make the argument that achieving and maintaining a representatively diverse student body is crucial in enhancing the academic interests of universities and the learning environment of university campuses as a whole, but the Latino groups more strongly emphasized that Latinos' distinct race and position in society help to provide unique contributions to university settings. In other words, the NAACP addressed the state's compelling interest in remedying the ill-effects of historical prejudices against blacks first, and argued that achieving racial diversity is paramount in learning environments second. The NCLR and LULAC addressed the importance of having a Latino presence (as opposed to the NAACP's argument regarding minority presence in general) on college campuses first and the state's compelling interest in remedying continuing effects of past racial discrimination against Latinos second.

Romer v. Evans (517 U.S. 620, 1996)

Romer v. Evans (1996) dealt with an issue not specific to black or Latino racial/ethnic concerns per se. The case involved Colorado's 1992 voter-approved amendment, Amendment 2, to the state's constitution which prevented government from extending protections based on sexual orientation. In a 6-3 decision, the Supreme Court ruled that this amendment violated the Equal Protections Clause of the Fourteenth Amendment of the U.S. constitution because it singled out homosexual and bisexual persons and imposed on them a broad disability by denying them the right to seek and receive specific legal protection from discrimination. Two aspects make the amicus briefs filed in this case important illustrative points. First, the case did not deal with racial/ethnic minority rights directly. Thus, ideological issues seem to explain minority advocacy groups' involvement with the courts in this instance. Second, a high degree of explicit cooperation between black and Latino groups is evident in that two of the three briefs were filed jointly by black and Latino groups.

The NAACP submitted two briefs in this case, one with the NCLR and one with MALDEF. In both briefs, the central argument was that all citizens, regardless of race, ethnicity, sex, sexual orientation, and other factors, are afforded equal protection of the laws as well as equal opportunities to participate in the political process and that Amendment 2 denies them such rights. In the NAACP/MALDEF brief, the groups argued that "Amendment 2 was adopted for [a] constitutionally impermissible purpose of preventing gay voters from participating equally in the political process." The NAACP/NCLR brief stated that "Amendment 2 walls off the political and judicial fora of the State of Colorado from its gay citizens, depriving them in a particularly flagrant fashion of the equal protection of the laws." Overall, the argument is that Amendment 2 infringes upon "the most important political right in any democratic society – the right to participate equally with all other citizens in the political process." Here, there is clear evidence of cooperative activity by black and Latino advocacy groups, as joint filings suggest more than reaching the same conclusion independently and from different perspectives. Moreover, this cooperation is based not on racial/ethnic group-specific interests, but on broader ideological orientations – concern over ensuring equal access to, and protections from, political and judicial institutions.

The NCLR did file an additional brief by itself that focused on the political and judicial processes that Amendment 2 unconstitutionally denied to homosexuals. In many ways, the NCLR brief and the NAACP/NCLR brief contained much of the same language and similar evidence for their general arguments (see Table 3.8). Thus, while technically filing their own brief, it is clear in this instance that the NCLR came to similar conclusions as the NAACP from essentially the same bases. Overall, the briefs filed in *Romer v. Evans* (1996) importantly illustrate black and Latino advocacy groups' involvement based on shared ideas of equity and the protections of the Fourteenth Amendment. While not surprising, the attention given to a case that arguably has little direct implications for blacks and Latinos (as such) may suggest that shared ideological orientations and lack of competing interests act as vehicles for cooperation as evidenced in the joint filings of black and Latino groups, and overlapping arguments from the NCLR's own brief.

Oklahoma City Schools v. Robert Dowell (498 U.S. 237, 1991)

Oklahoma City Schools v. Robert Dowell (1991) is a third illustrative case. In 1972, a federal district court issued an injunction imposing a school desegregation plan on the Oklahoma City Board of Education. In 1977, the court found that the school district had complied with the plan and the district had reached unitary racial composition, so the court issued an order terminating the plan. In 1984, the Oklahoma City Board adopted a Student Reassignment Plan (SRP), under which previously desegregated schools were becoming primarily one-race again because termination of the plan had lessened the busing efforts, as well as increased the travel burdens, of transporting black students to white schools. Black students and their parents as well as groups that originally protested de jure segregation, sought to restore the original court-ordered desegregation plan, claiming that the school system was becoming segregated once again. The basic question before the Supreme Court was "If a federal court deems that an injunction to desegregate schools has achieved its goals, can that court permanently dissolve the injunction?"[1] In a 5-3 decision, the Supreme Court ruled that a federal court could remove an injunction upon finding that a school system has demonstrated earnest compliance with an injunction. Since federal supervision of local school systems was intended as a temporary measure to remedy past discrimination, federal courts can consider removing such measures if it finds that the school system has operated in compliance with the Equal Protection Clause and that it is deemed unlikely that the school district would return to its former practices.

In support of respondents, the NAACP argued that where school segregation has substantially contributed to housing segregation, the school district must show that it has taken effective action to correct such discriminatory practices before the school district's remedial obligation is

---

[1] *Oklahoma City Schools v. Robert Dowell* 498 U.S. 237 (1991), www.oyez.org/cases/1990–1999/1990/1990_89_1080.

fulfilled. Even if the means the school district must use to accomplish this are difficult or time-consuming, it must show that it has taken all measures to ensure a successful desegregation process. The Courts have found that "racially-dual school systems" contribute to residential segregation and that segregated neighborhoods also tend to produce segregated schools because families must live in the school district of their children. This two-way development needs to be remedied and studies have shown that by effectively desegregating schools, housing desegregation can also be eliminated. Given the pressing need to remedy all lingering discriminatory practices and effects in society, effective actions must be taken to "remove housing vestiges of school segregation before a desegregation plan can be undone."[2]

The NCLR, among other minority groups with whom it submitted a brief in support of respondents, said courts must be hesitant to abandon supervision of school districts until a school district can demonstrate by "clear and convincing evidence that it has faithfully complied with the desegregation order, that it has taken no recent actions with segregative intent, and that all significant vestiges of past segregation have been eliminated."[3] However, the brief claimed that in the case of Oklahoma City Schools, its inner-city schools remain more than 90 percent black, indicating that they have not achieved "racial unitary" status. Furthermore, the brief stated that the Oklahoma City School Board had not demonstrated that the original court-imposed injunction had sufficiently fulfilled its purpose to allow its termination. The existing state of housing and school segregation proved that achieving and maintaining racial heterogeneity had not yet been realized and that the goal of the injunction had not been met. The brief said that school system must pursue "aggressive desegregation efforts" to ensure that inner city minority children have access to equal education opportunities because it improves minority student academic achievement and to "break the cycle of racial isolation in the lives of minority students and in our society as a whole."[4]

---

[2] Brief of National Association for the Advancement of Colored People and the Citizens' Commission on Civil Rights as Amici Curiae in Support of Respondents.

[3] Brief of the American Jewish Committee, the Asian American Legal Defense and Education Fund, the National Council of La Raza, the Puerto Rican Legal Defense and Education Fund, the Unitarian Universalist Association, and the YWCA of the U.S.A. as Amici Curiae in Support of Respondents.

[4] Brief of the American Jewish Committee, the Asian American Legal Defense and Education Fund, the National Council of La Raza, the Puerto Rican Legal Defense and Education Fund, the Unitarian Universalist Association, and the YWCA of the U.S.A. as Amici Curiae in Support of Respondents.

Both black and Latino advocacy groups shared the same position in arguing that desegregating school systems and neighborhoods is a pressing concern and that courts need to be unyielding in ensuring that school districts are doing all that they can to facilitate this process and achieve the outcome of racial unity. In the NAACP brief, the group appeared to hold courts to a stricter standard in ensuring that the school district has definitively shown it has taken essentially all possible actions to effectively correct discriminatory practices and segregation's effects in schools before the school district's obligation to do so can be said to be fulfilled and its injunction removed. The NCLR shared this position but its rhetoric did not appear as assertive as the language used by the NAACP. The NCLR also briefly raised the point that school desegregation would not only lead to housing desegregation but would also inevitably improve minority student academic achievement while the NAACP focused primarily on the imperative of achieving total desegregation in schools and neighborhoods as an end in itself.

U.S. Department of Commerce v. U.S. House of Representatives (525 U.S. 326, 1999)

Under the U.S. Constitution's Census Clause, Congress is authorized to conduct a census of the American public every ten years to provide a basis for the apportionment of congressional districts, among other things. The Census Act delegated this authority to the secretary of commerce. In 2000, the Census Bureau, a part of the Department of Commerce, announced a plan to use two new forms of statistical sampling for the 2000 Census to "address a chronic and apparently growing problem of 'undercounting' of some identifiable groups, including certain minorities, children, and renters."[5] U.S. residents, counties, and the U.S. House of Representatives challenged the constitutionality of the Bureau's new sampling methods. They argued that U.S. residents must be counted without the use of statistical and other noncounting methods, even though such scientific methods have been used in the past. The question before the U.S. Supreme Court was "Is the use of statistical sampling in the execution of the census inconsistent with provisions of the Census Act or in conflict with the Census Clause of the Constitution?" The Court ruled that the use of statistical sampling is not consistent with provisions of the

5 *Department of Commerce et al. v. United States House of Representatives et al.* 525 U.S. 326 (1999), www4.law.cornell.edu/supct/html/98–404.ZS.html.

Census Act because the Census Act prohibits the proposed uses of statistical sampling to determine the population for congressional apportionment purposes. Since it struck down the sampling provision of the Census Act, it did not need to address the constitutional question of whether it was inconsistent with the Census Clause.

The NCLR, among other minority groups with whom it submitted a brief in support of petitioners, claimed that the secretary of commerce's proposed use of statistical sampling is consistent with the Census Act and is not constitutionally prohibited by the Census Clause of the Constitution. They also argued that Congress lacked standing to bring this suit because it will not suffer an injury from the use of statistical methods to determine congressional apportionment. Thus, it is not a justiciable matter. Furthermore, past practices of counting have shown that the census has never depended solely on a strict enumeration, or one-by-one headcount, of every person who can be located. The secretary of commerce has discretion under the Census Act to use statistical sampling for the purpose of congressional apportionment and the Constitution also permits the use of statistical sampling to correct for inaccuracies and omissions in collected data. Taken together, the NCLR argued that the secretary's proposed methods should be allowed for use in the 2000 Census.

The NAACP supported the petitioners in this case and argued that the secretary of commerce has the power to conduct a fair and accurate census and has the authority to use sampling procedures to ensure that a fair and accurate census is taken. The Census Act must not be interpreted in isolation from its constitutional and statutory context; given that the government has the power and responsibility to assure political equality, the executive branch can use the method within its constitutional authority to achieve and maintain political equality, especially regarding a census for the purpose of congressional apportionment. The Urban League argued that the Census Act authorizes the secretary of commerce to use statistical sampling in conducting the census and that the Constitution also does not prohibit such uses of sampling in determining congressional apportionment. Activities taken with regard to the census should be focused toward the "goals of objectivity," "avoidance of political manipulation," and "the Constitutional goal of equal representation" rather than focusing on particular census-taking methods.[6] Furthermore, they

---

[6] Motion to File Brief as Amici Curiae in Support of Appellants and Brief of Jerome Gray, Sherman Norfleet, Gwendolyn Patton, Isaiah Sumbry, Dianne Wilkerson, American Jewish Committee, American Jewish Congress, and National Urban League as Amici Curiae.

stress the importance of protecting a minority voice in the political process and that prohibiting the use of the secretary's new methods would be at the severe disadvantage of minority groups.

Both black and Latino groups shared the same position in favor of allowing the secretary of commerce's new statistical methods in taking the 2000 Census. The NCLR addressed questions of whether the suit filed even presents a justiciable controversy satisfying Article III of the Constitution, whether the Census Act prohibits the secretary of commerce from using statistical sampling in determining the population for the purpose of apportioning representatives among states, and whether the Census Clause of the Constitution requires Congress to conduct an "actual enumeration" of the population and thus prohibits the use of statistical sampling in determining the population for the purpose of apportioning representatives among states.[7] The NAACP made similar arguments that addressed the constitutionality of the newly proposed methods but also briefly touched on past inaccuracies in counting and how its traditional undercount of minorities has denied certain groups access to the political process, particularly African Americans, Latinos, and Native Americans. Similarly, the Urban League addressed the danger of disallowing more accurate scientific sampling techniques because minorities will be undercounted significantly more than whites, thus placing African Americans and other minorities at a greater disadvantage than whites. African Americans and other minority groups will be deprived of accurate political representation in Congress and thus adversely affected. Both black groups emphasized the need for more accurate statistical methods to ensure that the "general undercount and the disparate undercounting of racial and ethnic minorities" does not persist.[8] While the NCLR's brief relied strictly on legal, historical, and constitutional evidence to argue in favor of the secretary's statistical methods, the NAACP and Urban League also emphasized the need to protect minority interests as a reason to allow the new statistical methods. For these minority groups, the Supreme Court ruling was seen as disfavoring the needs and interests of a protected class of citizens.

[7] Brief of Amici Curiae American Federation of State, County and Municipal Employees, State Legislative Policy Institute; NOW Legal Defense and Education Fund, Americans for Democratic Action, and National Council of La Raza in Support of Appellants.

[8] Brief of Amicus Curiae NAACP Legal Defense and Educational Fund, Inc. in Support of Appellants.

Wards Cove Packing Co. v. Atonio (490 U.S. 642, 1989)

Wards Cove Packing Co. primarily employed nonwhite workers for a certain unskilled seasonal job in canning fish. A group of nonwhite workers sued the company alleging that Wards Cove practiced discriminatory hiring practices in violation of Title VII of the Civil Rights Act of 1964. The group filing suit provided evidence for their claim by showing that there was a high percentage of nonwhites in unskilled work for the company and a high percentage of whites in skilled work for the company. The question before the U.S. Supreme Court was "Once employees present evidence of racial disparity among different classes of jobs, does the employer have to justify this disparity as a 'business necessity' in order to avoid a 'disparate impact' lawsuit under Title VII of the Civil Rights Act of 1964?"[9]

In a 5-4 decision, the Court ruled that the burden of proof does not fall on employers and they do not have to justify alleged disparities. The fact that one type of job at a firm has a higher percentage of nonwhites than other types of jobs does not by itself provide sufficient evidence that the firm has discriminatory hiring practices. However, Congress amended Title VII of the Civil Rights Act of 1964 with the Civil Rights Act of 1991 to counter the Court's holding in Wards Cove, thereby nullifying its precedent. Minority interests prevailed in the subsequent congressional action, which allowed that instances where more white workers are hired than nonwhite workers can be considered a "disparate impact" case. In other words, employers are prohibited from using hiring practices that might not necessarily appear to be discriminatory on their face but may be discriminatory in their application or effect and thus have an adverse impact on members of a protected class.

MALDEF and NAACP submitted a brief together. They argued that Title VII not only prohibits intentional, disparate treatment discrimination but also disparate impact discrimination. Thus, even if an employer is not intentionally discriminating against minority workers, the fact that an outcome results wherein more white workers are hired than nonwhite workers constitutes a violation of Title VII. Wards Cove Packing Co., the two minority advocacy groups argued, should have to justify its hiring practices which result in racial disparities to avoid a "disparate impact" lawsuit under Title VII. Both black and Latino groups submitted one brief together in support of the nonwhite workers and thus their

---

[9] *Wards Cove Packing Co. v. Atonio* 490 U.S. 642 (1989), www.oyez.org/cases/1980–1989/1988/1988_87_1387.

positions and the evidence they provide are identical. This jointly offered brief suggests they perceived that black and Latino workers were both affected in this case and thus they were able to come together and advocate for equal opportunities of all nonwhite workers, black or Latino, in the workplace.

Wygant v. Jackson Board of Education [of Jackson, Michigan] (476 *U.S. 267, 1986*)

The Jackson (Michigan) Board of Education and teacher's union had an agreement that (1) the board would not lay off teachers with the most seniority, and (2) the board would not lay off a percentage of minority personnel that exceeded the percentage of minority personnel employed at the time of layoff. The schools laid off some nonminority teachers with more seniority than other minority teachers who were retained. Wygant, a laid-off nonminority teacher, challenged the board's decision, holding that the board violated her equal protection rights. The question before the U.S. Supreme Court was "Did the collective bargaining agreement provision for race-based layoffs violate the 14th Amendment's Equal Protection Clause?"[10] In a 5–4 decision, the Supreme Court reversed a lower court decision and ruled that the collective bargaining agreement between the board and teacher's union did violate the Fourteenth Amendment's Equal Protection Clause, saying that Wygant's layoff stemmed from race and therefore violated her equal protection rights.

The NAACP argued that the petitioner (Wygant) does not state a claim on which relief can be granted. The NAACP argued that race conscious actions taken for the purpose of remedying past discrimination and achieving a fully integrated environment do not violate the Equal Protection Clause. Respondents rightfully filed a motion to dismiss because there is no claim on which relief can be granted if they were to prove that such motives did inspire the creation of Article XII. Therefore, the lower court decision had properly denied petitioners' motion. MALDEF argued that past discrimination has disproportionately affected the number of minority employees in the workforce and that efforts to remedy this have been slow to effect change. Therefore, on the whole, minority employees often have significantly less seniority than nonminority employees because past discrimination has prevented them from entering the workforce at the same

---

[10] *Wygant v. Jackson Board of Education* 476 U.S. 267 (1986), www.oyez.org/cases/1980–1989/1985/1985_84_1340.

rate as nonminority employees. Thus, strict application of a last-hired, first-fired seniority system has a significant disparate impact on minority employees and will substantially reduce the percentage of minority employees in the workforce. They argued that the Fourteenth Amendment does not require employers and unions to adopt such a seniority system for layoffs and that the board's policy did not provide an unconstitutional means of correcting the disparate impact of layoffs on the school district's minority employees. Furthermore, while race conscious, the board's policy does not create a preference for minority employees, does not immunize them from layoff, and does not require that minority employees be laid off at a slower rate than nonminority employees.

Both black and Latino groups agree that the board's policy does not violate the Fourteenth Amendment's Equal Protections Clause because it was an honest effort to remedy the effects of past discriminatory hiring/firing practices against minority employees and to avoid creating or allowing a disparate impact against minority employees even if hiring/firing practices appear or actually are nondiscriminatory upon application. However, the NAACP and MALDEF pose their argument in different ways. The NAACP addressed the questions of whether denial of petitioners' motion for summary judgment is appealable, whether courts correctly denied petitioners' motion for summary judgment, and whether petitioners' complaint was properly dismissed.[11] On the other hand, MALDEF addressed questions of whether a layoff provision that does not immunize minority employees from layoff but rather aims to correct the disparate impact of strict seniority constitutes a racial preference, whether the Fourteenth Amendment requires public employers to adhere to a last-hired, first-fired system for selecting employees for layoff, and whether the Fourteenth Amendment permits union and public employers to voluntarily adopt collective bargaining agreements that require racially proportional layoffs when without such a provision layoffs could be expected to have a substantially disparate impact on minority employees.[12] While both groups agreed that minority employees should be protected from possible disparate impacts of employers' hiring/firing practices, they expressed different reasons for sharing the same opinion.

[11] Brief Amicus Curiae for the NAACP Legal Defense & Educational Fund, Inc.
[12] Brief of Mexican American Legal Defense and Educational Fund, Amicus Curiae, in Support of Respondents.

Conclusion

This chapter began by identifying new issues and brought evidence to bear on describing and beginning to explain relations between the largest minority groups in the United States. Specifically, we examined whether and why minority advocacy (interest) groups, important to American pluralism and as mediating entities in the political system, compete, cooperate, or act independently in the processes of attempting to influence national policy making. The analysis of congressional testimony suggested independence and some compatibility in advocacy group activities, but there was no indication of conflict. The assessment of amicus briefs clearly indicated no conflict, some independence, and some notable signs of cooperation. Of the hearings examined (from 1970 to 2000) in which either black, Latino, or both types of advocacy groups testified, almost 90 percent of the time only black or Latino groups testified, but not both. This pattern held across decades for the bulk of the hearings on selected major subtopics. The aggregate data do not specify the direction of testimony, however, and determining agreement or congruence is thus difficult. In an effort to compensate for that limitation, we developed additional data from a random sample of congressional hearings, assessing the advocacy groups' positions and the degree to which they mentioned other groups when testifying on issues. This evidence reaffirmed the high level of separate or independent involvement of the groups but also provided no evidence of difference or conflict between the groups. In fact, in the random sample of cases we analyzed where both groups testified, they argued on the same general position. The key finding from our examination of congressional testimony is that independence is the norm and conflict is undetectable.

In the arena of legal advocacy, the analysis of amicus curiae briefs affirms that there is very little if any outright competition or conflict between black and Latino advocacy groups. In none of the cases examined from 1974 to 2004 did black and Latino groups included in the analysis file amicus briefs on opposing sides. Instead, groups signed on to amicus briefs together, or submitted separate briefs for the same side of the case, 23.4 percent of the time; here, there was, in fact, evidence of explicit cooperation. The remainder of the time, just over three-quarters of the cases examined, black and Latino groups simply filed briefs on their own, without signs of cooperation or conflict, suggesting another avenue for group advocacy that fits the description of independence and echoes the findings regarding congressional testimony.

The analyses of amicus filings revealed that independence versus cooperation varies by issue as well. Broad civil rights issues and education are the bases of cooperation, while other topics tend to be the focus of only one group, indicative of independence. There is even variation in activity prevalence across subtopics of civil rights issues; and this was found to be the case in both amicus filings and congressional testimony. Affirmative action was a topic of congruence and mutual cooperation in the briefs. In other policy areas, however, such as immigration, Latino and black groups tended to vary in terms of salience. There was consistently no evidence of conflict and some degree, though variation was present, in the cooperation of the advocacy groups' activities in the two institutions (congressional and judicial). In short, it seems that conflict is rather limited, if not nonexistent. Saliency and congruence are in part determined by the particular types of policies. Some of the congressional testimony and amicus filings indicate a low policy salience for one group; in these circumstances, a *non*-zero sum relationship would seem to occur virtually by default.

What, beyond what we have already discussed, might explain the intergroup relations we found? Several theories of minority group activity suggest that groups might cooperate or act similarly based largely on their ideological orientation toward civil rights and their constituencies' general experience with discrimination. In some respects, our evidence suggests this is the case, albeit limited to civil rights policy generally and affirmative action and discrimination, specifically. The variation in the amount of engagement across issues and sub-issues implies that there are not universal and/or intense dispositions to the point that groups expend resources on issues that are not predominant concerns to them, simply for the sake of avoiding conflict. Given different priorities and resource constraints, it may be that by not directly opposing each other, there is some degree of implicit (and perhaps quite intentional if not readily visible) cooperation or negotiation underlying the extensive degree of independence we found. However, the considerable evidence of apparent separate groups-based advocacy suggests that if this is the case, it is rare. In short, while the underlying sources for cooperation and independence may still vary, the lack of conflict suggests that some degree of latent cooperation may exist even when issue positions potentially diverge; and this is a story implied in later chapters.

A further question is how groups come to independent strategies or that foster cooperative strategies. This may be explained in part by more conventional interest group theories based on the rational use of scare resources. Cooperation is most likely to occur where ideas and interests overlap. Where interests do not appear to overlap, then groups lacking an intense or direct interest in the policy do not participate; that this interest divergence has not been manifested in conflict between the national advocacy groups is telling. Thus, minority advocacy groups may not always cooperate (based on similar ideology) because they do not have the same salient interests or constituencies. The counterpoint to this interpretation is that if groups do generally follow their interests, then why are there no instances of conflict? It seems quite unlikely that two sets of groups would never encounter a case in which their interests diverge. But the absence of evidence indicating conflict in the legal and the congressional arenas is striking and departs to some extent from the expectations of conventional interest group theory, and the findings of the urban-level research on black-Latino relations.

Table 3.9 summarizes our findings from this chapter in relation to the framework presented in Chapter 1 (particularly Table 1.1), highlighting the types of policies we expect would lead to particular types of intergroup relations. The findings suggest that affirmative action, civil rights, reapportionment, and employment discrimination are the most likely to lead to cooperation across black and Latino groups at the national level, and the least likely to have conflict. The independence or negotiation examples, where groups were "going it alone," include some obvious examples of distinct interests (District of Columbia issues for blacks, and employment of aliens and immigration for Latinos), but also some that show overlapping ideals *or* interests, but not both. Overall, the lack of conflict is most striking, especially when contrasted with the evidence of black-Latino conflict at the local level that we discussed in the previous chapter. The absence of conflict between the groups we found is, we think, partly explained by the types of policies and broad geographic arena in which the relations occur.

There is reason to expect that when issues such as civil rights, racial/ethnic equality, and the like are considered, and, further are considered in a national arena, more abstract, detached, and broadly ideologically driven purposive ideas and attendant political processes emerge, which in turn temper political competition or conflict between the minority groups (Schattschneider 1960). A related consequence is that national minority advocacy groups may be freer and better positioned to address issues in a way that moderates differences, and the outcomes we described earlier support this perspective. At the same time, while we found essentially no instances of conflict at the national level, and independence or other such

TABLE 3.9. *Summary of Empirical Findings on Congressional Testimony and Amicus Briefs, with Respect to the Analytical Framework*

Ideology and Interests	Expected Intergroup Relations	Empirical Observations[a]

Shared Ideology High
Shared Interests High
(less zero sum)
	Cooperation (ostensibly)
	(No conflict)
		Testimony:
		  Fair Housing
		  Census Implementation
		Amicus Briefs:
		  Civil Rights
		  Affirmative Action
		  Reapportionment
		  Employment Discrimination

Shared Ideology Modest to High
Shared Interests Low to Modest
	Independence or Possibly Negotiation[b]
	(No conflict)
		Testimony:
		  District of Columbia (Black)
		  Census (Latino)
		  Immigration (Latino)
		Amicus Briefs:
		  Criminal Procedure (Black)
		  Desegregation in Schools (Black)
		  Employment of Aliens (Latino)

Shared Ideology Low Shared Interests Low (more zero sum)	Conflict	No Incidences

[a] Observations from the entire congressional testimony data are provided only for the non-cooperation examples to highlight specific issues that are unique to each type of advocacy group. Congruence or conflict examples are derived from smaller random sample.

[b] It is possible for negotiation and tacit noncooperation to lead to the same empirical observations, and thus we include both behaviors and observations in the same cells. We expect that this is not the case, as discussed in the text of the chapter.

outcomes are the most common, the extent of clear-cut cooperation found is arguably modest, and seems to vary some by topic and institution.

On the whole, the interplay of ideology and interests and, related, the non-zero sum nature of the policies (at least as they affect blacks and Latinos) potentially play a role in helping us understand the interrelations of minority advocacy groups and the variation of those relations. This chapter's examination of activities of minority advocacy groups, in two national-level venues, demonstrates an independent and also nonconflictual quality. This is in stark difference to the conflict and competition often seen at the local level. Indeed, an absence of conflict seems universal in our findings here, though it commonly takes the form of independence rather than cooperation. Another area of minority advocacy group activities is found in the groups' evaluation of Congress, specifically, members of Congress, by rating' members' voting behavior in "scorecards." These ratings are the subject of Chapter 4 as we continue to explore the nature of black-Latino relations in national government processes.

4

Salience and Congruence in Policy Positions

*Black-Latino Advocacy Groups
and Congressional Scorecards*

Efforts to influence public policy occur in several forums in national politics. Along with congressional testimony and amicus filings, which we examined in Chapter 3, advocacy groups assess or monitor congressional behavior by selecting major issues the groups deem important, and rating members of Congress on their voting on the issues selected. These ratings are often called congressional scorecards and are used to both inform constituencies about and pressure members of Congress regarding the level of support a member gives to each groups' agenda. They allow groups to publicize the behavior of those members who agree or disagree with their positions, and ratings often serve as proxies for support of groups' interests in studies that seek to explain why members behave as they do. We use the ratings in a different way in this chapter to extend our analysis of black-Latino advocacy group relations.

Instead of the overall "rating" for each member, which is usually the item of interest in advocacy group ratings, our interest in this chapter is the policy and legislative issues from which groups derive their ratings. The contents of the ratings provide useful information for describing the issues of concern to minority advocacy groups, their positions on those issues, and from these, the degree to which cooperation, conflict, or non-conflict/independent behavior mark black-Latino relations. The analysis will examine the issues identified as salient (because of their inclusion on scorecards) as well as the policy positions of minority advocacy organizations in terms of the preferred vote (yes or no) on each issue. We thus address two basic questions: (a) what votes (or types of votes) in Congress are deemed most important, and (b) what is the degree of congruence or overlap of the votes identified in scorecards of black and Latino advocacy groups? This allows us to examine advocacy group behavior in terms of groups' efforts to affect the congressional arena through the identification of policy issues, and further address the central questions of this study: what is the nature of black-Latino intergroup relations as they occur in national politics?

Are the relations of these groups as suggested in their scorecards essentially the same as we found in the analyses of hearing testimony and amicus briefs, with no evidence of conflict and substantial independence characterizing black-Latino relations? Or, given the set of issues regarding roll-call votes in Congress, does more conflict emerge? We anticipate that given the breadth and types of national level policies, and our findings from Chapter 3, that conflict is minimal. However, compared to presenting congressional testimony or deciding to file amicus briefs, conflicting interests may be more likely when determinations are made about which are actually the most important policy votes and the preferred position on them in the congressional decision-making process. Thus, an analysis of the components of, and specified preferred positions indicated in, black and Latino ratings or scorecards provides an additional layer of empirical evidence on interminority group relations.

Prefatory Comments

As part of their efforts to influence policy, a number of groups developed scorecards that rate how members of Congress (MCs) vote on a number of issues selected by the groups. The NAACP and NHLA are among the many groups that regularly produce such scorecards, and our focus is on these two prominent black and Latino advocacy groups' scorecards. The scorecards typically include several pieces of information: the names of bills voted on in a congressional session which are selected by the advocacy group as being important; the group's preferred position on those votes; a record of how MCs actually voted on each; and the overall score that is assigned to each MC based on those votes. (The groups also commonly indicate the outcome, i.e., passage or nonpassage, of each piece of legislation as well.) We take these groups' scorecards as indicating their most *salient* policy *concerns* and their stated preferences on those policy *positions*. The use of such scorecards is not uncommon in political science research, and there are several precedents for drawing on these types of data from advocacy groups in assessing minority group representation in Congress (e.g., Welch and Hibbing 1984; Hero and Tolbert 1995; Grose 2005). Before turning to our overarching questions, certain theoretical, conceptual, and empirical issues deserve attention, however.

Some observers might question how much and how accurately advocacy groups speak for those they claim to represent, and some evidence indicates such questioning is warranted (Strolovitch 2007; Skocpol 2004; Marquez 1993). However, as we discussed in Chapters 1 and 2, we have little choice but to take the interest/advocacy groups and the larger system as they are, and we examine their interactions with and impacts on each other; we acknowledge, however, that some analysts see the contemporary interest group system as itself a problem in general (Skocpol 2004); and this is perhaps especially so for minority groups (Marquez 1993). But we will also provide evidence that suggests some of the criticisms about elite-mass divergence may be overstated.

We essentially accept that the NAACP and NHLA scorecards reasonably reflect accepted positions and are the most direct indicators available of black and Latino concerns, especially with respect to issues of political and economic equality. In short, an issue is basically treated here as a "black issue" if the NAACP sees it as such, as evidenced in the inclusion of the issue in the group's scorecard; similarly, an issue is viewed as a "Latino issue" if the NHLA sees it as such, as indicated by its inclusion in the group's scorecard. We recognize the potential bias this brings, but the group scorecards seem most appropriate to present analytical purposes, and we acknowledge possible limitations of these indicators. In any case, we believe there *is* ample evidence and related grounds for treating the NAACP and NHLA scorecards as appropriate, plausible indicators of black and Latino public opinion because the issues emphasized therein map reasonably well with views generally expressed by Latinos and blacks in mass surveys. For instance, Griffin and Newman claim that on average the attitudes of blacks and Latinos in the general population differ considerably from those of whites "on issues related to race, such as affirmative action, job discrimination, civil rights and somewhat less so on 'implicitly racial' issues like education, health care, and welfare spending" (Griffin and Newman 2008, 46; also see Canon 1999, 27–29). And the NAACP and NHLA scorecards have disproportionately high percentages of such items, as described later.

In addition to the observation that minority advocacy groups are "too conservative" in pursuing political and economic equality, there is another somewhat contradictory claim that is made about advocacy groups (and often about elected minority representatives as well) – that they are "too liberal," especially on social issues (such as gay rights and abortion, for example) or at least substantially more liberal than are those they are supposed to represent. To some degree we can understand both the "too liberal" and/or "too conservative" sets of criticisms by discussing self-definition in terms of liberal-conservative ideology. There are quite possibly several dimensions, or at least one alternative dimension, that captures the interests of minority groups and those that they represent. This dual nature of the critique of the use of minority advocacy groups and the issues they find salient and positions they take as proxies for the interests and positions of their constituents suggests that on the issues that are taken, there is probably some unique quality that allows for consensus. But, again, this is only tangential to our analysis that examines points of contention and cooperation between two groups and not the link between groups and their constituents.

With specific reference to Latinos, another matter arises that we note here and also address in subsequent chapters: the claim that Latino members of Congress (as well as advocacy organizations) are considerably more liberal than Latino constituents. Several pieces of evidence speak to, and potentially undermine, this claim. To begin with, Griffin and Newman (2008) find that Latinos represented by Latino MCs are closer to their MCs; a similar result was found for blacks. Also, attempting to understand the ideology of the mass of Latinos and blacks is not a simple matter. It has been argued that the concepts liberal and conservative do not capture the full or complex nature of Latino and black masses. It seems that many blacks and Latinos have what are often considered liberal views on issues of economic policy and the role of government in bringing about economic (and political) equality while they have what are often viewed as conservative positions on social issues such as gay rights. The conventional, single liberal-conservative continuum does not account for this split in the case of black and Latino public opinion, and probably for others as well. Furthermore, the very concepts of liberal-conservative appear not to resonate with a large number of blacks and Latinos. A "substantial portion of African Americans do not offer an ideological orientation when queried, so that liberal-conservative ideology may not be a useful construct for this group" (Griffin and Newman 2008, 46). It has been further claimed that (liberal-conservative) ideology is "useful in understanding Latino opinions" but its utility is limited (Griffin and Newman 2008, 46). For instance, respondents in the large (N = 8,600) Latino National Survey (LNS, Fraga et al., 2006) were asked "generally speaking, in politics do you consider yourself conservative, liberal, or middle-of-the-road, or don't you think of yourself in these terms?" The leading response, 32 percent, was "[I] don't think of [myself] in these terms" and another 17 percent of respondents answered "don't know"; thus, about 49 percent did not really directly answer the ideological question generally used in research and which is also the implicit reference in public intellectual discourse on such topics. Overall 21 percent answered "conservative," 13 percent "liberal," and 17 percent "middle-of-the-road." Compare these results to those of a national sample from the 2004 American National Election Study, which found that of all respondents (without breaking down race or ethnicity), only about 20% said that they did not know or have not thought about themselves in terms of a liberal-conservative ideological position. These patterns, along with the potential limitations of the concepts of liberal-conservative in tapping both economic and social dimensions, suggest a need for much caution when discussing black and Latino public opinion in conventional ideological terms. When it comes to ideology in terms of mass public opinion on specific questions and issues in relation to representation, the evidence indicates some mapping. And given these caveats and the blurred relevance of broader ideological orientations, for our analysis we essentially defer to the NHLA and NAACP to identify particular issues as Latino and black concerns in congressional roll-call voting.

Analyzing Salience and Congruence

We begin the empirical analysis by evaluating the types of issues that are salient to minority advocacy groups and then move to the degree of congruence across groups by examining the votes included in the congressional scorecards of the National Association for the Advancement of Colored People (NAACP) and the National Hispanic Leadership Council (NHLA) since these are the two major interest groups representing the largest racial/ethnic minority groups in the nation and have consistently produced scorecards over an adequate period of time. (The NHLA is technically an umbrella coalition representing a number of Latino advocacy groups.) The data are compiled for the 105th through the 108th Congresses (1997–2004). Since the NHLA began distributing scorecards in the 105th and we are seeking comparisons that require consistent time-frames, our starting point is determined by available data. Unfortunately, there are no other groups out of the set we included in the analyses in the previous chapter that have regularly published scorecards that cover similar time periods. But given the high profile nature of these two groups, the coalitional nature of the NHLA (it includes MALDEF, LULAC, and the

NCLR, which were the main Latino advocacy groups we investigated in Chapter 3), and the reality that valid comparisons of scorecards require that they apply to the same time period, we are confident that, besides being the most readily available, the two groups selected are appropriate examples of black-Latino advocacy groups for our purpose here.

Regarding policy concerns or *saliency*, the question, is what issues are most important to minority advocacy groups? What do they choose to single out from the vast number of votes taken in Congress over the course of legislative sessions? We consider the issues selected for inclusion in scorecards and the extent to which the different advocacy groups *identify the same policy issues* as the salient issues. Specifically, we identify the frequency with which the groups place similar issues on scorecards. This strategy is much the same as the one used in identifying issues in the amicus and congressional testimony analyses in Chapter 3. The degree of activity and of overlap in policy issues on which groups engage can thus be determined.

Second, policy *congruence* follows evidence of saliency and considers whether the groups take the same positions on those issues they have in common on their scorecards. That is, do the groups have *congruent* views on the issue's desirability? Are they in agreement or "on the same side" in either support or opposition when they do identify the same issues? What are the aggregate patterns, and what do they suggest? And, of course, do the patterns that emerge indicate a competitive, cooperative, or independent relationship? Delineating the frequency and the substantive policies or issue areas the groups identify provides a starting point for understanding how broad versus narrow interests can affect the several forms of intergroup relations. We coded the issue topic of each vote so we can determine the nature of the underlying relationships – that is, if there are particular topics that tend to foster more or less cooperation, independence, or conflict. The policy topics are coded to reflect the topics included in the Baumgartner and Jones Congressional Testimony Dataset used in the previous analysis so there is a good degree of continuity between this analysis and that presented in Chapter 3.

Figure 4.1 displays the frequency distribution of votes categorized by policy topic for all four Congresses we examine. We collapse the data in this way initially since the frequency of any particular topic can be quite low for some of the Congresses, and thus the bigger picture can emerge from this approach. When we examine congruence, we look more closely at Congress to Congress variation.

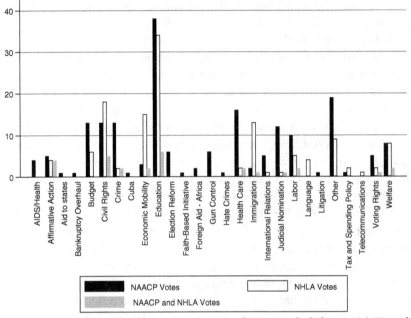

FIGURE 4.1. Salient Votes by Topic: Counts of Votes Included on NAACP and NHLA Scorecards (105th–108th Congresses: 1997–2004)

Two aspects of the distribution of salient topics stand out in Figure 4.1. First, votes included in the scorecards of both groups are distributed across a variety of topics, confirming that while these groups serve specific constituencies, policies salient to minority interests are rather broad and diverse. Issues ranged from welfare, to gun control, to labor, to Cuba, to name just a few topics of the roll-call votes on which these groups took a position. Second, while variation exists, there are topics that take up larger portions of the groups' agendas. The four topics most frequently addressed in NAACP scorecards during this period were education (23 percent of the votes), crime (7 percent of the votes), civil rights (7 percent of the votes), and health care policy votes (7 percent of the votes). Together these topics accounted for about 45 percent of the NAACP's scorecard items. The NHLA's major topics shared two with the NAACP: education and civil rights. The most frequent topics included in NHLA scorecards were education (27 percent of the votes), civil rights (14 percent of the votes), economic mobility (12 percent of the votes), and immigration (10 percent of the votes). Together, the four policy areas accounted for 63 percent of the NHLA scorecard votes. In terms of overall salience, the scorecards reveal that while broader issue concerns were shared between the groups, the particular foci of the groups arguably diverge. Education and civil rights, both issues that have immediate effects on the two groups, maintained high levels of salience over the period examined for both groups. More specific problems faced by their respective constituencies – particularly crime, AIDS, gun control, and health care for the NAACP and immigration and economic mobility for the NHLA – demonstrate some difference in policy focus. While votes selected in these areas tended to distinguish the groups in terms of policy areas of interest, another important part of the story in the salience analysis is the wide array of policies represented, and in most cases, most major general topics were included by both advocacy groups. However, specific votes did not often overlap.

While there are indeed broad similarities in policy salience by topic, describing the nature of black-Latino relations requires us to consider the extent to which individual votes were jointly salient or salient to both groups, and if these groups shared the same position (congruence) on the issues salient to both. This is the next step in the analysis. Overall, as Table 4.1 highlights, there are relatively few votes that were included in both NAACP and NHLA scorecards. Of the 293 total votes included in the groups' scorecards, which includes votes in both the House and Senate, less than 10 percent (only 28) of the specific votes were chosen by both groups. In other words, there is a good deal of independence on the issues chosen. It is also clear from this finding that the two groups' scorecards diverge a great deal in terms of the importance each places on specific roll-call votes. This divergence suggests that the two groups do provide unique sets of priorities that may be interpreted as representative of the difference in policy issues emphasized by the NHLA and the NAACP. One implication is that there is likely to be little or no conflict if/when the two groups fail to focus on, or are not equally intensely interested in, the same issues. Independence and/or an absence of conflict implies that various policies are inherently not zero sum for the two groups. Indeed, they differ quite substantially in the issues in which they engage in the congressional voting arena. (This should be kept in mind when we evaluate support for these groups' positions in later chapters.)

In terms of congruence, Table 4.1 also displays the number of votes in each scorecard and the number of shared votes (shared salience) by Congress. The degree of commonality fluctuates as does the percentage of one group's scorecards that overlap with the other. However, in all Congresses, the percentage of overlap was relatively low compared to the percentage of votes that were identified independently by each group. In

TABLE 4.1. *Policy Salience and Congruence of Minority Advocacy Groups' Agendas (Number of Cases Included in Congressional Scorecards and Degree of Salience and Congruence)*

Congress	NHLA	NAACP	Shared Salience (% of NHLA Total; % of NAACP Total)	Congruence (% of Shared)
105th (1997–1998)	33	23	7 (21.1%; 30.4%)	7 (100%)
106th (1999–2000)	36	30	6 (16.67%; 20.0%)	6 (100%)
107th (2001–2002)	34	50	12 (35.3%; 24.0%)	12 (100%)
108th (2003–2004)	24	63	3 (12.5%; 4.8%)	3 (100%)
Total	127	166	28 (22.1%; 16.9%)	28 (100%)

Note: NAACP = National Association for the Advancement of Colored People; NHLA = National Hispanic Leadership Agenda.

general, neither group had votes that overlapped to the point that they made up more than about one-third of the total votes and the overlap for all Congresses was well below the one-third mark. For all roll-call votes included, about 22 percent of the votes included in the NHLA scorecards were also included in the NAACP's scorecards, while about 17 percent of the votes included in the NAACP scorecards were also included in the NHLA scorecards.

Yet *where the groups did include the same votes, they were entirely congruent in their position.* Table 4.1 also shows that in all twenty-eight of the votes that both groups deemed salient, the groups agreed on the preferred outcome. As Figure 4.1 demonstrates, shared salience and congruence were most likely observed in votes regarding affirmative action (100 percent of votes on this topic were congruent), civil rights (20 percent of votes on this topic were jointly salient, and 100 percent of those were congruent), and labor (18 percent of votes in this area were jointly salient and 100 percent of those were congruent). These votes were also distributed across both the House and the Senate.

The remaining common votes identified were spread across a number of topics as presented in Table 4.2. This table also shows that some of the congruent votes are massed in one chamber and in a particular Congress. For instance, three out of four of the affirmative action votes

TABLE 4.2. *Overlapping Votes as Identified by NAACP and NHLA Congressional Scorecards (Votes Categorized by Topic)*

House of Congress Session of Congress	House of Representatives 105 106 107 108				Senate 105 106 107 108				TOTAL
Civil Rights/Voting Rights	1	1	2	0	0	0	2	0	6
	4 total				2 total				
Affirmative Action	3	0	0	0	1	0	0	0	4
	3 total				1 total				
Education	0	0	0	1	1	0	4	0	6
	1 total				5 total				
Welfare	0	0	1	0	0	0	0	1	2
	1 total				1 total				
Health care	0	0	1	0	0	0	1	0	2
	1 total				1 total				
Labor	0	1	0	0	0	1	0	0	2
	1 total				1 total				
Economic Mobility	0	0	1	1	0	0	0	0	2
	2 total				0 total				
Crime	0	1	0	0	0	1	0	0	2
	1 total				1 total				
Immigration	0	0	0	0	1	0	0	0	1
	0 total				1 total				
Judicial	NA				0	1	0	0	1
					1 total				
TOTAL per Congress	4	3	5	2	3	3	7	1	28
Total per Chamber	14				14				

Note: NAACP = National Association for the Advancement of Colored People; NHLA = National Hispanic Leadership Agenda.

were identified in the House of Representatives in the 105th Congress, and four of the five congruent votes for education were in the Senate in the 107th Congress. This suggests that particular agenda items that spur cooperation may be driven by the legislative context (chamber) as well. Across Congresses, and across chambers, the issues vary that subsequently lead to votes that are deemed more important to mutual interests and ideas of black and Latino groups.

Congruence – A Winning Strategy?

Does congruence pay off? If both the NHLA and NAACP identify the same vote and hold the same position (which are one in the same as we

TABLE 4.3. *Congruence and Success: Percentage (and Number) of Favored Outcomes of Votes Included in Congressional Scorecards by the NAACP and NHLA, 105th–108th Congresses*

Congress	Vote Identified by NAACP Only	Vote Identified by NHLA Only	Vote Identified by Both NAACP and NHLA
All Congresses (105th – 108th)	47.83% (66 of 138)	29.29% (29 of 99)*	**64.29%** (10 of 28)
105th Congress	37.50% (6 of 16)	42.31% (11 of 26)	**71.43%** (5 of 7)
106th Congress	58.33% (14 of 24)	23.33% (7 of 30)*	**66.67%** (4 of 6)
107th Congress	44.74% (17 of 38)	22.73% (5 of 22)	**50.00%** (6 of 12)
108th Congress	48.33% (29 of 60)	28.57% (15 of 21)*	**100%** (3 of 3)

Note: Cells report the percentage of roll-call votes where the outcome was the result favored by the NAACP, NHLA, or both as indicated by their congressional scorecard ratings. The number of favored vote outcomes and total number of votes identified for each category are presented in the parentheses. **Bold** indicates highest percentage in each row. * signifies a significant ($p < .05$) difference between the individual group's success rate and when the votes were included in the ratings of both groups based on a chi-square test of difference in proportions. NAACP = National Association for the Advancement of Colored People; NHLA = National Hispanic Leadership Agenda.

show above), are roll-call results more likely to result in outcomes that reflect the positions of the two groups compared to when they identify issues separately? The analyses above show that on a vast majority of items on their scorecards, the NHLA and NAACP engage in independent behavior, so even if there is a benefit, it is not clear that it is the only driving factor in deciding to include a specific roll call in their ratings. These groups serve distinct constituencies and thus pursue distinct agendas. But there may not only be overlapping ideas and policy interests, but also victories, associated with congruence. If so, then it may be a coalitional strategy of pushing broad agendas that partially explains movements to cooperation as suggested in many of the theories that underlie the prediction of broad and sustained coalitions.

Table 4.3 reports the percentage of roll-call items included only in the NAACP or NHLA scorecards that resulted in an outcome favored by each organization in the second and third columns for the individual Congresses as well as aggregated for all four Congresses. In the fourth column, this winning percentage is reported for votes that both groups included in their scorecards (the congruent votes). The column categories are mutually exclusive. The data do suggest that cooperative behaviors are more successful. The percentage of favored outcomes for the votes identified by both groups ranges across Congresses, with a low of 50 percent success in the 107th Congress to 100 percent success in the 108th Congress. For all Congresses combined, when both groups identify the same vote and take the same position they are successful just under two-thirds of the time (64.3 percent). In every Congress and in aggregate, the preferred outcome was less likely when the NAACP or NHLA identified votes that the other did not. In short, going it alone tended to result in relatively fewer successful outcomes than did cooperation.

But there are some nuances and caveats that should be noted. Given the low number of cases of congruent votes, there is little evidence of statistically significant differences across the categories. The NAACP's independence success rate is not lower from a statistically significant perspective. And only in the 106th, 108th, and the aggregation of all Congresses were statistically significant differences found between the likelihood of NHLA-only identified votes ending favorably for the group versus the congruent votes. Yet, it is still striking that favorable outcomes were more likely for congruent positions, and this effect was clearest (from a statistically significant standpoint) for the Latino advocacy group (NHLA). It seems that the benefit of cooperation is most pronounced for the NHLA.

It may also be the case that when the two groups took the same position, they were reflecting a much wider level of support for their position by various other groups and interests. The result thus might be that wide coalitions are driving success, not simply cooperation by these two groups. The groups both simply picked winners. This suggestion, however, does not seem to undermine the basic intuition of these or the rest of the results we present. First, if cooperation occurred only on winning votes, then the assumption that large coalitions held the same position on the issue is certainly compatible with overlapping interests and non-zero sum policies between NHLA and NAACP constituents. Moreover, it suggests that such large coalitions can emerge in the national arena and the breadth and nature of the policies at this level of government may be driving this. And such a phenomenon is consistent within our general arguments. However, it is really the evidence that many roll-call items were not congruent or jointly included in NAACP and NHLA issues that suggests the importance of congruence.

If groups were simply picking winners, then why go it alone when there is generally less likelihood of a favored outcome relative to cooperation? The answer seems to be that distinct interests tend to drive issue salience, and that congruence occurs when both groups share similar interests (and perhaps even share those interests with other groups). And finally, it is still and perhaps especially important to keep in mind that there were no instances of conflict. Conflict may further reduce the likelihood of favorable outcomes, although since there are no incidences of conflict, we cannot infer this from our evidence. Moreover, it may be that conflict jeopardizes cooperation on other issues and/or in future Congresses. If this is the case, the lack of conflict may be a result of both groups desiring to keep the possibility of the beneficial cooperative strategy alive and well. These are interesting points of speculation that we hope future research will address.

Conclusion

The evidence in this chapter suggests that conflict does not emerge across national minority advocacy organizations in the identification of, and position on, important congressional roll-call votes. Yet, there are relatively little obvious specific similarities or incidences of cooperation in the process of identifying pertinent roll-call votes either. Groups tend more often to follow a path of independence or nonconflict, pursuing different sets of priorities (e.g., immigration vs. AIDS), and identify different key decisions as salient even within the same general policy area. When they do identify the same sets of votes as priority issues, there is a complete absence of competition or position divergence. Instead, in each of the twenty-eight votes jointly identified as priorities, the NHLA and the NAACP always took the same position.

Table 4.4 provides a selection of examples of topics for votes that fell in the categories of independence or cooperation for the scorecard analysis in this chapter. In several ways, the results are strongly consistent with those found in the previous chapter. For Latino groups, independence was noticeable on the issue of immigration. Given the potential for immigration to conflict with black groups' interests, particularly the interests of poorer low-skilled workers, lack of conflict on this topic is striking. For black groups, independence emerged around AIDS and gun control. Cooperation, however, was evident in areas where both groups shared similar interests, particularly on votes dealing with civil rights, affirmative action, and labor. And again we note that as our findings on

TABLE 4.4. *Summary of Empirical Findings from Scorecards with Respect to the Analytical Framework*

Nature of Interests	Expected Intergroup Relations	Empirical Observations[a]
Shared Interests High	Cooperation (No conflict)	Scorecards: Civil Rights Affirmative Action Labor
Non-Zero Sum Policies Shared Interests Low to Modest	Independence or Possibly Negotiation[a] (No conflict)	Scorecards: Immigration (Latino) AIDS (Black) Gun Control (Black)
Zero Sum Policies Shared Interests Low	Conflict	No Incidences

[a] It is possible for negotiation and independence to lead to the same empirical observations, and thus we include both behaviors and observations in the same cells.

congressional testimony and amicus briefs demonstrated, there are no incidences of conflict in roll-call votes identified in NAACP and NHLA scorecards.

These findings highlight several points that contrast with those of previous research on urban politics and the perception of group conflict, or cooperation, common in much scholarly as well as popular discourse. First, the congressional scorecard data analysis indicated modest levels of overlap among the issues identified by the Latino and black advocacy groups; that is, specific issue salience differs considerably between the groups. This may come as a surprise to some or many observers who assume a uniform (liberal) policy agenda among these groups, but our suggestion is that the geographic breadth and types of policy responsibility at the national level are possible reasons for the relatively small number of mutually salient issues, and congruence on those that are mutually salient. At the same time, we found no evidence of conflict in the positions taken by the groups. In the roughly 10 percent of votes identified by both groups as salient, there was complete congruence in positions. The conflict between blacks and Latinos often apparent in studies examining urban/local settings is certainly not replicated in the activities of minority advocacy groups in the national political processes we have examined.

Our analyses in the next two chapters move from minority interest/ advocacy groups, which seek to influence government but are technically not government officials per se, to constitutionally elected officials, that is, minority members of the U.S. Congress, acting within the formal institutions of government. Whether black and Latino officeholders in the national legislative body, and who exercise formal authority, display behaviors suggestive of conflict, cooperation, or something else in their policy decisions is another major question within our larger investigation.

5

Black-Latino Relations in the
U.S. House of Representatives

Thus far, we have examined relationships between minority advocacy groups as they seek to influence Congress and the Supreme Court. Most significantly, there was no evidence of conflict between blacks and Latinos in those endeavors, in contrast to what is widely portrayed in previous studies focused on urban politics. Instead, the evidence pointed to the general independence of policy positions, punctuated by cooperation on a relatively small set of policy issues when minority interest groups advocated on behalf of their constituents in the legislative and legal arenas. National advocacy groups represent a national geography of interests, of course. And thus the lack of conflict we have found so far may be dampened when localized interests pull policy advocates away from the singular national interests of the advocacy groups we have examined in Chapters 3 and 4. In this chapter we expand our investigation in important ways, focusing the analysis on another dimension of black-Latino relations – the voting behavior of members of Congress (MCs) on a distinct set of roll-call votes. That is, we shift from the role of important, though informal actors, advocacy groups, and examine significant actors who play fundamental roles in a major formal institution of the national government as elected representatives – members of the U.S. House of Representatives.

The electoral connection that purportedly dominates MCs' behavior is one potential source that links mass-based conflict sometimes found in local geographic districts to national level politics (Mayhew 1974). Thus, it may be that MCs' attention to mass preferences will reflect the conflict suggested in local level studies, even when national policy issues are addressed. Conflict could emerge as MCs are more influenced by, or beholden to, localized geographic interests than are national minority advocacy groups. On the other hand, it is arguable that MCs are at least partly removed or detached from certain direct local influences because of the different geographic breadth and the types of policy authority they have, along with the role of political parties and/or ideology in national governance – and these contrast considerably with the situation of local governments (and of mass attitudes). These various possibilities underscore the importance of closely examining minority (and white) MCs' behaviors as part of our assessment of black-Latino relations at the national level. As we shall see, the findings on minority MCs' voting within this formal institution of government closely approximate the findings on advocacy groups in the informal (or mediating) institutional arena of interest group politics. That is, we see no or very little clear evidence of conflict, some evidence of compatibility, and a number of null findings suggestive of independence or nonconflict.

An evaluation of the scorecards created by national minority advocacy groups in the previous chapter showed there is little overlap in the salience of votes identified on the NAACP and the NHLA House scorecards in the 105th to the 108th Congresses.[1] That is, the two groups differ considerably in the salience they attach to various issues. Also recall that when the roll-call votes did overlap, the black and Latino advocacy groups always took the same position on the issue; in other words, there was extremely high congruence on the few overlapping issues. This small degree of overlap suggests that the scorecard ratings are specific to each group's agenda and not a reflection of an underlying black-Latino policy focus or preference that is identical to both. (Appendix 5.1 illustrates the range of policy issues addressed, as well as the lack of substantial overlap in salient roll calls.) The scorecards are particularly useful because they allow for separate indicators of MCs' support for black and for Latino interests as defined by the advocacy group measures. And in turn, we can examine the degree to which descriptive representation (representational effects) and minority populations (mass effects), first and foremost, along with other factors, such as partisanship, lead to independence or cooperation in the support of individual MCs for black and Latino interests.

[1] The National Hispanic Leadership Agenda is a coalition of Latino organizations that had published scorecards on congressional votes for its members since the 105th Congress. Scorecards can be accessed at www.lulac.org/advocacy/scorecard.html. Scorecards for the NAACP, and included votes, can be found at www.naacp.org. There were 140 unique House votes identified by the two groups, with 14 of those votes identified on both the NAACP and the NHLA scorecards.

The central questions in this chapter concern several aspects of minority group politics as they relate to intergroup relations. The first is the degree to which descriptive representation, or the representation of minority groups through racial/ethnic group members, affects the voting records regarding minority interests and intergroup relations. That is, are racial/ethnic minority MCs more likely to have scorecard ratings reflecting less conflict, or compatibility, with the concerns of the "other" minority group's issues, and in comparison nonminority MCs? In a related sense the question is, do the minority MCs act not only as delegates for their specific congressional districts and their own racial/ethnic groups, but also as trustees for minority interests broadly (see Juenke and Preuhs, forthcoming)? The second, closely related, issue addressed in this chapter concerns whether the racial/ethnic composition of a congressional district affects the voting behavior of the MC for their own and for the other minority group? For instance, if Latino constituents oppose black interests, as reflected in the contention that conflict characterizes black-Latino relations, then we might expect to find a negative relationship between Latinos in an MC's district and that MC's support for black interests. Conversely, a positive relationship signifies cross-group cooperation. Finding no relationship between the racial/ethnic composition of a district and the MC's support for minority group interests echoes a common finding in previous chapters, that black-Latino relations are predominantly characterized by independence. In addition, parties in Congress act as broad-based coalitions that can dampen conflict and heighten cooperative dispositions; and we note later that the party organizations can play an important role in mitigating conflict, and are broad mechanisms (and whose impact is not as widespread, consistent, or clear-cut in local politics, Trounstine 2010).

Addressing these issues provides fuller understanding of the nature of MCs' intergroup relations, as well as suggesting paths that affect them. Since the policies deal with national issues and a wide geographic set of interests, but representation is often seen as local and responsive to the smaller geographic interest of the congressional district, examining intergroup relations through MC voting behavior provides an important context from which to examine our claims. Indeed, if there is conflict in black-Latino relations at the national level, we might well expect to find it in the behavior of representatives formally elected from the districts that collectively constitute the premier legislative body of the U.S. government, Congress (and especially, here, the House of Representatives). We begin our assessment with a discussion of previous scholarship as a background for the analysis in this chapter, and then examine how MCs vote as recorded on black and Latino advocacy group legislative scorecards.

Intergroup Relations in Congressional Voting

A good deal of research relevant to the specific concerns of this chapter has addressed the extent of influence of black and Latino members of Congress on policy, assessing issues of both descriptive and substantive representation (Griffin and Newman 2008; Canon 1999; Whitby 1997; Casellas 2007; Grose 2005; Hero and Tolbert 1995; Cameron, Epstein and O'Halloran 1996; Espino 2007; Fleisher 1993; Hood and Morris 1998; Hutchings 1998; Lublin 1997; Overby and Cosgrove 1996; Sharpe and Garand 2001; Welch and Hibbing 1984; Whitby and Krause 2001). Many of these studies consider whether minority members actually vote differently from others. There has also been a handful of parallel studies of descriptive and substantive representation in *state* legislatures (Preuhs and Juenke 2011; Juenke and Preuhs 2012; Casellas 2007; Bratton and Haynie 1999; Haynie 2001; Preuhs 2005, 2006, 2007; Owens 2005). The focus of these studies is the degree to which black or Latino representatives support black or Latino interests, respectively. To this point, however, there has not been a systematic analysis of black and Latino legislative voting patterns on issues of direct concern to each other. There has thus been no way to gauge the effect of descriptive or substantive representation on conflict or support in the congressional arena. The particular scorecards we draw on offer what in our view is the best, most direct, and most sufficiently large base of evidence available for and appropriate to our specific analytical purposes.

The NAACP and NHLA seek to influence the public policy decisions of Congress that are particularly important to blacks and Latinos in part through the scorecards they create. Examining votes on those scorecards thus seems a good way to assess whether there is conflict or something else in black and Latino MCs' relations in Congress. Most of the previous studies examining a group's representatives use much broader indicators of civil rights scores rather than examining a set of votes of more specific interest to racial/ethnic minority groups. For example, the Leadership Conference on Civil Rights' (LCCR) scorecard is commonly used as an indicator of minority interests. However, LCCR is a broad coalition comprising a wide variety of groups and thus the LCCR scorecards include votes regarding religious minorities, women, and people with physical disabilities. Other indicators sometimes used in the study of racial/ethnic concerns are even broader, such as NOMINATE scores, which are a general measure of MC liberalism (see Canon 1999, 290–291; Crespin and Rohde 2007; Burden 2007 for criticisms of these; for exceptions to these practices, see Baker and Cook 2005; Hero and Tolbert 1995). Policy concerns especially germane to blacks and Latinos are underrepresented in these indicators. There is certainly a substantial degree of compatibility with black or Latino interests and general liberalism (versus conservatism) as suggested by our broader argument about shared interests in non-zero sum contexts at the national versus state level; but there are differences as well (e.g., see Banting and Kymlicka 2006, chapter 1). Further, the composition of votes included in scorecards from the NHLA and NAACP diverge considerably (as seen in Chapter 4) and this can be leveraged to examine the nature of minority MCs' intergroup voting behavior.

How members of Congress vote on actual governance decisions is a substantive, policy-focused basis for assessing relations between groups. It is thus useful to consider how members of Congress vote and the factors that explain the votes on issues identified by minority advocacy groups. Of particular interest are how racial/ethnic minority members vote and, specifically, how Latino MCs rate on the NAACP (black) scorecard, and how blacks rate on the NHLA (Latino) scorecard. Similarly important is whether constituent populations – the size of black and Latino populations within each congressional district – affect support of the MCs on the "other" group's scorecard rating. Finally, nonminority MC voting behavior, particularly Democrats who share party affiliation with most of the minority MCs, is analyzed to provide a reference point and add to previous findings about the degree to which political parties provide collective substantive representation (Hero and Tolbert 1995; Lublin 1997).

Representatives' voting decisions can be influenced by numerous factors, of course. A member's political party and/or ideology are consistently shown to explain much of roll-call voting. One claim is that disposition of the party more directly attentive to liberal concerns about racial/ethnic equality – Democrats since (at least) the 1960s – is one and likely the major instrument for addressing minority group policy concerns (Grose 2005; Hero and Tolbert 1995; Lublin 1997). Consistent with this, blacks and to a lesser degree Latinos in the electorate have been much more likely than the general population to affiliate as Democrats; furthermore, the black and Latino members of Congress were disproportionately, indeed almost entirely (among blacks), Democrats during the period under study. Thus, considering political party as a primary source of cross-group representation is an element of our analysis. (Some scholars have argued, however, that the American party system, including the Democratic Party, has *not* strongly advocated racial equality for various reasons or has done so only in very limited ways (see Frymer 1999; Minta 2009).

Certain questioning notwithstanding, the strong evidence that members' party affiliation has a major impact on their voting on legislation must be acknowledged, and this is indeed broadly consistent with our general argument. But is there some part of MC voting on and support for minority advocacy groups explicable by something other than party, such as their racial/ethnic background and/or the racial characteristics of their constituency? Again, previous research does not examine the extent to which minority officeholders vote in ways consistent with the preferences of "other" minority groups. Thus our central question remains: do we find conflict (or something else) in black-Latino relations in national politics – in this instance, in the voting of members of the U.S. House of Representatives?

Analysis of Minority MCs' Voting

With data from NAACP and NHLA ratings of MCs over five Congresses – specifically during the 104th (1995–96) to 108th (2003–04) for the NAACP, and the 105th to the 108th for the NHLA (the 105th was the first Congress in which the NHLA rated members) – we first describe and discuss the aggregate patterns of black and Latino members as well as of nonminority Democrats and Republicans. These two are arguably the most visible of the several minority advocacy groups associated with the questions we are investigating, and, for the purposes of our analysis, these groups' scorecards are useful because they consistently rate MCs over time. (We refer the reader to discussions in Chapter 3 regarding the basic background of these groups as ample bases for assessing support for minority group interests with these scorecards.)

General Patterns

To examine general trends in support for black and Latino interests, we provide in Tables 5.1 and 5.2, respectively, the average vote score and additional summary statistics on NAACP and NHLA scorecards of MCs, categorized by their party affiliation and racial group background. This initial evidence indicates that black Democrats had consistently high

TABLE 5.1.   *NAACP Ratings by Party and Racial/Ethnic Background,*
104th–108th Congresses

Congress	Member Type	Mean	Median	Standard Deviation	Cases
104th	Black Democrats	82.91	77.78	9.14	39
(1995–1996)	Latino Democrats	68.69	66.67	17.79	11
	White Democrats	51.08	55.56	17.86	159
	Black Republicans	22.22	22.22	11.11	3
	Latino Republicans	16.67	16.67	7.86	2
	White Republicans	15.76	11.11	12.11	232
105th	Black Democrats	96.85	100	8.18	37
(1997–1998)	Latino Democrats	89.29	91.67	11.98	14
	White Democrats	86.88	83.33	10.21	162
	Black Republicans	25.00	25.00	11.79	2
	Latino Republicans	36.11	33.33	20.97	3
	White Republicans	17.92	16.67	14.85	226
106th	Black Democrats	94.44	92.86	6.18	36
(1999–2000)	Latino Democrats	84.82	89.29	17.86	16
	White Democrats	84.08	85.71	15.17	162
	Black Republicans	21.43	21.43	n/a	1
	Latino Republicans	44.65	50.00	16.88	4
	White Republicans	32.42	28.57	14.18	221
107th	Black Democrats	92.37	94	6.37	35
(2001–2002)	Latino Democrats	93.25	94	6.44	16
	White Democrats	84.04	89	12.78	159
	Black Republicans	22	22	n/a	1
	Latino Republicans	26	28	3.46	3
	White Republicans	26.62	28	6.02	211
108th	Black Democrats	93.89	97	5.56	35
(2003–2004)	Latino Democrats	91.83	93	6.58	18
	White Democrats	88.07	90	9.78	152
	Black Republicans[a]	n/a	n/a	n/a	n/a
	Latino Republicans	30.6	30	2.51	5
	White Republicans	31.91	30	6.99	225

Note: Cases represent numbers of members of Congress (MCs) where data were available
and do not necessarily add up to 435. NAACP = National Association for the Advancement
of Colored People.
[a] No black Republicans served in the 108th Congress.

NHLA ratings, including the highest average ratings on NHLA scorecards in the 105th and 106th Congresses. As would be expected, black
Democrats rate very highly on the NAACP scorecard, with the average
support score ranging from 82.9 percent in the 104th Congress (the only

TABLE 5.2. *NHLA Ratings by Party and Racial/Ethnic Background,*
105th–108th Congresses

Congress	Member Type	Mean	Median	Standard Deviation	Cases
105th	Black Democrats	92.31	96	7.38	35
(1997–1998)	Latino Democrats	84.83	92	23.64	12
	White Democrats	83.15	83	11.84	160
	Black Republicans	20.50	20.50	17.68	2
	Latino Republicans	47.33	42	17.62	3
	White Republicans	19.05	13	15.04	223
106th	Black Democrats	88	91	6.45	36
(1999–2000)	Latino Democrats	82.81	86.50	12.19	16
	White Democrats	74.96	82	14.91	162
	Black Republicans	0	0	n/a	1
	Latino Republicans	22.75	4.50	39.73	4
	White Republicans	5.50	0	8.27	221
107th	Black Democrats	83.03	83.33	8.07	37
(2001–2002)	Latino Democrats	83.68	83.33	4.74	16
	White Democrats	71.06	72.22	13.42	158
	Black Republicans	11.11	11.11	n/a	1
	Latino Republicans	22.22	22.22	0.0	3
	White Republicans	12.39	11.11	7.54	222
108th	Black Democrats	96.62	100	14.09	37
(2003–2004)	Latino Democrats	99.67	100	1.41	18
	White Democrats	93.94	100	15.19	156
	Black Republicans[a]	n/a	n/a	n/a	n/a
	Latino Republicans	33	33	10.42	5
	White Republicans	19.91	17	10.63	232

Note: Cases represent numbers of members of Congress (MCs) where data were available and do not necessarily add up to 435. NHLA = National Hispanic Leadership Agenda.
[a] No black Republicans served in the 108th Congress.

Congress for which the mean was below 90 percent) to 96.8 percent in the 105th. Latino Democratic MCs generally rate quite high on the NAACP indicator (with one exception, the 104th Congress), and in one instance (the 107th Congress), Latinos actually rate slightly higher than black Democrats on this measure. Latino Democrats also have higher NAACP ratings than white Democrats, though not always by a large amount, averaging 6.6 percentage points higher across the five Congresses (104th to 108th). Overall, this preliminary evidence indicates that Latino and black Democrats do not diverge in their support for the other group's interests. Instead, minority MCs are generally more supportive of *both* black and Latino interests than are white Democrats.

Another point is noteworthy. Though few in number, Latino Republican MCs rate substantially higher than *white* Republicans on the NHLA scorecards; the former average over 17 percentage points higher than the latter over the four Congresses (105th to 108th). Hence, while Latino Republicans are broadly similar to white Republicans and have much lower ratings than Latino Democrats overall, they nonetheless initially appear to have somewhat higher scores on Latino-salient issues than do white Republicans. Latino Republicans also rate somewhat higher than white Republicans on the NAACP scores in the 105th and 106th Congresses, though Latino Republicans are essentially the same as white Republicans on the NAACP scores for the other three Congresses (104th, 107th, and 108th). In any event, even among Latino Republicans, there seems to be an absence of conflict as defined by being less supportive than partisan ties would suggest. It is also important to acknowledge the consistent difference in average ratings across parties for both NAACP and NHLA with Democratic MCs more supportive of both groups' agendas than Republican MCs. This initial glimpse of intergroup voting patterns clearly reinforces the interpretation that intergroup relations show essentially no conflict at the national level and provides some limited and mixed evidence of cooperation between the minority groups.

Multivariate Analysis

To examine the independent effects of the racial/ethnic characteristics of the representative, district-level constituency characteristics, and partisanship, several multiple regression analyses were undertaken. The variables used to capture each of these factors included in the models and their associated alternative explanations are as follows. To assess the effects of descriptive representation, or the racial/ethnic background of the MC, two dichotomous variables were constructed. *Black Representative* is coded as 1 for MCs who are black, and 0 otherwise, and *Latino Representative* is coded as 1 for Hispanic/Latino representatives, and 0 otherwise. While very few black and Latino Republicans served during the Congresses included in our analysis, there is the distinct possibility that partisanship conditions the effects of descriptive representation (cf. Baker and Cook 2005), which we address in two ways. We measure partisan affiliation as a dichotomous variable, *Republican*, which codes all Republican MCs as 1, and 0 otherwise. We also include interaction terms between the black and Latino Representative variables and the party (Republican) variable to capture the potential for a conditional effect of descriptive representation, and conduct a separate set of analyses following the full models that limit the sample to only Democrats to further control for partisan effects.

One of our main concerns is to examine whether responsiveness to certain preferences of constituencies might draw MCs away from advocacy for cross-group interests as the localized conflict influences national decisions through the electoral connection. Thus, racial/ethnic group constituency size is the first of the district characteristics to be considered. We include four racial/ethnic group measures in the models. We also use an array of district-level characteristics (from the U.S. Census Bureau) that have been shown to affect, or are plausibly related to, support for minority advocacy group interests (see Grose 2005; Hero and Tolbert 1995; Lublin 1997). *Proportion Latino* is the proportion of the district population that is of Latino or Hispanic origin. *Proportion Black* is the proportion of the population that is black, and *Proportion Asian* is the proportion of the population that is of Asian background.[2] Additionally, since Latino issues and the NHLA scorecards often include matters of immigration, we include the *Proportion Foreign Born* as an additional control. The size of the white population is excluded and serves as the baseline group.

The relative size of these groups, however, might lead to either positive or negative pressures on levels of support. If racial backlash is a mechanism driving legislative voting behavior, or the propensity to vote in ways deemed inconsistent with minority interests increases as minority population size increases, higher levels of minority population size would be negatively associated with NAACP and/or NHLA scores (see, e.g., Giles and Evans 1986; Fellowes and Rowe 2004; Preuhs 2007). It might also indicate conflict if one group's size is negatively related to the other group's scorecard ratings. Conversely, minority population size may increase representative support for minority issues as MCs respond to the interests of their minority constituents (Baker and Cook 2005; Grose 2005; Hero and Tolbert 1995; Lublin 1997). Given the potential for diverging effects, we test these and all the other coefficients with a two-tailed test of significance.

[2] We examined a number of specifications of these racial/ethnic constituency variables, including a curvilinear relationship, by including the raw and squared terms of each in all the models presented later in the chapter. Alternative specifications were not consistent across Congresses, nor did they change the substantive or statistical results of the main independent variables. Given a degree of covariance in racial/ethnic variables already included in the models, we opt to include only the raw term to avoid further threats to the validity of the results.

In addition to the racial and ethnic background of the MC, the racial/ethnic attributes of the MCs' constituents, and the MCs' political party affiliation, we also account for a variety of demographic and political factors that have been shown to influence MCs' voting behavior. The first, *Democratic Presidential Vote*, is a proxy for the ideological and partisan leanings of the district's constituency and is measured as the percentage of the vote for the Democratic candidate in the most recent general election. *Education* is the proportion of the district population with a college degree, *Urban* is the proportion of the population living in an urban area; both of these have been shown to be positively associated with support for general liberalism (Baker and Cook 2005; Grose 2005; Lublin 1997), and that is our expectation as well. *Poverty* is the proportion of the population living below the poverty level and *Income* is the median income of the district; these two variables capture district wealth. While wealth has been shown to be positively associated with support for general civil rights legislation, it is less clear that it is associated with liberalism defined more broadly (Grose 2005). Nevertheless, given the disproportionate presence of blacks and Latinos in the lower income and socioeconomic strata generally, these two measures serve as useful proxies for economic interests that may overlap with minority interests and ultimately affect MC support for minority group concerns.

More formally, we model support for NHLA and NAACP scores as a function of the ascriptive characteristics of the House member, his or her party affiliation, and district characteristics. The regression analysis is based on the following model:

Level of Support (NHLA or NAACP) = α + β_1 (Black
Representative) + β_2(Black Representative X
Republican) + β_3(Latino Representative) +
β_4(Latino Representative X Republican) +
β_5(Republican) + β_6(Proportion Latino) +
β_7(Proportion Black) + β_8(Proportion Asian) +
β_9(Proportion Foreign Born) +
β_{10}(Education) + β_{11}(Urban) +
β_{12}(Poverty) + β_{13}(Income) + error.

We are most interested in examining two questions with this model that relate to our overarching questions about what lead MCs to their

TABLE 5.3. *Predicted Effects of Black and Latino Representation and Population on NAACP and NHLA Scorecards*

Variable	Cooperation/ Compatibility (no conflict)		Independence (no conflict)		Conflict	
	NAACP Scorecard	NHLA Scorecard	NAACP Scorecard	NHLA Scorecard	NAACP Scorecard	NHLA Scorecard
Representation						
Black Representative	Positive	Positive	Positive	No Effect	Positive	Negative
Latino Representative	Positive	Positive	No Effect	Positive	Negative	Positive
Population						
Proportion Black	Positive	Positive	Positive	No Effect	Positive	Negative
Proportion Latino	Positive	Positive	No Effect	Positive	Negative	Positive

Note: Cell entries report the direction of the expected effect. No effect indicates there is an expected null relationship. NAACP = National Association for the Advancement of Colored People; NHLA = National Hispanic Leadership Agenda.

positions on minority agendas, and, by extension, interminority group relations. The first is the degree to which descriptive representation and racial/ethnic group constituencies as well as party (and other factors) explain voting patterns on issues important to specific minority groups. If the coefficients for the black and Latino (and partisan) background variables ($\beta_1 - \beta_4$) are positive and significant, there is evidence to support the claim that descriptive representation matters in inducing support, or at least mitigating conflict. The coefficient for the Republican dummy variable (β_5) should be negative and significant if party is a factor affecting substantive representation. The argument that substantive representation is driven by the racial/ethnic composition of the constituency, and thus substantive representation of minority groups is driven by electoral concerns, will be supported if $\beta_6 - \beta_9$ are significant. Conflict would be indicated by negative coefficients for the size of the black, Latino, Asian, or foreign born variables, but if these are positive, increasing support for minority concerns is implied.

Another important issue is the degree to which racial and ethnic descriptive representation mitigates conflict, suggests independence, or may even indicate higher scorecard ratings and thus support for other minority racial/ethnic group interests. The various expectations about the effects of descriptive representation and population size are summarized in Table 5.3. To explore the nature of intergroup relations indicated by the evidence, we examine the coefficients across different scorecard models. If β_1 and β_2 are positive in the NAACP models, but negative in the NHLA models, and β_3 and β_4 are positive in the NHLA models, but negative for NAACP models, conflict is indicated. If black and Latino MCs support each other's positions, the coefficients $\beta_1 - \beta_4$ should be positive and significant across both scorecards, and at a higher degree than whites, indicating compatibility (which is also "not conflict"). If black and Latino descriptive representation only matters regarding support for their own group's policy positions, meaning there is neither conflict nor compatibility across groups associated with descriptive representation, then we should see a pattern of black MCs having significantly higher support on NAACP issues only (β_1 and β_2 are positive only in the NAACP models) and the same for Latino MCs for NHLA models (β_3 and β_4 are positive only in the NHLA models). This would suggest "independence" associated with the distinct effects of descriptive representation, but not outright cooperation (but not conflict, either). While the average scores suggest that both groups tend to be more supportive of minority advocacy group positions than whites (as was shown in Tables 5.1 and 5.2), it is possible that black MCs' support for NHLA positions and Latino MCs' support for NAACP positions are lower than white support for each after controlling for district and party effects.

We further assess intergroup relations at the congressional district level by examining the racial and ethnic minority *constituency size* variables. In line with the previous discussion, if larger Latino populations are positively associated with higher ratings on NHLA positions, but negatively associated with ratings on the NAACP scorecard, and if black population size is positively associated with support for NAACP positions, but negatively associated with support for NHLA positions, competition, channeled through racial/ethnic constituency factors, is suggested. If both Latino and black population variables are positively associated with NAACP *and* NHLA scores, then there is evidence of not only substantive representation, but "cross-group" support (beyond an absence of conflict). Finally, independence is suggested if positive coefficients for the population variables are present only for each group's respective scorecard and are not significant in the other group's model. These several expectations are also summarized in Table 5.3. Our research and findings here contribute to the research on the impact of descriptive representation on the substantive policy representation of minority interests. More than that, however, our analytical approach enables us to provide the first exploration of underlying dynamics of relationships *between* racial/ ethnic groups and their descriptive representatives in congressional decision making.

Table 5.4 presents the analyses of MC ratings on NAACP scorecards for the 104th through the 108th Congresses and Table 5.5 presents the NHLA models for the 105th–108th Congresses.[3] For both the NAACP and NHLA analyses and for each Congress, two models are presented. The first excludes the descriptive representation variables while the second provides the results for the full model. Since minority population and descriptive representation are highly correlated, this approach allows us to examine the degree to which descriptive representation alone accounts for some of the variation in support for NAACP and NHLA policy positions; we do this by comparing the significance of only district minority population effects to the significance of the effect of descriptive representation once it is added to the model.

The results show that party affiliation is the most consistent explanation, reflecting previous research findings, and is also compatible with our general arguments (and we return to these points shortly). The next most consistent factor was the racial background of the MC. And we discuss and emphasize the nature and general importance of this finding first, followed by some more specific points. Most relevant is that in no Congresses were black representatives (statistically significantly) less likely to support NHLA positions, nor did any Congresses reveal that Latino MCs are less likely to support NAACP positions. In short, there is no evidence of conflict. If conflict arises in interminority group

---

[3] We also pooled cases for all Congresses in a single model to address the potential that small variations in each Congress would hide significant findings. The pooled design included controls for each Congress, but essentially double-counted most members as House turnover is rare. The results were indeed stronger for the effect of descriptive representation (both black and Latino MCs were significant), but the remaining findings reported in our Congress-by-Congress analysis remain. We found, essentially, a lack of conflict even with the pooled model. However, we choose to focus on the individual Congresses for two main concerns. First, there is a reasonable argument that the scores (our dependent variables) are incompatible across Congresses in that different issues are used to measure support and we do not want to mask real variation if it exists. Second, pooling technically requires independence across years and within MC observations in order to avoid biased estimates. We do not have enough variation to adequately deal with this issue. Given these two concerns and the general consistency in the finding that minority group conflict is not reflected in congressional voting patterns, we opt for the Congress-by-Congress approach for our analysis.

TABLE 5.4. *Ordinary Least Squares Model Estimates of NAACP Scorecard Ratings, 104th–108th Congresses*

Independent Variables	104th Congress		105th Congress		106th Congress		107th Congress		108th Congress	
Black Representative	27.26*** (4.41)		4.16 (4.03)		−0.64 (4.33)		7.27* (3.01)		1.41 (2.48)	
Proportion Black	−12.82 (9.44)	27.20*** (7.13)	−16.43+ (8.77)	−10.29+ (6.21)	−3.61 (9.21)	−4.35 (6.59)	−13.42* (6.53)	−3.31 (4.81)	−2.32 (5.55)	−0.20 (4.11)
Latino Representative	9.27+ (5.15)		0.36 (4.66)		−5.28 (5.21)		7.31* (3.64)		1.63 (2.77)	
Proportion Latino	4.36 (9.92)	12.01 (9.79)	−4.84 (9.57)	−0.91+ (8.50)	4.92 (10.99)	4.73 (9.29)	3.80 (7.67)	12.37+ (6.46)	9.05 (5.99)	10.05+ (5.24)
Republican	−32.23*** (2.29)	−26.77*** (2.31)	−64.25*** (2.13)	−64.37*** (2.11)	−40.46*** (2.33)	−43.74*** (2.24)	−51.95*** (1.60)	−50.76*** (1.57)	−47.96*** (1.34)	−47.45*** (1.29)
Black Rep * Republican	−19.70* (9.01)		6.69 (9.70)		−7.32 (13.81)		−9.87 (9.47)		n/a	
Prop. Black * Republican	39.99** (13.21)	4.50 (12.34)	3.32 (12.54)	−2.19 (11.10)	−13.98 (13.51)	−11.08 (11.94)	−0.29 (9.55)	−9.54 (8.60)	−8.29 (8.06)	−10.35 (7.07)
Latino Rep. * Republican	−4.42 (12.01)		3.12 (9.37)		19.01 (10.37)		−1.64 (7.87)		0.63 (5.66)	
Prop. Latino * Republican	4.84 (14.95)	4.36 (9.92)	30.24** (9.84)	20.18 (12.31)	−9.14 (11.98)	−27.74* (14.08)	−1.43 (8.84)	−3.55 (10.10)	−6.59 (7.37)	−1.70 (8.08)
Proportion Asian	40.45* (18.15)	41.82* (17.35)	−18.08 (15.90)	−20.88 (15.87)	−15.18 (16.66)	−14.27 (16.44)	7.58 (11.83)	8.09 (11.87)	8.45 (9.61)	6.66 (9.55)
Proportion Foreign Born	4.91 (14.89)	−3.13 (13.09)	−10.80 (11.94)	−16.55 (12.84)	−5.29 (13.65)	−14.92 (14.06)	14.23 (9.61)	−15.11 (9.97)	11.67 (7.66)	−9.76 (7.97)
Prop. Foreign Born * Republican	−26.45 (21.47)		21.64 (18.49)		61.60** (20.27)		−2.93 (15.21)		−9.64 (12.68)	

Education	11.23	14.15	-3.82	-11.05	75.06*	68.60*	35.48	34.41	12.98	11.55
	(33.51)	(32.14)	(29.60)	(29.68)	(31.39)	(31.65)	(22.17)	(21.94)	(15.21)	(15.16)
Urban	1.21	4.64	-0.34	0.54	-3.81	-1.64	-2.72	-1.69	-5.53+	-5.63+
	(4.67)	(4.58)	(4.26)	(4.37)	(4.50)	(4.60)	(3.31)	(3.31)	(3.10)	(3.11)
Poverty	7.72	24.01	-2.56	4.42	-2.85	9.98	-19.28	-15.96	-10.99	-11.32
	(30.84)	(29.75)	(27.32)	(27.48)	(29.03)	(29.53)	(20.02)	(19.97)	(13.36)	(13.45)
Income	0.01	0.01	0.01	0.01	-0.00	0.01	-0.01	0.00	0.01**	0.01**
	(.01)	(.01)	(0.01)	(.01)	(0.01)	(0.01)	(0.01)	(0.01)	(0.00)	(0.00)
Democratic Presidential Vote	0.62***	0.43***	0.73***	0.69***	0.79***	0.75***	0.47***	0.44***	0.48***	0.48***
	(.09)	(.09)	(.08)	(.09)	(.09)	(.09)	(.06)	(.06)	(.05)	(.05)
Constant	3.93	13.64	64.51***	43.06***	34.22***	28.17***	62.24***	63.38***	60.03***	60.59***
	(8.87)	(8.58)	(7.86)	(7.79)	(8.43)	(8.54)	(5.84)	(5.80)	(3.81)	(3.90)
N[b]	445	445	443	443	441	441	426	426	422	422
F	95.89***	87.06***	292.29***	236.65***	156.29***	124.18***	367.24***	303.67***	543.50***	469.00***
Adjusted R^2	.73	.76	.90	.90	.82	.82	.92	.92	.94	.94

Note: + indicates $p < .10$, * $p < .05$, ** $p < .01$, *** $p < .001$ in a two-tailed test of significance. Unstandardized OLS coefficients are reported, along with standard errors in parentheses. NAACP = National Association for the Advancement of Colored People.

[a] The base category are white Democrats for all models.

[b] N's reflect all members of Congress (MCs) holding office during the span of the Congress and available data.

TABLE 5.5. *Ordinary Least Squares Model Estimates of NHLA Scorecard Ratings, 105th–108th Congresses*

Independent Variables	105th Congress		106th Congress		107th Congress		108th Congress	
Black Representative	9.26* (4.49)		7.82* (3.82)		8.26** (3.17)		-3.53 (3.91)	
Proportion Black	-23.61** (9.51)	-9.71 (6.67)	-2.88 (8.11)	8.07 (5.89)	-16.16* (6.92)	-5.12 (5.21)	-14.48+ (8.79)	-20.16** (6.41)
Latino Representative	-3.59 (5.21)		4.67 (4.59)		7.76* (3.94)		-3.02 (4.42)	
Proportion Latino	0.54 (10.34)	3.93 (9.54)	7.88 (9.68)	13.13 (8.32)	3.72 (8.32)	13.67+ (7.05)	16.40 (9.52)	11.77 (8.35)
Republican	-57.87*** (2.27)	-58.51*** (2.26)	-62.25*** (2.05)	-61.78*** (2.01)	-52.31*** (1.73)	-52.25*** (1.71)	-63.74*** (2.09)	-65.57*** (2.03)
Black Rep * Republican	-3.98 (10.34)		-12.29 (12.16)		-8.61 (10.28)		n/a	
Prop. Black * Republican	1.76 (13.47)	-10.37 (11.85)	-8.35 (11.90)	-17.11 (10.68)	-1.91 (9.90)	-11.27 (8.92)	3.82 (12.81)	-11.83 (11.25)
Latino Rep. * Republican	25.94** (10.16)		10.89 (9.12)		10.32 (8.59)		18.73* (8.95)	
Prop. Latino * Republican	7.72 (10.72)	3.04 (13.88)	-1.16 (10.55)	3.87 (12.60)	-2.36 (9.06)	-8.44 (11.06)	-11.12 (11.50)	2.31 (12.48)
Proportion Asian	-15.29 (16.88)	-13.63 (17.09)	29.48* (14.66)	27.88+ (14.72)	11.02 (13.73)	8.23 (13.73)	-1.12 (15.30)	-5.50 (15.28)
Proportion Foreign Born	-2.99 (13.23)	-12.36 (14.46)	-16.01 (12.02)	-14.55 (12.58)	-22.28* (10.62)	-24.27* (11.05)	-23.50+ (12.20)	-18.56 (12.78)
Prop. Foreign Born * Republican		34.62+ (20.63)		2.98 (18.14)		17.76 (16.74)		-5.70 (19.74)

Education	-26.01	-39.33	76.99**	73.73**	-14.56	-20.27	-39.50	-36.75
	(32.07)	(31.87)	(28.08)	(27.86)	(24.28)	(23.94)	(24.28)	(24.09)
Urban	-3.08	0.28	-3.50	-1.60	0.76	2.56	2.73	4.31
	(4.59)	(4.65)	(4.03)	(4.05)	(3.58)	(3.56)	(4.85)	(4.87)
Poverty	2.61	12.69	-41.75	-32.04	-6.48	2.01	-23.69	-21.28
	(29.51)	(29.45)	(25.98)	(25.99)	(22.03)	(21.82)	(21.31)	(21.29)
Income	0.03+	0.03**	-0.02+	-0.02	0.00	0.00	0.00	0.01
	(0.01)	(0.01)	(0.01)	(0.01)	(0.01)	(0.01)	(0.00)	(0.01)
Democratic Presidential Vote	0.71***	0.62***	0.57***	0.51***	0.52***	0.48***	0.74***	0.73***
	(.09)	(.09)	(.08)	(.08)	(.06)	(.06)	(.07)	(.07)
Constant	34.24***	33.60***	51.00***	61.34***	46.90***	45.35***	56.47***	54.44***
	(8.44)	(8.33)	(7.54)	(7.53)	(6.43)	(6.33)	(6.07)	(6.18)
N^b	435	435	441	441	438	438	435	435
F	218.57***	180.57***	337.20***	278.04***	338.32***	282.89***	376.10***	328.75***
Adjusted R^2	.87	.87	.91	.91	.91	.91	.92	.92

Note: + indicates $p < .10$, * $p < .05$, ** $p < .01$, *** $p < .001$ in a two-tailed test of significance. Unstandardized OLS coefficients are reported, along with standard errors in parentheses. NHLA = National Hispanic Leadership Agenda.

[a] The base category are white Democrats for all models.

[b] N's reflect all Members of Congress (MCs) holding office during the span of the Congress and available data.

relations in Congress, and it does *not* appear to, it is not through the voting behavior among minority descriptive representatives. Indeed, it seems that descriptive representation might provide at least a limited basis for "cross-group" support; these results offer modest confirmation for descriptive representation as both a vehicle for minority group advocacy and a vehicle for cross-group advocacy.

Black representatives were significantly more supportive of both NAACP and NHLA votes when compared to the baseline category of white representatives in many of the Congresses, or at least to a greater degree than the other possible explanations. In two of the five models of the NAACP ratings, black representatives were significantly more supportive than white MCs. In the 104th Congress, black MCs were 27 percentage points more supportive than whites, while they were about 7 percentage points more supportive than whites in the 107th Congress. In one instance for the NAACP ratings, the 104th Congress, black Republicans were less supportive than their fellow white partisans. For NHLA ratings, black representatives were more consistently supportive in three Congresses, ranging from 7.8 percentage points more supportive of the Latino agenda in the 106th Congress to 9.26 percentage points more supportive in the 105th Congress. And it is important to note that black MCs never exhibited a significant negative coefficient (which would have indicated less support for NHLA positions than given by their non-black counterparts).

Latino representatives were less consistent supporters of NHLA and NAACP positions than blacks, but were *never* significantly *less* supportive of NHLA positions than non-Latino counterparts. In three of the nine full models (in Tables 5.4 and 5.5 combined), Latino representatives were significantly more supportive of minority positions than were whites. Latino Democrats displayed cross-group support with higher ratings than white representatives on the NAACP scorecards in two of the five Congresses examined (104th and 107th) and own-group support on NHLA scorecards higher than white support once, in the 107th. Furthermore, in the 105th and 108th Congresses, Latino *Republicans* were more supportive of NHLA positions than their Republican colleagues. There were no other instances of significant effects of descriptive representation.

What is the impact of racial demographics in the MC's district? Comparing the black and Latino population coefficients in the models excluding the descriptive representation variables (see the second and fourth rows of Tables 5.4 and 5.5, the first column for each Congress) to the full models (the second column for each Congress) reveals that in most of the Congresses examined, the racial background of the representative has a more consistent positive effect than the racial composition of the constituency alone. Black population is only positive and significant in one of the five Congresses for NAACP ratings, and never positive and significant in the four Congresses for NHLA models, compared to positive and significant effects of the black representative variable in two Congresses for the NAACP models and three of four Congresses for NHLA models. Latino populations similarly exhibit limited effects. The Latino population variable is significant in three of the NAACP models – a negative effect in the 105th Congress and positive effects for the 107th and 108th – and only one of the NHLA congressional scorecard models excluding descriptive representation variables. Moreover, when black population size exerts a significant effect in the full NAACP models, the coefficients are *negative*. The Latino population variable never exerts an independent effect on NHLA models. While there is ample evidence from previous research to support the contention that racial/ethnic population is a key factor in the *election* of minority MCs, and thus there is presumably a positive indirect effect on MC voting behavior, minority population size does not have an independent (positive and direct) effect on MC voting patterns in most models.

There is some evidence that minority population size can lead MCs to reduce support for the other group, and thus constituency-induced conflict may be reflected in MC voting decisions. Note that the size of the black population exerts a negative and significant effect on support for NHLA scores in three Congresses (the 105th, 107th, and 108th). All else equal, MCs from districts with larger black populations tended to support Latino interests less than MCs from districts with fewer black constituents. However, this effect is offset by descriptive representation. In these initial findings it seems that though conflict may emerge from mass or population-based preferences in some instances – for instance, from black constituents on Latino issues – a black MC (elite) mitigates these effects. The moderating mechanism, then, seems to be the commonly supportive or cooperative orientation of minority elected, "elite" officials, MCs, and not simply a reaction from population characteristics and in turn presumably mass opinion.

Additionally, when minority population size is a factor in same-group advocacy, it suggests "backlash" (Giles and Evans, 1986) to group-specific interests. In the 105th and 107th Congresses, large black populations were associated with less support for NAACP positions. This may indicate that without a large black population and subsequent descriptive representation, black interests face a backlash effect. Efforts to control for curvilinear effects in the models demonstrated that this pattern was not simply a function of population, but also of descriptive representation. On the whole, however, there is little evidence beyond racial/ethnic background and partisan explanations of factors that consistently suggest support for minority issues. (We further explore the ideological elements later in this chapter as well as in Chapter 6.)

The coefficient for Republicans is negative and significant in every specification in both NAACP and NHLA models, and indicates that Republicans' ratings are about 28 to 72 percentage points lower than Democrats' ratings on the NHLA and NAACP scorecards. While there is no consistent pattern, for the 105th through the 108th Congresses, where comparable data are available, the Republican coefficient averaged −56.67 in the full NAACP models and −64.85 in the full NHLA models. The largest differences were found in the 106th and 108th Congresses. And the proxy for district ideology and partisan strength is also a significant factor in every model. Here, again, the effects vary a good deal by Congress and advocacy group, but the effect is generally quite strong. For every 1 percent increase in support for the Democrat candidate, NAACP ratings rose from between .43 percent (in the 104th Congress) to .75 percent (in the 106th Congress), all else equal. The NHLA effects were similar, with a one point increase in support for the Democratic Presidential candidate leading to ratings increases between .48 in the 107th Congress to .78 in the 108th Congress.

Clarifying the Analysis of the Intersection of Descriptive Representation and Party

To present the results more clearly, Figure 5.1 displays the 95% confidence intervals (CIs) for the estimated levels of support from Black and Latino Democrats relative to White Democrats from Tables 5.4 and 5.5. The large background bars reflect the typical level of support expected from a white Democratic MC, while the smaller bar and capped lines represent the estimated level of support from black and Latino Democrats, respectively. Each is estimated holding all other factors at their mean.[4]

---

[4] The results presented in Figure 5.1 are based on the results of the full models presented in Tables 5.4 and 5.5. The mean values and CIs are estimated using Clarify (Tomz, Whittenberg, and King 2001).

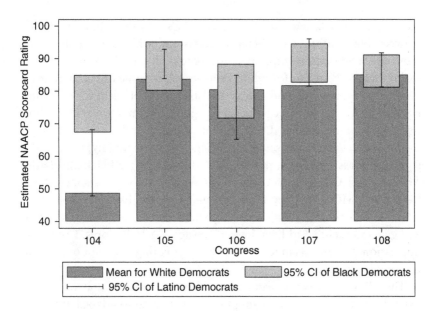

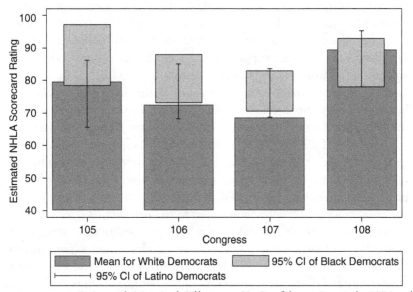

FIGURE 5.1. Estimated Marginal Effects, 95% Confidence Intervals (CIs), of Black and Latino Democrats on NAACP and NHLA Scorecard Ratings

Support for black interests by Latino MCs generally lies somewhere between black support for black interests and white support for black interests. While Latino support could potentially dip into the 'negative' realm (below the mean for white Democrats), in none of the analyses of NAACP support score models was the estimated coefficient for the Latino representative variable negative and significant; moreover, we cannot reject the hypotheses that the black representative and Latino representative coefficients were the same according to F-tests (null hypothesis: $\beta_1 - \beta_3 = 0$). This is evident in the large overlap in CIs for black and Latino MCs in most Congresses. Latino MCs were not always distinguishable from white MCs. But they were *also* indistinguishable from black MCs who were distinctly strong policy advocates in two of the Congresses and generally tended to have higher average NAACP scores. Conflict or opposition does not seem to be evident in the voting behavior of minority Congressional elites.

The NHLA scorecard segment of Figure 5.1 shows that in general, black Democrats were more supportive of the Latino advocacy groups' positions and, again, a good degree of overlap tends to occur in the estimated marginal effects across black and Latino Democrats. Latino Democrats, across both sets of scorecards, were more similar to their white partisan counterparts than black Democrats. Thus, the most plausible interpretation is that support across racial/ethnic groups consistently emerges more from black MCs than Latino MCs. Most notably for our larger argument, however, there is no statistically discernible evidence of interminority group conflict. None of the Congresses studied revealed that black or Latino MCs were significantly less likely than whites to support the NHLA or NAACP, respectively. Rather, the evidence suggests some modest levels of compatibility that vary by Congress but are most pronounced in black voting regarding Latino concerns. And when population characteristics tended to move support away from minority interests, descriptive representation acted to mitigate this effect.

Since most of the black and Latino MCs included in the analyses presented here are Democrats, and the party variable accounts for much of the variation in support for NAACP and NHLA positions, further clarification of the independent effects of, and cross-group support through, minority representatives can be gained by examining only Democratic MCs.[5] Furthermore, it may be that the "backlash' found with the

---

[5] When party is the sole independent variable included in a model of NAACP or NHLA scores, the adjusted R^2s range from .61 to .91.

full sample is primarily a result of partisan differences in reactions to minority population size and/or a residual effect from the relationship between minority population size and the descriptive representation variable. Accordingly, Tables 5.6 and 5.7 present models of NAACP and NHLA scorecard ratings, respectively, that restrict the sample to only Democratic MCs and thus allow us to disentangle the effects of population and descriptive representation. Two model specifications are presented for each Congress. One includes only the population variables and district characteristics included in the previous models and the other adds the descriptive representation variables to the models.

Note that the proportion black variable by itself is never significant in the NAACP models and compare this to the significant positive effects of black representatives in three Congresses for NAACP ratings. Latino population size is significant in only one of the NAACP models (a positive effect in the 108th). However, unlike the previous analysis, Latino MCs do not exert independent effects when we evaluate only Democratic MCs. In the NHLA models (Table 5.7), proportion black is negative once again in the 105th and 107th Congresses. However, the black representative variable also exerts a significant positive effect in those Congresses (and in the 106th Congress, the black MC variable is close to being statistically significant [p<.101]). Though proportion Latino exerts a slightly significant effect in the 107th NHLA scores when we do not control for Latino representatives, the Latino population variable no longer exerts a significant effect when descriptive representation is taken into account. The results presented in the full sample models in Tables 5.4 and 5.5, along with these results for the models including only Democrats, affirm the independent role of descriptive representation in cross-group support. It is clear that party has a substantial role in providing cross-group support and dampening conflict as the effects of descriptive representation are diminished in these analyses.

While party clearly plays the major role, sometimes offsetting the effects of minority representation (particularly in NHLA ratings), descriptive representation is a more significant factor in explaining both minority group support and cross-group support than many of the nonparty related factors. There still remains, however, some evidence of backlash emerging from localized geographic interests even after confining the analysis to Democrats. Black population is negatively associated with NAACP scores in two Congresses and the size of the foreign-born population is negatively related to NHLA scores in the 107th Congress. Surprisingly, but again underscoring the role of descriptive representation and party

TABLE 5.6. *Ordinary Least Squares Model Estimates of NAACP Scorecard Ratings, Democrats Only, 104th–108th Congresses*

Independent Variables	104th Congress (1995–1996)		105th Congress (1997–1998)		106th Congress (1999–2000)		107th Congress (2001–2002)		108th Congress (2003–2004)	
	NAACP	NAACP	NAACP	NAACP	NAACP	NAACP	NAACP	NAACP	NAACP	NAACP
Black Representative		20.22***		5.42+		1.31		6.93+		1.81
		(5.03)		(3.15)		(4.58)		(3.59)		(2.49)
Proportion Black	6.79	−18.89+	−3.28	−11.54	4.03	0.81	−9.77	−18.33*	0.58	−1.41
	(9.25)	(11.04)	(5.69)	(7.40)	(8.09)	(10.37)	(6.75)	(8.49)	(4.64)	(5.87)
Latino Representative		8.67		−0.46		−6.40		6.99		2.89
		(5.45)		(3.63)		(5.41)		(4.34)		(2.80)
Proportion Latino	8.15	−0.76	0.26	0.02	8.53	15.92	11.78	2.34	12.87*	9.55
	(11.86)	(12.25)	(7.57)	(8.64)	(11.01)	(12.84)	(8.74)	(10.20)	(6.09)	(6.80)
Proportion Asian	52.90*	46.48*	−2.57	2.14	.02	2.00	12.78	9.77	14.06	14.13
	(20.95)	(20.31)	(13.27)	(13.36)	(18.91)	(19.01)	(15.00)	(14.95)	(10.23)	(10.28)
Proportion Foreign Born	−12.66	−10.03	7.06	−14.82	−14.31	−18.89	−26.16	−20.80	−19.54*	−17.65*
	(17.06)	(16.52)	(31.19)	(11.14)	(15.97)	(16.45)	(12.86)	(13.17)	(8.73)	(8.89)
Education	−75.49	−55.44	−1.82	5.39	96.94*	97.74*	−2.01	−0.61	20.09	20.97
	(51.12)	(49.70)	(4.51)	(31.22)	(43.18)	(43.22)	(33.92)	(33.63)	(19.87)	(19.96)
Urban	6.54	12.56+	−1.82	−0.14	−6.28	−5.78	0.83	2.67	2.90	3.08
	(6.72)	(6.65)	(4.51)	(4.61)	(6.41)	(6.55)	(5.35)	(5.39)	(4.53)	(4.54)
Poverty	−35.24	−10.88	−7.00	−1.08	10.06	12.87	−10.06	−5.03	−18.03	−20.66
	(44.27)	(43.02)	(28.09)	(28.60)	(39.79)	(40.18)	(31.54)	(31.46)	(16.97)	(17.20)
Income	0.00	−0.00	−0.00	−0.00	0.00	0.00	0.00	0.01	0.01	0.01
	(0.22)	(0.02)	(0.01)	(0.02)	(0.01)	(0.02)	(0.01)	(0.02)	(0.01)	(0.01)

Democratic Presidential Vote	1.19*** (.14)	0.88*** (.15)	0.55*** (.10)	0.51*** (.10)	0.59*** (.13)	0.59*** (.14)	0.58*** (.09)	0.51*** (.10)	0.43*** (.06)	0.42*** (.07)
Constant	-11.70 (13.94)	-2.28 (13.77)	58.01*** (8.63)	58.84*** (8.65)	40.27*** (11.98)	39.80*** (12.10)	52.03*** (9.29)	53.36*** (9.24)	57.90*** (4.90)	59.07*** (5.01)
N[b]	209	209	212	212	214	214	210	210	200	200
F	25.82***	24.43***	8.03***	6.89***	7.06***	5.91***	8.91***	7.92***	17.66***	14.53***
Adjusted R^2	.52	.55	.23	.23	.20	.20	.25	.27	.43	.43

Note: + indicates $p < .10$, * $p < .05$, ** $p < .01$, *** $p < .001$ in a two-tailed test of significance. Unstandardized OLS coefficients are reported, along with standard errors in parentheses. NAACP = National Association for the Advancement of Colored People.

[a] The base category are white Democrats for all models.

[b] N's reflect all members of Congress (MCs) holding office during the span of the Congress and available data.

TABLE 5.7. *Ordinary Least Squares Model Estimates of NHLA Scorecard Ratings, Democrats Only, 105th–108th Congresses*

Independent Variables	105th Congress (1997–98)		106th Congress (1999–2000)		107th Congress (2001–2002)		108th Congress (2003–2004)	
	NHLA	NHLA	NHLA	NHLA	NHLA	NHLA	NHLA	NHLA
Black Representative		10.48**		7.16		8.42*		-2.18
		(4.13)		(4.36)		(3.79)		(4.31)
Proportion Black	-2.48	-18.42*	-1.24	-10.58	-6.52	-16.90+	-15.08+	-12.14
	(7.24)	(9.35)	(7.73)	(9.87)	(7.29)	(8.96)	(7.88)	(10.18)
Latino Representative		-4.87		4.51		7.26		-1.53
		(4.75)		(5.14)		(4.71)		(4.89)
Proportion Latino	4.69	8.34	7.33	0.89	18.38+	8.49	15.21	17.25
	(10.01)	(10.90)	(10.52)	(12.22)	(9.53)	(11.09)	(10.54)	(11.81)
Proportion Asian	17.38	18.53	8.67	6.78	22.15	18.58	3.90	4.30
	(16.88)	(16.74)	(18.06)	(18.09)	(17.60)	(17.53)	(17.83)	(17.98)
Proportion Foreign Born	-11.65	-14.79	-14.67	-11.32	-38.95**	-33.29*	-27.84+	-29.28
	(14.56)	(14.46)	(15.25)	(15.66)	(14.29)	(14.63)	(15.24)	(15.55)
Education	1.02	2.42	45.46	46.01	-25.91	-24.71	-26.16	-26.07
	(39.93)	(39.36)	(41.24)	(41.14)	(37.38)	(37.00)	(34.55)	(34.82)
Urban	-7.66	-4.90	3.12	5.10	5.03	7.20	17.33*	16.98*
	(5.77)	(5.78)	(6.12)	(6.23)	(5.91)	(5.93)	(7.60)	(7.67)
Poverty	15.33	19.18	-28.13	-20.56	-14.18	-7.64	-36.84	-35.51
	(36.04)	(36.06)	(38.00)	(38.24)	(34.74)	(34.58)	(29.56)	(30.04)
Income	0.01	0.02	-0.01	-0.01	0.01	0.00	-0.00	-0.00
	(0.02)	(0.02)	(0.01)	(0.02)	(0.02)	(0.01)	(0.01)	(0.01)

Democratic Presidential Vote	0.51*** (.12)	0.44*** (.13)	0.68*** (.13)	0.59*** (.14)	0.57*** (.11)	0.49*** (.11)	0.58*** (.11)	0.59*** (.11)
Constant	61.67*** (10.90)	50.75*** (10.90)	57.20*** (11.63)	41.24*** (11.51)	42.72*** (10.28)	44.18*** (10.19)	56.96*** (8.51)	56.12*** (8.70)
N^b	207	207	214	214	211	211	206	206
F	4.46***	4.51***	8.89***	7.59***	9.05***	8.14***	10.45***	8.50***
Adjusted R^2	.13	.16	.25	.25	.26	.27	.29	.29

Note: + indicates $p < .10$, * $p < .05$, ** $p < .01$, *** $p < .001$ in a two-tailed test of significance. Unstandardized OLS coefficients are reported, along with standard errors in parentheses. NHLA = National Hispanic Leadership Agenda.

a The base category are white Democrats for all models.

b N's reflect all members of Congress (MCs) holding office during the span of the Congress and available data.

affiliation, there are no models where minority group size is positively related to same-group advocacy when descriptive representation is added into the model. It appears that party affiliation and the racial/ethnic background of the MC (descriptive representation), and to a lesser degree the member's constituency, are the primary ingredients of intergroup compatibility. Moreover, note that the black population, when negatively associated with scorecard measures, is associated with *both* NAACP and NHLA scores. This suggests a general antiminority backlash rather than interminority conflict emerging from minority constituency preferences.

Finally, while some models' effects of descriptive representation seem to hold even after the sample is restricted to only Democratic MCs and after controlling for the partisan composition of the constituency, it is possible that these results are simply driven by similar Black-Latino general ideological orientations beyond party affiliation, and that controlling for ideology is needed to accurately estimate the effect of descriptive representation on cross-group advocacy.

Further Exploring the Links of Minority Representatives and Ideology

Since the overall interest group scores and common indicators of ideology are highly correlated, including both in a single model is methodologically problematic.[6] And, given our focus on minority interests, NAACP and NHLA scores are more proximate measures of our central concern than broader measures of ideology. Nevertheless, to examine minority MC cross-group advocacy while controlling for ideology, we analyze the various individual roll-call votes to gauge the general nature of the effects of descriptive representation. This approach mitigates the collinearity issue in evaluating the robustness of the general argument that there is little cross-group conflict and that descriptive representation can lead to cross-group advocacy at the national level.

The analysis consisted of examining the 138 regression models for all votes included in the 105th–108th House NAACP and NHLA ratings. (We

---

[6] Including NOMINATE scores, a common measure of MC ideological voting patterns, in the full models presented in Tables 5.4 and 5.5, but excluding the percent Democratic vote variable, does diminish some of the effects of black or Latino representatives scorecard ratings for the "other" group. However, the effects remain in the 107th Congress (all significant at the p <.02 level) and significant effects of black representatives on Latino scores occur in the 106th Congress and Latino effects on black issues in the 108th (p <.05). Thus, the independent effects of descriptive representation do hold in a variety of contexts, even with a high level of collinearity present.

exclude the 104th since we do not have NHLA scores for this Congress and we seek to compare both black and Latino cross-group advocacy.) The models include all independent variables from Tables 5.4 and 5.5, with the exception of the "Democratic" vote variable as it is highly collinear with the first dimension NOMINATE score, which is the common measure of ideology we utilize (Poole and Rosenthal, 1997). Roll-call votes are classified as "cooperative votes" if black representatives from the Democratic Party (a) unanimously support the position of the NHLA when Democratic MCs do not unanimously support the NHLA position, or (b) when black representatives exert significant and positive independent effects on the probability of supporting the NHLA position. Votes are similarly classified if (a) Latino Democrats unanimously support the NAACP position or (b) have independent effects on the probability of an MC taking the NAACP position. Thus, all strict party-line votes, votes where ideology renders the descriptive representation coefficient not statistically significant, or completely unanimous votes, are considered "independent votes." "Conflict votes" are those where blacks or Latinos unanimously oppose the NHLA or NAACP position, respectively, or their respective coefficient is both statistically significant and in the opposite direction of the position of the NHLA or NAACP, respectively.

Overall, the pattern that emerges from these individual roll-call analyses supports the general conclusions from the broader analyses presented earlier, and thus we will summarize them only briefly here. Of the 138 votes analyzed, only 2 (1.45 percent) were classified as between-group conflict votes. These included a vote supported by the NAACP to award Rosa Parks the Congressional Gold Medal in the 106th Congress, and a resolution in the 108th Congress regarding Senate amendments for the child tax credit (which the NHLA opposed). The former still had support from 87 percent of the Latino Democrats, while the latter garnered support from 92 percent of black MCs. Thus, conflict is actually more a minor deviation from very high support levels than suggestive of any systematic opposition. More telling, over 56 percent of the votes, 78 in all, could be classified as between-group "cooperative" votes. Cooperation was highest in the 105th (69 percent cooperative) and the 107th (71 percent cooperative), and lowest in the 108th (44 percent cooperative). Note that the 105th and 107th Congresses are where we found evidence of black MC support for NHLA issues among Democrats (refer to Table 5.6). The remaining 42 percent (or 58 of the 138 roll calls) were classified as independence primarily due to party-line votes or where there was not a significant effect of the racial or ethnic background of the MC.

In short, there is virtually no between-group conflict while descriptive representatives, even after controlling their ideology, commonly heighten between-group support.

Finally, while there is no significant relationship between cooperative/ independent votes and topics, voting rights (100 percent cooperative) and civil rights (81 percent cooperative) are two high frequency topics with the most cooperation while budget (44 percent cooperative) and international relations (17 percent cooperative) exhibit the most "independence." Even immigration, a topic that might be expected to foster cross-group conflict had more cooperative votes than independent nonconflict votes. In short, while general ideology may be a legitimate factor for consideration, controlling for it underscores the basic finding that descriptive representation can dampen potential conflict, and the general conclusion that intergroup relations at the congressional level is dominated by commonality or independence – conflict is almost completely absent.

Moreover, conspicuous by their absence is the lack of consistent effects of most of the other control variables. From education levels in the district to poverty rates, few control variables seemed to exert significant effects in any consistent way and, parenthetically yet significantly, also suggest that socioeconomic factors frequently thought, and often found, to be significant in analyses of similar issues in fact demonstrate little or no effect here.

Conclusion

This chapter is likely the first effort to pose and to systematically assess the question of interminority group relations between blacks and Latinos in Congress by examining roll-call voting patterns on salient minority issues (defined by minority advocacy organizations). There is little or no evidence of conflict, which echoes the findings on the dimensions of black-Latino relations delineated in previous chapters. Consistent with our expectations, minority intergroup relations appear to vary according to the specific geography of interests or level of government and the policy issues related to those levels. In congressional roll-call voting on national policies, blacks have voting records somewhat compatible with salient concerns of Latinos (as defined by the NHLA scorecard), and Latino Democrats in Congress have voting records generally supportive of the most salient concerns of blacks (as defined by the NAACP scorecard). It appears that black and Latino representatives have voting dispositions consistent with support of the "other" minority group to the same degree, and occasionally higher, than their party affiliation (and ideology in a number of roll calls) alone would suggest. The current findings reveal essentially no conflict and, indeed, a modicum of mutual support – a finding that contrasts clearly with much of the recent literature on intergroup relations at lower/ urban levels of the political system (see Chapter 2; Rocha 2007a, 2007b; Vaca 2004). Moreover, the compatibility is driven, in part, by descriptive representation. Constituency characteristics have limited independent effects, though in a few instances there is a suggestion of a slight negative or racial resentment interpretation of representatives' behavior. These effects generally seem to apply across group interests and thus they do not reveal a strong intergroup conflict interpretation. Nevertheless, when we found that black population size was negatively associated with support for Latino issue concerns, elected representatives' behavior still indicates no conflict and even a bit of positive inclination toward the other group's interests. We can then add to other studies' conclusions that descriptive representation matters in that the current findings show that the impacts of substantive representation of minority interests are not wholly specific to minority representatives' "own" group. The inclusion of Latino *or* black *legislators* may well increase substantive representation for either black *or* Latino *constituents*.

At the same time, a good deal of evidence we found is consistent with the partisan model of support for minority interests. Support for both black and Latino votes are to a great extent determined by party affiliation of the MC, and the district's partisan tendencies also seems important (Hero and Tolbert 1995; Lublin 1997; Grose 2005). Parties are a key coalitional factor that influences between-group support. These findings on the impact of ideology and party are *also* consistent with our larger arguments in that we have argued throughout that broader-based ideas, often reflected in party and ideology, have more substantial impacts at the national level of government. The nature and extent of the impact of ideology and party are considerably different at the various levels of the political system (Trounstine 2010), which are associated with the breadth and substance of policy in the American federal system. Ideology and party seem to dampen potential conflict and promote at least independence, and sometimes cooperation, among minority officeholders.

Overall, then, our results add to understanding minority intergroup relations in several ways. First, black and Latino relations in congressional roll-call voting are not characterized by conflict; instead, there is some evidence of compatibility, which can go at least a bit beyond what party affinities and ideology alone would lead us to expect. Yet the finding of the importance of party and ideology is itself consistent with the broader claims of our study. Moreover, these relationships seem to have been more or less in place over at least the period studied here (from the mid-1990s to 2004). Minority intergroup compatibility seems more common and ongoing than urban-based studies would lead us to believe. This takes on added significance when combined with the findings that congressional scorecards of minority advocacy groups show very little overlap in what are taken to be salient issues, while there is complete congruence on the ideas that do overlap (see Chapter 4).

It remains to be seen whether the ostensible compatibility of black and Latino interests demonstrated here will continue to be the case among national elites and MCs under circumstances where some potentially conflicting issues – for instance, immigration – persist; a bit of our evidence hints that mass views about interminority group support are less strong than among (national) elites. On the other hand, even recently, members of the congressional black, Hispanic, and Asian Pacific caucuses joined to establish a Congressional Tri-Caucus which seems to be a formalization of the coalitional nature of interminority group relations suggested in the evidence we saw from the 104th to 108th Congresses. With minority voter mobilization increased due to co-ethnic candidates (Barreto 2007), will the informal cooperation among minority lawmakers indicated earlier, and subsequently codified in a formal caucus, change due to increasing constituency pressures? And to what degree will the policy compatibility between minority constituents and minority representatives (Griffin and Newman 2007) change due to these dynamics? These are worthy questions for future research.

The questions posed and theoretical approach used here have focused on analytical issues not emphasized in other studies and have produced novel findings on groups whose political interrelations are markers of American democratic pluralism and issues of equality more generally. Descriptive representation of minority groups in the national-level legislature, linked to substantive representation of policy concerns across groups, are significant aspects of evolving minority intergroup politics. It bears repeating, then, that the absence of conflict and the independence of minority MCs' voting behavior we have shown contrasts considerably with findings on black-Latino relations in the local realms of the American political system.

Appendix 5.1

Frequency of Roll-Call Votes Included in NAACP and NHLA Scorecards for the 104th–108th Congresses, by Topic

Topic	Exclusive NAACP Identified Roll-Call Votes					Exclusive NHLA Identified Roll-Call Votes				Roll-Call Votes on Both NHLA and NAACP Scorecards			
	Congress					Congress				Congress			
	104	105	106	107	108	105	106	107	108	105	106	107	108
Affirmative Action										3			
Budget	3	2			3		3		3				
Civil Rights	1		1	1	3	1	1	4	3		1	2	1
Crime	1	1	4	1	1						1		
Education		2	2	3	4	3	5	5					
Health Care	2	1	1		1		1					1	
Immigration					1	5	1		4				
International Relations		1	3		1		1						
Language						3							
Welfare	1				3	2	1					1	
Other	2	1			7	3	5						
Tax and Spending Policy				1									
Faith-Based Initiative				1									
Telecommunications								1					
Economic Mobility								3	5			1	1
Foreign-Aid-Africa				2									
Voting Rights				2		1				1			
Labor	1			1	1				1		1		
Gun Control					2								
AIDS/Public Health					1								
Total	11	8	12	13	28	18	18	13	16	4	3	5	2

6

The Role of Group Interests and Ideology
in Cross-Group Support

We saw some evidence, in Chapter 5, that minority lawmakers act as both strong advocates for their own group's interests and also as conduits for interminority group support. Specifically, black and Latino members of Congress (MCs) tended to support NAACP and NHLA positions at least as much, and in some Congresses to a greater extent, as their white counterparts (even after accounting for other f actors). A central conclusion of that chapter is present throughout this study: there is virtually no evidence of conflict or competition between advocates for black and Latino concerns; there is much evidence suggesting independent group advocacy, and some evidence of cooperation across minority groups at the national level.

In this chapter we extend this analysis in related, but different, directions. Rather than directly examining advocacy we seek to identify the source(s) of cross-group support that may help us understand the lack of interminority group conflict at the national level. We again focus on the behavior of members of Congress and their support for NHLA and NAACP legislative positions. The results suggest several important points consistent with larger themes in our analysis regarding (a) the importance of broad (versus narrower) interests in national politics (especially when compared to local politics) and its implications for dampening conflict and (b) the frequently independent behavior and/or unique foci or orientation of blacks and of Latinos (both advocacy groups and MCs) in national politics relative to each other and to white elites. We find that black and Latino MCs appear to have different cues or heuristics that magnify support for their *own* group's positions compared to what shapes their views on the other group's positions. Specifically, ideology (in terms of a standard, general liberal/conservative conception) plays a lesser role regarding support for representatives' *own* racial/ethnic group's policy positions; those are significantly animated by within-group considerations. However, ideology is the major basis for support of other groups in determining minorities' (and liberal whites') support for other groups in national politics (and this impact of ideology is lacking and/or less clear and consistent in local/urban politics [cf. Trounstine 2010]). The analysis and findings presented in this chapter suggest that minority representatives are distinct in how they think about and support their own group's concerns. But they are also influenced by the more standard ideological orientations in voting decisions. Moreover, for black MCs, minority descriptive representation adds a further level of liberalism to their policy orientation, which increases support across minority group interests. These orientations, in turn, help explain the lack of conflict at the national level where broader ideology plays a prominent role (as is also the case with political party, as we have seen), while also highlighting the independent or distinct within-group concerns; both of these point to less minority intergroup conflict.

Ideology as a Bridging Mechanism

In Chapter 5 we acknowledged the role of ideology per se but we did not emphasize it at that point, in part because our view is that general indicators of ideology both understate concerns particularly relevant to minority groups and dominate and overlap with measures of minority interest to such an extent that they may obscure any relationship between descriptive representatives and NHLA and/or NAACP scorecard ratings. (Ideology was not completely overlooked, however, as we also found evidence of the effect of descriptive representation and party in an analysis of individual roll calls for each of the votes included in the NHLA and NAACP scorecards.) Here, we address ideology and clarify its impact on cross-group support to evaluate whether it acts as a bridging mechanism across black and Latino concerns to (at minimum) reduce interminority group conflict, and perhaps even foster cooperation.

Our argument is that general ideology affects the nature of intergroup relations at the national level. (And ideology's impact is substantially different than at lower levels of government.) Minority lawmakers in Congress, then, not only most often share partisan attachments (see the discussion in Chapter 5) but also have a similar placement on the standard liberal-conservative ideological spectrum. Black and Latino lawmakers may be especially liberal, and that level of liberalism then fosters commonality and bridges group-specific policy preferences. Minority descriptive representatives are more supportive of other groups' interests, in part, since they are also more liberal than other representatives. Their shared ideology dampens intergroup conflict and potentially raises levels of support beyond that of nonminority counterparts in Congress.

Previous studies on the distinct ideological orientations of minority lawmakers provide ample evidence of a unique level of advocacy (see Chapter 5). While we focus our analysis on evidence from periods that coincide with our data, it is also useful to summarize some of the previous evidence again. Studies of local- and state-level legislative institutions generally show a positive impact of the overall racial/ethnic diversity on policies that help minority constituents. The policy effects of racial/ethnic diversity range from better educational outcomes for minority students (Meier and Stewart 1991; Meier et al. 2005) to more funds for social services and crime prevention (Browning, Marshall,and Tabb 1984 ; Marschall and Ruhil 2007) at the local level, to more generous state-level social welfare provision (Owens 2005; Preuhs 2006 and 2007). Latino incorporation into the legislative power structure is also associated with preventing passage of measures targeted at Latinos, such as Official English, or English Only laws (Preuhs 2005). Though such studies provide evidence that greater racial diversity in lawmaking bodies affects public policies, they do not directly address how minority representatives differ from nonminority representatives.

A second set of research on minority descriptive representation is more relevant to the immediate question of the differences in minority versus nonminority lawmakers' policy dispositions. This line of inquiry focuses on individual-level legislative behavior and has produced mixed results. At the state level, black legislators introduce more "black interest" legislation than nonblack legislators – the types of legislation identified were social welfare, health care, and education policy (Bratton and Haynie 1996; Haynie 2001) – while both black and Latino legislators tend to have more generally liberal voting patterns (Preuhs and Juenke 2011; Juenke and Preuhs 2012). A larger scholarly debate involves the behavior of descriptive representatives in the U.S. Congress. Several studies found that black legislators support liberal and black interests at higher levels than do nonblack legislators (Baker and Cook 2005; Canon 1999; Grose 2005; Whitby 1997). These studies all test the effect of a black representative dummy variable on a dependent variable measuring "black interests" while controlling for a variety of factors. The most common measure of black interests is NOMINATE scores, which are derived from an index that includes all competitive roll-call votes in a particular Congress, and are generally considered a measure of overall, relative ideology (Poole and Rosenthal 1997); these are said to reflect the core liberal-conservative ideological dimension as generally understood in American politics (see Canon 2005, 291). We have contended that such measures are inadequate to our purposes of evaluating advocacy or support for minority concerns because the measures are simply too general to capture specific minority group policy concerns, though those scores may be valid measures of overall ideology.

The initial focus here is whether minority MCs exhibit a degree of ideological coherence that sets them apart from nonminority lawmakers and thus establishes a higher degree of liberalism that, in turn, facilitates cross-minority group support. To determine this, we extend the analyses presented in Chapter 5 to consider the effect of minority descriptive representation on broader measures of ideology. Instead of evaluating how minority descriptive representatives differ in terms of support for black (NAACP) and Latino (NHLA) advocacy groups, we examine the effect of descriptive representation on NOMINATE scores, which measure a general liberal/conservative orientation of members of Congress. NOMINATE scores are coded such that more liberal members have lower (negative values) scores than conservative members (who have more positive values). The analysis includes two dummy variables, coded 1 for *Black Representative* and *Latino Representative*, respectively, and zero otherwise, as well as a variety of control variables that we utilized in the analyses of NAACP and NHLA scores.[1] We also limit this analysis to Democratic MCs only since we have already established the effect of party on support for minority group interest legislation and want to control for this potentially confounding factor given a very small set of black and Latino Republicans serving in the House of Representatives. Because we will rely on the results of the analysis to determine overall support for minority policy positions, we also limit the analysis to the

---

[1] The control variables included in this analysis are based on district characteristics and are the following: Latino Population, Black Population, Asian Population, Foreign-born Population, Education, Urbanization, Poverty, Income, South (a dummy variable coded 1 if the MCs district is in the South) and Democratic Presidential Vote. Each of these variables is measured at the district level and more fully described in Chapter 5.

105th through the 108th Congresses since the NAACP and NHLA both prepared scorecards for these sessions.

Table 6.1 presents the results of the regression analyses of the ideology of individual Democratic MCs. The negative coefficients for black representatives indicates that black (Democrat) MCs are more liberal than white Democrats in each of the four Congresses; these are statistically significant (p <.05, two-tailed tests) in all four Congresses as well. Black representatives are more liberal than their white counterparts, even after a variety of common district-level characteristics are controlled. The extent to which black representatives are more liberal can be gauged by the number of standard deviations, or average distances from the mean, in NOMINATE scores represented by the coefficient. The coefficients reflect effects of black representatives that are .53 standard deviations more liberal than white Democrats in the 106th Congress to .82 standard deviations more liberal than white Democrats in the 107th Congress. The effects of black representation in the 105th (.58 standard deviations) and the 108th (.75) fell between these ranges in magnitude. Measuring the relative magnitude from a different perspective, the additional liberalness of black representatives in the 105th Congress, for instance, is equivalent to the effect of moving support for the Democratic presidential candidate in the previous election from 50 percent of the vote to 60 percent of the vote (a .10 point change in the NOMINATE score). Thus, while not overwhelming, the liberalness of black descriptive representatives is significant.

Latino MCs do not show a more liberal position than white MCs, and this is a consistent finding in each of the Congresses. After controlling for a variety of other factors, particularly generally significant factors such as the Democratic presidential vote share, we found that Latino representatives do not seem to have a higher level of liberalism than white Democratic MCs. These results are in line with previous research which has found that party is a key mechanism for Latino substantive representation (Hero and Tolbert 1995) and suggests that Latino MCs are often similar in their ideological orientation to other nonminority Democrats.

If ideology is a factor that leads to cross-group support and advocacy that bridges group-specific interests, then the results of these analyses suggest that blacks will be more likely to support Latino interests than will white Democrat MCs. However, the results also indicate that the level of support for black interests from Latino MCs will not be so different from the support by white Democrats. These results thus support

TABLE 6.1. *Effects of Descriptive Representation on Ideology for Democrats in the 105th–108th Congresses. Dependent Variable: DW Nominate Scores (Higher Values Indicate More Conservative Ideology)*

Independent Variables	105th Congress		106th Congress		107th Congress		108th Congress	
	Coefficient	SE	Coefficient	SE	Coefficient	SE	Coefficient	SE
Black Representative	−0.10*	0.04	−0.09*	0.04	−0.14***	0.04	−0.12**	0.04
Latino Representative	0.05	0.05	0.01	0.05	0.01	0.05	0.03	0.04
Latino Population	−0.14	0.12	−0.17	0.12	−0.08	0.13	−0.14	0.11
Black population	0.14	0.11	0.05	0.11	0.29*	0.12	0.29**	0.11
Asian Population	−0.32	0.17	−0.27	0.17	−0.29	0.18	−0.05	0.16
Foreign-Born Population	0.32	0.14	0.29	0.15	0.32*	0.16	0.22	0.14
Education	−0.30	0.44	−1.08*	0.42	−0.63	0.43	−0.16	0.34
Urbanization	−0.07	0.06	0.01	0.06	0.01	0.07	0.02	0.07
Poverty	0.15	0.37	0.16	0.36	−0.15	0.37	0.29	0.27
Income	0.00	0.00	0.00	0.00	0.00	0.00	0.00	0.00
South	0.01	0.03	0.06*	0.03	0.04	0.03	0.03	0.03
Democratic Presidential Vote	−0.01***	0.00	−0.01***	0.00	−0.01***	0.00	−0.01***	0.00
Constant	0.30	0.13	0.20	0.12	0.15	0.12	0.09	0.09
N	212		214		215		206	
Adjusted R²	.52		.50		.48		.54	
F	17.14***		16.49***		15.04***		17.93***	

Note: Unstandardized OLS coefficients and standard errors (SE) reported. * p <.05, ** p <.01 and *** p <.001 in a two-tailed t-test.

the general conclusions of Chapter 5, where we found that black MCs, to a greater extent than Latino MCs, tended to support the other group's interests more than party affiliation alone would imply.

This finding is important but only part of the explanation for the effect of descriptive representation. Descriptive representatives may be influenced by both general ideological orientation as well as (other) unique attributes in minority representatives' considerations of minority policy concerns. As we will discuss later in the chapter, the degree to which ideology or individual attributes serve as factors influencing policy leanings depends on whether descriptive representatives are assessing the interests of their own group or of the other group. The former is shaped more by particular attributes of descriptive representation; the latter is where general ideology plays an important role in bridging minority group interests. We develop these points and discuss their implications for our larger arguments further in the sections that follow.

Minority Members of Congress and Their Unique Ideological Orientations

Black and Latino legislators view policy issues from unique backgrounds, but they are situated within the broader ideological conceptualizations of the political system as well. Some evidence of the unique advocacy provided by minority representatives was presented in Chapter 5, and we explore this further in this chapter. Notably, minority representatives not only display heightened advocacy for their own group's interests and generally support (or at least do not undermine) the interests of other groups. They also see policy issues in different ways than would be expected by the usual ideological categories only; that is, the standard ideology accounts do not tell the whole story (Minta 2011). An example of this is suggested in the first vote on the financial bailout bill to deal with the economic crisis that arose in September 2009; that vote took place in the U.S. House of Representatives on September 29, 2008. As the full force of the financial meltdown caused by a variety of factors related to home mortgages became apparent, the Democratic-controlled House of Representatives initially voted down a proposal supported by (Republican) President George W. Bush as well as Democratic leadership. The bill would have provided $700 billion to rescue the financial industry and stave off what supporters feared would be an economic "calamity that would drag down not just Wall

TABLE 6.2. *Racial/Ethnic and Partisan Differences in the Vote in the U.S. House on the First Bailout Bill, September 29, 2008*

	Latino Democrats	Black Democrats	Latino & Black Democrats	White Democrats	Latino Republicans	White Republicans
Number	20	39	59	176	3	195
YES	8	18	26	150	0	65
NO	12	21	33	26	3	130
% YES	40	46	44	85	0	33
% NO	60	54	56	15	100	67

Street investment houses but possibly the savings and portfolios of millions of Americans" (Hulse and Herszenhorn 2008). Some opponents of the bill argued that it was unfair because it used taxpayer money to pay for the mistakes of the financial industry with little help for average Americans hurt by the crisis. Others opposed it on the grounds of excessive government intrusion into the free market. Though a second attempt eventually led to passage, the initial vote seems consistent with our point that minority lawmakers sometimes view policy issues, and eventually vote, in different ways than their co-partisans. And there are numerous examples of this in other aspects of Congressional activities, such as oversight (Minta 2011).

Table 6.2 shows the breakdown of yes and no votes by party and by the racial/ethnic background of the House members for this first bailout vote. Contrary to what might be expected by black and Latino MCs' overwhelming party affiliation as Democrats, the pattern of support for this bill among these minority representatives differed considerably from white Democrats. While 85 percent of white Democrats supported passage of the legislation, support among Latino and black Democrats was only 40 percent and 46 percent, respectively. In other words, though a vast majority of white Democrats supported the financial sector bailout in this first vote, a majority of black and Latino Democrats opposed the bill. There were few Latino Republican representatives, but all voted against the bill, diverging a bit from the two-thirds opposition by white Republicans.

Though the bill later passed the chamber in an amended form, the difference in support between minority MCs and white MCs within the ranks of the Democratic Party is telling in two ways. First, it suggests similarities between black and Latino members' orientations in certain circumstances; greater opposition to the bailout by minority members indicates a perceived commonality of interests across the two groups. Second, and an intriguing point for this chapter, is that while this was ostensibly a partisan vote reflecting some general ideological orientations about the proper role of government, minority members apparently drew on some other source than party and ideology in dealing with this issue. The degree to which, and how, unique cues may influence minority lawmakers as they act as advocates for minority interests is the focus of the next section of this chapter.

As mentioned earlier, the basic thesis is that when minority lawmakers consider their own group's interests, they rely on cues apart from the general liberal-conservative ideological orientation. However, when it comes to support for other groups, minority lawmakers (and whites) draw on the usual ideological orientations that act as their main reference for cross-group support. This argument is fleshed out later, but we preface it by examining some of the scholarship on descriptive representation that demonstrates why we might expect that different influences affect minority lawmakers as they consider their own group's interests, on the one hand, versus those of other groups, on the other hand.

The potential value of minority descriptive representation is that these officials will not only look different, but will also *act* different from nonminority representatives and, thus, presumably, be more forceful advocates for minority concerns (Mansbridge 1999). This difference between racial and ethnic minority versus nonminority legislators is ostensibly driven by shared experiences that are unique and particularly important to minority groups. The value of descriptive representation is said to be most pronounced as shared experiences lead to the identification and advocacy of issues that are important to minority group members, but are uncrystallized in dominant political discourse and/or by dominant social groups (Mansbridge 1999). Descriptive representation matters, then, not only or primarily as a means to ensure more advocacy of issues that are already addressed in political debates, but in how representatives understand and/or frame public policies and the unique perspectives brought forth as these representatives advocate positions that address minority needs.

This conception of the importance and potential consequences of descriptive representation underlies the (normative and) empirical theoretical assumptions of a growing body of research. But congressional-level analyses of the effects of descriptive representation seldom employ research designs that capture the (potential) uniqueness of descriptive representation conceived this way (Mansbridge 1999; cf. Canon 1999; Grofman, Handley, and Niemi 1992; Grofman and Handley 1989). In short, the bulk of the recent research addresses the degree to which racially descriptive representatives are more liberal, meaning more supportive of minority positions; we did as well, in Chapter 5 in the brief analysis of ideological voting. We know less about whether and how these representatives differ in their basic conceptualization or understanding of policy issues. One result is a continued debate about whether having racial/ethnic descriptive representation instead of simply electing (white) representatives who are (very) liberal in standard ideological terms matters much for substantive policy representation (cf. Swain 1995). Our contention is that such studies largely miss or inadequately examine the argument that descriptive representatives have distinct perspectives and approaches to racial/ethnic substantive representation and minority group advocacy (Mansbridge 1999; Minta 2011; Canon 1999).

One way descriptive representation matters is by modifying the standard ideological frame as the major touchstone on advocacy decisions among minority representatives. Whereas white lawmakers seem to use the dominant ideological (liberal-conservative) framework in their thinking about minority interests, unique perspectives of minority officeholders, including perhaps a sense of racially linked fate (Dawson 1994), show how a subtler perception of minority concerns affects their outlook on their own minority group's circumstances. Consequently, the effect of the dominant political ideology on minority representatives' voting behavior on policies that are especially important and specific to minority groups is partly overridden or surpassed by these other references. Nonetheless, the standard liberal/conservative orientation still plays an important role in that it is a basis for *cross*-group support and coalitions if groups share similar or have especially high levels of a particular ideological orientation (the latter is the case for black MCs' liberalism). The contemporary liberal-conservative spectrum thus provides a baseline for liberal MCs, both minority or nonminority, as they advocate for the specific concerns of individual minority groups, because of their shared ideology. When minority group MCs, blacks in this case, *also* have especially high levels of liberalism, one outcome is stronger cross-group support for Latino interests.

While a good deal of evidence has examined the effects of descriptive representation in legislative bodies, here we are particularly interested in

how minority MCs come to act as advocates for their own group's interests and how other cues or heuristics seem to bridge or foster advocacy
for other groups' positions. Ideological similarity plays a role in explaining why there is almost a complete lack of conflict in black and Latino
relations at the national level, where ideology is often a major component
influencing representatives' behavior.

A "Conditioning Effect" and a Different Kind of Descriptive Representation?

If minority representatives are unique, they may not only exhibit more
liberal voting, but would *also* be expected to exhibit a different kind
of representation from nonminority lawmakers. Again, the benefit of
minority descriptive representation is alleged to emerge when policy
concerns of minority constituents lie outside established political cleavages and discourse, or those concerns remain uncrystallized (Mansbridge
1999; also see Canon 1999; Gutman and Thompson 1996; Kymlicka
1995). If there is no difference in the way minority lawmakers reflect
upon and arrive at their decisions, then nonminority lawmakers could
very well be equally strong advocates for minority constituents for a
given electorate. Thus, one important way that minority descriptive representatives differ from white representatives is in the distinct ideas they
hold, advance, and emphasize in political decisions. There is, we suggest, a difference in the cues minority and nonminority representatives
use in the decision-making process regarding advocacy for their *own*
groups. General ideology plays the role of bridging *across* these different
perspectives.

The grounds for legislative decisions are varied, of course, but if minority lawmakers are distinct it is likely linked to perspectives they bring to
politics from a social milieu and worldview different from that experienced by nonminority lawmakers. Because of their shared background
and familiarity with minority constituents, they evaluate decisions based
on a set of concerns or ideological dispositions that are at least somewhat apart from or outside the 'regular' ideological cleavages in society and its legislative institutions (cf. Hero 1992, ch. 10; Minta 2011;
Burden 2007).

Though minority groups share many of the same concerns as other
groups, there is considerable evidence that a number of social problems
are somewhat unique and/or very disproportionate in their impacts
on minority groups and that there is likely a (perceived) critical racial

component beyond that attributable to class or economic factors alone. Racial minority representatives are likely to be attuned to the racial dimension (as well as economic), while white representatives are likely to be influenced by economic dimensions primarily if not solely (these patterns are suggested by the notion of two-tiered pluralism; Hero 1992). Thus, minority representatives may not draw cues on minority issues only with reference to the liberal/conservative dimension in congressional voting (Poole and Rosenthal 1997), but from the uniqueness of racial group interests that are not fully encompassed in the standard ideology. And this may be the case even though blacks exhibit especially strong liberal leanings to begin with, beyond what can be explained simply by party affiliation (as demonstrated earlier). This likewise accords with Mansbridge's (1999) conception of concrete minority concerns that are generally uncrystallized in the absence of minority representation (also see Dawson 2001). Minority officeholders thus not only provide new information to the deliberative process but also think about policy concerns in a different way.

Understandings based on experience with discrimination, for instance, rather than an abstract understanding of social inequality, is a possible basis for decision making and is in line with the idea that minority representatives have unique knowledge in this regard; stated otherwise, there are qualitative as well as quantitative differences. It is not just ideological consistency with minority (or even liberal) constituents, but an ability to directly relate to the specific types of difficulties disadvantaged minorities face that can drive minority representatives to support their own group concerns. The unique quality that descriptive representatives bring to legislative bodies may not only be manifested in more support for a particular group's positions, speeches, minority staff, or other observable behavior, but in how they engage in those behaviors.

If it is the case that minority descriptive representatives are unique and conceive of minority interests differently from nonminority lawmakers (and in different ways across minority groups), the role of the conventional ideological cleavage would be expected to be supplemented and even supplanted as a major influence on minority lawmakers when making decisions regarding support for their own group's interests. Nonminority lawmakers, however, who are less likely to have such alternative perspectives, will conceive of minority issues primarily through the standard ideological lens. To test these claims we compare the support of Democratic members of the U.S. House of Representatives for black and

Latino policy priorities (as measured by advocacy groups' ratings), with specific attention to how black, Latino, and white MCs differ in the way conventional liberal-conservative ideological dimensions influence voting regarding minority issues; we focus on the relationships between three key indicators.

DW-NOMINATE scores for individual MCs provide a widely accepted measure of the standard liberal-conservative ideological cleavage in the U.S. Congress (Poole and Rosenthal 1997). As in previous chapters, MCs' NAACP ratings are used to measure support for black concerns, while support for Latino issues are measured with NHLA scores for the 105th through the 108th Congresses. Examining the behavior of both black and Latino MCs allows us to more carefully examine differences between minority group members' behaviors. If descriptive representation matters, then it is the racial/ethnic background of the MC and the MCs' racial/ethnic group's specific concerns that most influence their decisions. Even if groups such as Latinos and blacks share general backgrounds and social disadvantages, the distinction between these two groups (see, e.g., Hero 1992, ch. 10) should manifest itself in differences in the types of factors that influence their decision making. In other words, blacks and Latinos should approach black and Latino issues differently (as will whites), depending on whether the issues are germane to their own group's rather than another group's policy positions, even if there is ultimately little difference in overall levels of support (as indicated by the NOMINATE scores).

We specifically test several hypotheses based on the implications of the theoretical propositions focusing on the relationships between the NOMINATE score, as a general indicator of MC ideology, and measures of black and Latino advocacy group positions, the NAACP ratings, and NHLA ratings. If minority representatives are affected more than are other representatives by different influences in forming policy positions significant to their own group's concerns, the liberal-conservative dimension should play a more muted role in black MCs' support of NAACP positions and in Latino MCs' support of NHLA positions. Conversely, in the absence of a similar background or alternative perspectives on the salience of minority concerns, MCs will draw on the conventional political ideology as the primary cue for their policy positions; this is where ideology acts as a bridge across racial/ethnic groups and their policy advocates. We first examine how minority groups differ from whites in this respect; specifically, the hypothesis is that correlations between NOMINATE scores and NAACP ratings, as well as NOMINATE scores and NHLA ratings, will be stronger for white MCs than they are for black and Latino MCs, respectively.

One implication of the argument is that the distinct approaches to policy advocacy based on shared group background among minority representatives means they will make use of different cues when considering their own ethnic group compared to other minority groups. White MCs are informed by the conventional ideological concepts regarding *both* black and Latino concerns; black and Latino MCs, each drawing on distinct situated knowledge, when considering their own group's concerns, will diverge in the degree to which the liberal-conservative cue affects their behavior. Minority Democrat MCs are influenced by cues from the standard ideological parameters when considering matters relevant to groups other than their own advocacy group, and thus this ideology can foster cross-group support; in short, ideology bridges intergroup issues. However, minority Democrat MCs will also be substantially influenced by shared social experiences, and their views will be shaped less by general ideology when considering issues most germane to their co-ethnics. Hence, a second hypothesis is that for white MCs the correlation between NAACP and NHLA scores will be stronger than the correlation between NAACP and NHLA scores for black and Latino MCs.

Furthermore, if the effects of descriptive representation are based on specific racial/ethnic issues, then MCs who are *not* of the same racial/ethnic background would think in terms of the conventional liberal/conservative continuum when deciding about support for other minority groups' positions. A third hypothesis emerges from this logic. If cues are within-group specific, the effect of NOMINATE scores on NAACP ratings should be dampened for black MCs but not for Latino or white MCs; similarly, the effect of NOMINATE scores on NHLA ratings should be dampened for Latinos, but not for black or white MCs. In short, when MCs do not share the same racial/ethnic background with a particular minority group, the more general ideological orientation is the primary influence on cross-group support, and this ultimately encourages less conflict, as we found in the previous chapters.

This and the previous hypotheses are important tests of the effect of descriptive representation as a cuing or heuristic device as well as allowing for the evaluation of the role of ideology as a factor that bridges minority group interests regarding policy issues in national politics (and especially so when contrasted to local government). We now present analyses that directly assess the assumption that descriptive representation is about beliefs and policy orientations specific to particular minority groups, and are not solely about the also important broad issues of poverty, education, or other disadvantages that could be experienced by both minority and nonminority groups.

We begin by examining simple bivariate correlations (Pearson's r) between NOMINATE, NHLA, and NAACP scores. Again, if minority representatives are guided by concerns for those of their own racial/ethnic backgrounds and white MCs take their cues from the prominent economic liberal/conservative lens, the magnitude of the correlation between NOMINATE scores and minority interest group ratings should be lower for minority lawmakers (our first hypothesis). Recall that since NAACP and NHLA ratings increase as support increases, while NOMINATE scores are coded such that negative values indicate a more liberal stance, a negative correlation between group ratings and NOMINATE scores indicates that more liberal members tend to have higher minority group ratings.

Figure 6.1 presents the correlations between NOMINATE scores and NAACP scores for white and black MCs (Figure 6.1a) and the correlations between NOMINATE scores and NHLA scores for white and Latino MCs (Figure 6.1b). In each Congress, the correlation between NOMINATE and NAACP scores is considerably stronger for white MCs than for black MCs (Figure 6.1a), with correlation coefficients for white MCs ranging from –0.656 to –0.765, while the range for black MCs is between –0.024 and –0.552. And in each of the four Congresses, the correlation is significant (p <.05) for white MCs but is significant for blacks in only one Congress, the 107th. For NHLA scores (Figure 6.1b), the correlation coefficients are uniformly stronger for white MCs in all the congressional sessions (ranging from –0.583 to –0.728) than for Latino MCs (ranging from –0.038 to –0.492) and are significant (p <.05) in each Congress for white MCs but do not reach statistical significance for Latino MCs in any of the four Congresses. Thus, consistent with our first hypothesis, for both black and Latino MCs the relationship between NOMINATE scores and support for their respective groups' roll-call preferences is consistently (much) weaker than the relationship for white MCs. White MCs apparently do take their cues regarding positions on minority issues from the conventional ideological paradigm, while Latino and black MCs ostensibly derive their support for their respective group's positions from some other sources.

The correlations between NAACP and NHLA scores are displayed in Figure 6.1c. The data fit the expectations of our second hypothesis. Across

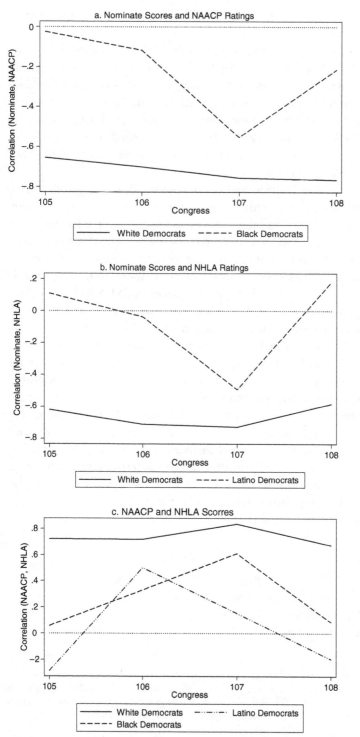

FIGURE 6.1. Correlation Coefficients (Pearson's r) between NOMINATE, NAACP, and NHLA Scores for Democratic Members of the House of Representatives by Racial/Ethnic Background, 105th–108th Congresses

all four Congresses, the correlation between NAACP and NHLA ratings is higher for white MCs than for black or Latino MCs. And with one exception (black MCs in the 107th Congress), the correlation for black and for Latino MCs is not statistically significant. These findings suggest that white MCs apply the same underlying ideological heuristic in considering black and Latino issues. But, as predicted, distinct and varying sources influence black MC and Latino MCs' support for NAACP and NHLA issues, respectively.

The analysis now turns to a more rigorous multiple regression analysis of the first and third hypotheses using the NHLA and NAACP scores as separate dependent variables. We model support for minority group concerns (NAACP and NHLA scores) as a function of general ideology, descriptive representation, and demographic characteristics of the congressional district. (These variables were more fully described in Chapter 5 and reintroduced in our analysis of NOMINATE scores presented in Table 6.1.) NOMINATE scores are again used as the measure of each MCs' (general) liberal-conservative ideology. Minority descriptive representation is defined in two dichotomous variables; *Black Representative* and *Latino Representative*. Since we propose that the effect of ideology on support for minority group interests is conditioned by the racial/ethnic background of the MC, we also include two interaction terms in the model (*Black Representative X Ideology* and *Latino Representative X Ideology*) which are simply the products of the two variables. Additionally, the model includes a set of variables regarding congressional district-level constituency characteristics that have been associated with support for minority interests or with ideology more generally and which we also employed in Chapter 5.[2] Formally, the following general model is estimated for each of the four.

Level of Support (NHLA or NAACP) =
$\alpha + \beta_1$(Ideology) + β_2(Black Representative X Ideology)
+ β_3(Latino Representative X Ideology) + β_4(Black
Representative) + β_5(Latino Representative) + $\beta_{6\text{-}n}$
(Controls) + error.

[2] Note that we do not include the Democratic Presidential Vote in the analyses presented here since it is highly collinear with the ideology (NOMINATE) variable. It turns out that including this variable does not change the substantive results we report nor is the effect of the Democratic Presidential Vote score statistically significant in the models.

The first hypothesis is that ideology has a consistent effect on MC support for minority group positions but is altered for minority representatives in models of their (own) respective group ratings. We thus expect that β_1 will be negative and significant in models of both NAACP and NHLA ratings as liberal white MCs are more supportive of NHLA and NAACP positions than conservative white MCs. However, since minority representatives' policy positions are hypothesized to be less affected by the liberal-conservative ideological continuum in votes on these measures, the effect of ideology is conditioned by the racial/ethnic background of the MC. Our third hypothesis suggests that because the orientation of minority group MCs is linked to their own group, the conditioning effect should only be found for blacks in the NAACP models, and for Latinos in the NHLA models. And in the other models, where black support for NHLA or Latino support for NAACP positions is examined, general ideology ought to remain the dominant influence on minority representatives' scores, and this is how ideology acts to dampen conflict or induce support.

To test these propositions, the coefficients for the interaction terms between ideology and the two descriptive representative dummy variables are examined. In the NAACP model, β_2 should be positive and significant, while β_3 should not be statistically significant. In the NHLA model, β_3 should be positive and significant, while β_2 should not significantly differ from zero. Though we are particularly interested in the degree to which the racial/ethnic background of the MC conditions the effect of general ideology, descriptive representation may increase an overall liberal orientation (as we discussed in the previous analyses, in Chapter 5); hence, we still might expect that the coefficient for black representatives (β_4) and Latino representatives (β_5) will be positive and significant in the NAACP and NHLA models, respectively. However, given what we found in Chapter 5, black MCs are the most likely source for group-specific support and therefore we offer this prediction though we recognize it may not occur across all the models.

Table 6.3 presents the results for the Ordinary Least Squares (OLS) regression analysis of NAACP ratings for the 105th through the 108th Congresses. The first set of models, the four columns under *Descriptive Representation and Ideology*, exclude the interaction terms. These findings indicate the consistent and dominant impact of the standard ideological variable on support for black interests. In each case, not only is the general ideology coefficient highly significant, but the direct effect of ideology overwhelms the direct effects of all of the remaining variables (cf.

TABLE 6.3. *The Conditioning Effects of Descriptive Representation on Ideology's Explanatory Power of NAACP Scorecard Ratings, 105th–108th Congresses.* (Dependent Variable: NAACP Rating)

Independent Variables Member Characteristic	Descriptive Representation and Ideology				Conditioning Effects of Descriptive Representation			
	105th	106th	107th	108th	105th	106th	107th	108th
Ideology	-41.81***	-63.09***	-57.26***	-34.19***	-45.08***	-67.46***	-60.40***	-39.06***
	(4.29)	(6.02)	(4.51)	(3.63)	(4.74)	(6.14)	(4.66)	(3.71)
Ideology X Black Representative					44.18***	58.74***	27.87*	37.35***
					(13.24)	(17.85)	(13.21)	(8.47)
Ideology X Latino Representative					-0.23	-19.53	28.28	7.05
					(10.73)	(31.07)	(22.76)	(14.63)
Black Representative	1.05	-4.39	0.53	-2.11	23.76***	24.71**	13.57*	15.84***
	(2.72)	(3.77)	(2.81)	(2.21)	(7.28)	(9.46)	(6.93)	(4.59)
Latino Representative	2.98	-5.65	6.26	4.02	2.86	-14.89	18.41	6.49
	(3.13)	(4.72)	(3.48)	(2.47)	(4.82)	(14.63)	(10.67)	(6.46)
District Characteristics								
White Population	-17.73	1.12	18.17	-3.34	-16.98	12.35	10.36	-6.73
	(14.99)	(21.44)	(14.85)	(10.28)	(14.89)	(24.58)	(16.15)	(10.61)
Latino Population	-11.33	6.72	8.77	5.85	-9.31	17.08	2.27	3.43
	(11.02)	(16.55)	(11.77)	(8.05)	(10.79)	(19.28)	(13.34)	(8.33)
Black population	-16.61	7.81	15.29	12.09	-13.63	23.85	9.18	7.88
	(17.24)	(24.34)	(17.06)	(11.86)	(17.03)	(27.13)	(18.22)	(11.94)
Asian Population	-35.72	-13.86	17.66	7.16	-34.22	2.70	6.49	0.03
	(23.84)	(33.90)	(23.75)	(16.47)	(23.46)	(38.82)	(25.20)	(16.92)
Foreign-Born Population	-1.62	0.12	-3.50	-9.74	-3.25	-2.83	0.90	-7.11
	(9.13)	(13.09)	(9.53)	(7.46)	(9.13)	(13.49)	(10.07)	(7.44)
Education	17.16	38.88	-27.10	33.46	24.19	44.19	-27.31	30.85
	(28.73)	(39.41)	(28.11)	(18.71)	(28.58)	(38.63)	(28.02)	(17.94)

Urbanization	−3.96	−5.58	2.30	3.48	−4.76	−6.79	1.95	3.35
	(4.17)	(5.60)	(4.24)	(3.95)	(4.09)	(5.48)	(4.21)	(3.78)
Poverty	7.02	23.76	−2.48	−10.19	2.47	12.28	−5.57	−11.82
	(23.66)	(32.50)	(24.05)	(14.77)	(23.20)	(32.03)	(23.93)	(14.13)
Income	−0.08	0.14	0.05	0.02	−0.10	−0.00	0.02	0.00
	(0.13)	(0.17)	(0.12)	(0.05)	(0.13)	(0.17)	(0.12)	(0.05)
South	−2.27	2.25	−1.03	−2.04	−2.89	1.28	−1.23	−2.17
	(1.85)	(2.57)	(1.92)	(1.48)	(1.83)	(2.53)	(1.91)	(1.41)
Constant	95.73***	54.89*	46.13**	70.87***	95.59***	45.96	54.25***	73.77***
	(15.44)	(22.18)	(15.33)	(10.62)	(15.30)	(24.56)	(16.49)	(10.89)
N	212	214	210	200	212	214	210	200
F	16.39***	14.28***	21.66***	21.21***	13.34***	13.74***	19.46***	21.39***
Adjusted R²	0.45	0.45	0.56	0.58	0.47	0.47	0.57	0.61

Note: Unstandardized OLS coefficients are reported, with standard errors in parentheses. * $p < .05$, ** $p < .01$, and *** $p < .001$ in a two-tailed t-test.

Poole and Rosenthal 1997). Moreover, it seems to fit the claims by critics of descriptive representation that descriptive representation itself does not explain much, after accounting for general ideology. It also underscores the nonsignificant findings we reported in our initial analyses of cross-group support in Chapter 5. Over all, these models thus suggest that ideology provides an underlying mechanism for support of minority interests. That said, here we are more interested in *how* minority MCs differ in the way they formulate their thinking and policy positions than in how much *more* support they express relative to white MCs. In other words, is there a *difference in the factors* leading to black MCs' support of NAACP positions versus white and Latino MCs' support of NAACP positions?

The second set of models for the 105th through the 108th Congresses (see columns labeled *Conditioning Effects of Descriptive Representation*) include the interaction terms and they reveal general support for the argument that factors other than conventional ideology affect minority representatives' advocacy for their co-ethnic minority issues. Nevertheless, conventional ideology remains a prominent factor when the other group's concerns are considered, thus facilitating cross-group support. All models are jointly significant and the increase in the amount of variance explained (R^2) over models without the interaction suggests the usefulness of including the interaction terms.

In the interaction models, coefficients for ideology remain negative and significant. Thus, the NAACP ratings for white MCs continue to be affected by the standard liberal-conservative considerations. So, ideology plays a consistent role in white MC support for black interests. However, the coefficient for the interaction term between ideology and a black representative is positive and significant, which means that the effect of general ideology is reduced for black representatives, as predicted. Further evidence of the unique effect of co-ethnic descriptive representation is that the interaction term between Latino MC and ideology is small and not significant in these models of NAACP ratings. Latino MCs see these issues through the liberal-conservative heuristic when considering black interests in a manner that is very similar to white MCs. This highlights the distinctiveness of descriptive representation from each group (toward other groups) and also demonstrates the impact of ideology in fostering support across racial/ethnic minority group legislators.

Do the hypotheses also hold regarding positions on Latino interests? The results of models of NHLA ratings, in Table 6.4, echo those just noted in the NAACP ratings. The models are all jointly significant and the level of explained variation increases when the interaction terms are included. Without the interaction terms, ideology is the dominant explanation for NHLA ratings. But once the interaction terms are included, our hypotheses are modestly supported by the results in that each of the interaction terms for Latino and ideology are positive, though they are only significant in the 105th and 107th Congresses. Additionally, the interaction terms for ideology and black MC are also significant in the 106th and 107th Congresses, raising some doubt about the distinctiveness of Latino MCs' views of NHLA concerns when compared to black MCs; but they support the notion of some unique contribution of black descriptive representation that is apart from general ideology.

However, in these results in Tables 6.3 and 6.4 the effect of ideology and the standard errors of the interactions are *conditional* on whether the representative is black or Latino. In other words, the standard error for the interaction coefficients reported in these tables do not tell us precisely the statistical significance of the effect of ideology when we compare a nonminority to a minority representative. To assess the effects of ideology on white, black, and Latino MCs, and whether there are statistically significant differences, the conditional effects and conditional standard errors must be examined (Brambor, Clark, and Golder 2006; Friedrich 1982).

Table 6.5 presents the conditional coefficients for ideology, along with 95 percent confidence intervals based on the conditional standard errors, for white, black, and Latino MCs for each Congress studied. The conditional coefficients measure the magnitude and direction of the effect of ideology for each group, while the 95 percent confidence intervals help gauge the statistical significance for those coefficients; if the confidence intervals (CIs) cross zero, then the effect is not statistically different from zero. First, note that in each Congress, general ideology has a smaller effect on their respective group's rating for black and for Latino MCs than it does for white MCs. For example, in the 105th Congress' s NAACP ratings, the coefficient for ideology for white MCs is −45.08 (p <.05) while the coefficient for blacks is only −0.90 and is not significant. For NHLA ratings in the 105th, the coefficient for ideology is −46.76 for white MCs (p <.05) while it is actually a positive 27.95 for Latino MCs and is significant but in the opposite direction. And except for the 107th Congress, the 95 percent confidence intervals for the coefficients for ideology for black MCs in the NAACP models and Latino MCs in the NHLA models are not significant, or they fall completely in the positive range and are all thus in the opposite direction of what a liberal-conservative ideological explanation would predict. In short, in these four Congresses, general liberalism had no effect on black MCs' support for NAACP positions, and

TABLE 6.4. *The Conditioning Effects of Descriptive Representation on Ideology's Explanatory Power of NHLA Scorecard Ratings, 105th–108th Congresses. (Dependent Variable: NHLA Rating)*

Independent Variables	Descriptive Representation and Ideology				Conditioning Effects of Descriptive Representation			
Member Characteristic	105th	106th	107th	108th	105th	106th	107th	108th
Ideology	-41.35***	-60.07	-58.12***	-38.47***	-46.76***	-66.58***	-62.55***	-43.80***
	(6.22)	(5.81)	(4.90)	(6.99)	(6.41)	(5.86)	(4.99)	(7.42)
Ideology X Black Representative					33.44	52.56**	47.18***	26.86
					(18.14)	(17.03)	(14.33)	(17.05)
Ideology X Latino Representative					74.71*	81.25**	22.77	46.48
					(30.45)	(29.65)	(25.68)	(30.10)
Black Representative	5.06	2.26	0.24	-5.19	21.02*	26.56**	22.83**	6.86
	(3.87)	(3.63)	(3.06)	(4.36)	(9.84)	(9.03)	(7.56)	(9.20)
Latino Representative	-6.10	4.44	5.62	-1.07	27.27	40.32**	15.02	17.69
	(4.56)	(4.55)	(3.86)	(4.88)	(14.44)	(13.96)	(12.08)	(13.28)
District Characteristics								
White Population	9.68	15.02	29.81	26.58	-8.17	-15.93	21.73	13.09
	(21.87)	(20.67)	(17.91)	(20.27)	(22.97)	(23.46)	(19.81)	(21.74)
Latino Population	10.52	-2.59	23.71	20.46	-0.66	-26.66	19.32	9.90
	(15.32)	(15.96)	(13.48)	(15.89)	(16.01)	(18.39)	(15.47)	(17.08)
Black population	3.28	7.77	34.36	29.90	-13.56	-19.22	29.56	16.80
	(24.58)	(23.46)	(20.23)	(23.38)	(25.67)	(25.88)	(21.87)	(24.44)
Asian Population	18.82	10.55	42.80	35.90	-9.51	-39.16	32.16	13.88
	(34.00)	(32.67)	(26.71)	(32.51)	(35.70)	(37.04)	(28.42)	(34.70)
Foreign-Born Population	1.48	8.92	-14.80	-10.21	3.87	19.94	-11.54	-2.54
	(12.83)	(12.62)	(10.75)	(14.78)	(12.66)	(12.87)	(11.06)	(15.32)
Education	-2.81	-18.01	-57.08	-24.16	0.33	-23.29	-52.69	-28.94
	(39.52)	(37.99)	(31.35)	(36.73)	(38.86)	(36.86)	(30.93)	(36.60)

	(1)	(2)	(3)	(4)	(5)	(6)	(7)	(8)
Urbanization	-8.82	6.67	4.00	22.63**	-8.65	6.08	3.04	22.12**
	(5.60)	(5.40)	(4.74)	(7.56)	(5.51)	(5.23)	(4.65)	(7.53)
Poverty	19.36	-4.50	-18.47	-8.87	18.81	-4.49	-25.79	-10.91
	(32.13)	(31.34)	(27.03)	(29.23)	(31.65)	(30.56)	(26.54)	(29.07)
Income	0.07	-0.07	-0.01	-0.01	0.05	-0.07	-0.06	-0.03
	(0.18)	(0.17)	(0.14)	(0.11)	(0.17)	(0.16)	(0.14)	(0.11)
South	-2.27	2.84	-0.39	-1.05	-2.06	2.71	-0.81	-1.03
	(2.49)	(2.48)	(2.16)	(2.89)	(2.46)	(2.42)	(2.13)	(2.88)
Constant	60.19**	41.58*	27.51	39.94	76.59***	70.39**	36.63	52.84*
	(22.32)	(21.29)	(18.24)	(20.90)	(23.11)	(23.44)	(19.94)	(22.28)
N	207	214	211	206	207	214	211	206
F	7.49***	15.54	20.60***	8.15***	7.33***	15.46***	19.44***	7.44***
Adjusted R²	0.29	0.47	0.55	0.31	0.32	0.50	0.57	0.32

Note: Unstandardized OLS coefficients are reported, with standard errors in parentheses. * p <.05, ** p <.01, and *** p <.001 in a two-tailed t-test.

TABLE 6.5. *Estimated Coefficients of Ideology on NAACP and NHLA Ratings and Confidence Intervals Based on the Conditional Standard Error, by Congress and Member Type*

Congress		Effect of Ideology on NAACP Ratings		Effect of Ideology on NHLA Ratings	
		Conditional Coefficient	95% Confidence Interval	Conditional Coefficient	95% Confidence Interval
105th Congress	White	−45.08*	−54.37 to −35.79	−46.76*	−59.32 to −34.20
	Black	−0.90	−9.21 to 7.41	−13.32*	−25.30 to −1.34
	Latino	−45.31*	−53.53 to −37.09	27.95	15.97 to 39.93
106th Congress	White	−67.46*	−79.49 to −55.43	−66.58*	−55.09 to −78.07
	Black	−8.72	−20.25 to 2.81	−14.00*	−25.01 to −2.99
	Latino	−86.99*	−98.52 to −75.46	14.97	3.96 to 25.98
107th Congress	White	−60.40*	−69.53 to −51.27	−62.55*	−72.33 to −52.77
	Black	−32.53*	−43.53 to −21.53	−15.37*	−24.43 to −6.31
	Latino	−32.12*	−43.12 to −21.12	−39.78*	−48.84 to −30.72
108th Congress	White	−39.06*	−46.33 to −31.79	−43.80*	−58.34 to −29.26
	Black	−1.71	−8.51 to 5.19	−16.94*	−30.56 to −3.32
	Latino	−32.01*	−38.81 to −25.21	2.68	−10.94 to 16.30

Note: Cells report the conditional coefficients based on the results displayed in Tables 6.1 and 6.2, and are simply the summation of the baseline ideology coefficient and the coefficient for the respective interaction term. Confidence intervals are based on the conditional standard error for the conditional coefficients (Friedrich 1982). The confidence intervals are calculated by multiplying the conditional standard errors by 1.96, and then subtracting and adding these values to the coefficients, respectively, to determine the lower and upper bounds.

*Coefficient is negative and significant (p <.05, two-tailed).

the effect of general ideology on Latino MCs' support for NHLA positions was often not even in the same direction as its effect on white MCs;
the latter finding is one that is masked by the results presented in Table
6.2. Thus, the effect of ideology differs across racial/ethnic backgrounds
of MCs. Moreover, in all of the models, including those for the 107th
Congress, the CIs for the effect of ideology on NAACP ratings for black
MCs do not cross the CIs for white MCs, nor do the CIs for ideology's
effect on NHLA ratings for Latino MCs cross the confidence intervals for
white MCs. In other words, MCs' support for minority group positions
is based on ideology except when minority representatives are considering their own group's positions. Support across groups in national-level,
congressional voting seems to be driven by ideology.

As our third hypothesis calls for, with the evidence in Table 6.5 we
can more closely assess the degree to which general ideology influences
Latino MCs' and black MCs' support for the other minority group's concerns. In the 105th, 106th, and 108th Congresses, the effect of ideology
for Latino MCs is negative and significant on NAACP ratings, and the
effect of ideology is likewise negative and significant for black MCs on
NHLA ratings. In these Congresses, minority lawmakers use the same
cues as whites with regard to the other group's interests. Descriptive representation's influences on voting and advocacy do not necessarily trans-
fer from one minority group to another. Instead, ideology acts to bridge
common interests regardless of minority group representation. The 107th
Congress is the exception to this, but that is probably due to the higher
degree of overlap across the roll-call votes included by the NHLA and
NAACP in their ratings of this Congress.[3] Indeed, this actually bolsters
the argument that group-specific concerns determine policy positions,
and suggests again independence in interminority group relations. If both
minority groups share concerns, there should consequently be less difference across minority groups in terms of the moderating effect of ideology; and this seems to be the case for the 107th Congress.

What can be said about more or increased *levels* of support for
minority interests, which was the central concern of Chapter 5? We can
assess the effect of descriptive representation on NAACP and NHLA
ratings based on the results in Tables 6.3 and 6.4, but we need to recognize that the effects are conditioned by, or depend in part on, the

---

[3] Five of the thirty-four separate roll-call votes included in both scorecards were included in
both NAACP and NHLA ratings calculations. This was a higher percentage than in other
Congresses, but still accounts for less than 15 percent of the roll-call votes.

TABLE 6.6. *Estimated Coefficients of Descriptive Representation on NAACP and NHLA Ratings and Confidence Intervals Based on the Conditional Standard Error for Mean NOMINATE Scores, by Congress*

Congress		Effect of Descriptive Representation on NAACP Ratings		Effect of Descriptive Representation on NHLA Ratings	
		Conditional Coefficient	95% Confidence Interval	Conditional Coefficient	95% Confidence Interval
105th	Black	−0.10	−23.86 to 29.63	2.96	−34.94 to 40.86
Congress	Latino	2.95	−19.77 to 25.66	−0.37	−65.16 to 64.41
106th	Black	−7.01	−29.32 to 15.61	−1.30	−36.86 to 34.27
Congress	Latino	−6.88	−72.47 to 58.70	7.01	−55.48 to 69.59
107th	Black	−0.92	−17.50 to 15.66	−2.18	−32.08 to 27.73
Congress	Latino	−6.88	−54.90 to 41.13	5.68	−48.51 to 59.88
108th	Black	−2.09	−12.82 to 8.64	−6.03	−42.42 to 30.36
Congress	Latino	3.60	−26.99 to 34.19	−1.37	−63.21 to 60.48

Note: Cells report the conditional coefficients based on the results displayed in Tables 6.1 and 6.2, and are the effect of the descriptive representation dummy variable interacted with the mean ideology for the each group. For instance, the coefficient and standard error for a Black Representative in the 105th NAACP model equals 23.76 + 58.74*(1 * −.54), where 23.76 is the dummy variable coefficient, 58.74 is the coefficient for the interaction term, and −.54 is the mean ideology score for blacks in the 105th Congress. The mean ideology scores for black Representatives were −.54, −.53, −.52, and −.48 for the 105th, 106th, 107th, and 108th Congresses, respectively. The mean ideology scores for Latino Representatives were −.37, −.41, −.41 and −.41 for the 105th, 106th, 107th, and 108th Congresses, respectively. Confidence intervals are based on the conditional standard error for the conditional coefficients (Friedrich 1982) based on the means for each group. The confidence intervals are calculated by multiplying the conditional standard errors by 1.96, and then subtracting and adding these values to the coefficients, respectively, to determine the lower and upper bounds.

degree of liberalism. That is, the change in the basic level of support for minority concerns attributable solely to the racial/ethnic background of the representative varies across values of ideology. Table 6.6 reports the conditional coefficient and 95 percent CIs for the black and Latino representation variables for the average values of black and Latino ideology. The results show that there is no significant effect of descriptive representation when compared to white Democratic MCs with the same ideological orientations. In essence, if one were simply concerned about predicting levels of support for NAACP or NHLA positions among generally liberal Democrats, there is little difference between liberal white versus liberal black or Latino MCs. While not reported in the table, extending the scale of liberalism to include the range of NOMINATE scores for each group results in only modest, and again statistically insignificant, differences in estimated NAACP and NHLA scores particularly at the liberal end of the ideological spectrum. A liberal ideology moves all of these groups toward support for minority interests. This underscores that a major effect of descriptive representation is manifested in how black and Latino MCs' understandings are rooted in sources other than the conventional ideology. So, even if or when liberal whites vote like blacks and Latinos, or when blacks support Latino interests, and vice versa, that *similar behavior* may be *attributable to different sources*. On the one hand, a general ideological outlook rooted in economic/class factors acts to bridge *cross*-group support (or mitigate conflict) for all groups (cf. Minta 2011, 115–6). On the other hand, perspectives shaped by particular racial/ethnic group considerations, apart from just economic/class factors, shape blacks' and Latinos' perspectives when they consider their own group. In some ways, this finding highlights our suggested explanation for the different findings in our study and those at the local level (cf. Minta 2011, 117). Where a broad and clear ideological context is less present, such as occurs at the local level, group-specific interests play a prominent role that may lead to less cooperation relative to national-level politics where broader ideological perspectives more often play a more prominent role in policy debates and decisions.

Accounting for the Direct and Indirect Effects of Descriptive Representation

While MCs with similar (liberal) ideologies may tend to support minority concerns regardless of the representatives' racial/ethnic backgrounds, it is not likely that all groups hold similar ideological orientations. And, of course, without the assumption that ideologies are basically similar, the degree to which black and Latino MCs support their own group's concerns and the concerns of the other group are less clear from the analysis. In other words, there are both direct and indirect effects of minority descriptive representation on advocacy of minority group issues. The previous analysis suggests that the key difference here, after accounting for ideology, is that minority MCs are influenced by different cues when considering policy positions depending on whether those positions are relevant to their own group or to another group's preferences. However, we argued in Chapter 5 that black and Latino MCs may be an additional source, beyond ideology and partisanship, for fostering support across minority groups. These two findings at first seem incompatible, until we take into account the results in Table 6.1 which demonstrated that black MCs are more liberal than white or Latino MCs (even after controlling for other district characteristics). Black MCs are more liberal and with that unique ideological intensity also act as a conduit for the cross-group support for Latino interests. Black MCs do not always support Latino issues at higher rates, of course, but there is an indirect effect to be accounted for to adequately describe the role of descriptive representation in cross-group support.

Figure 6.2 illustrates the effect of descriptive representation on support for NAACP and NHLA positions that accounts for both the indirect effect of minority representation (especially black representation) on ideological intensity and the direct effect of ideology. Specifically, the graphs depict the estimated 95 percent confidence intervals for NAACP ratings (upper portion of the figure) and NHLA ratings (lower portion of the figure) for each of the two groups based on the results of the analyses in Tables 6.3 and 6.4, but adjusting for the effect of each group's different ideological orientations (as measured by NOMINATE scores) from Table 6.1. The adjusted ideology score is the ideology score for whites, but adjusted for differences found in Table 6.1 according to the coefficients for the respective minority representative. For example, when estimating the 95 percent confidence interval range for NAACP ratings for the 105th Congress for MCs with an adjusted −.2 ideology score, that basic score (−.2) is what is used to estimate NAACP ratings for white MCs. For black MCs, we subtract −.1 from the ideology score when estimating the effect since that is the coefficient for black representatives in the NOMINATE models (Table 6.1). Thus, the adjusted ideology is actually the white baseline, with adjustments made for black and Latino MCs. The effects on NAACP and NHLA ratings presented in Figure 6.2 account for both the direct effects of ideology and descriptive representation on support scores as well as the indirect effects of descriptive representation on these scores as it acts on ideology.

The confidence intervals present the range of scores we would expect 95 percent of the time for each level of adjusted ideology. (The estimates were made with Clarify which uses a simulation and sampling technique

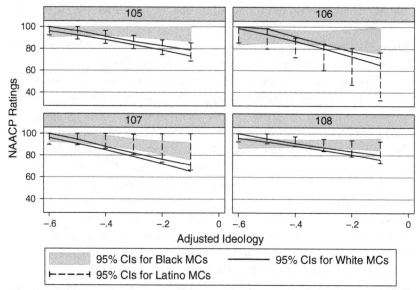

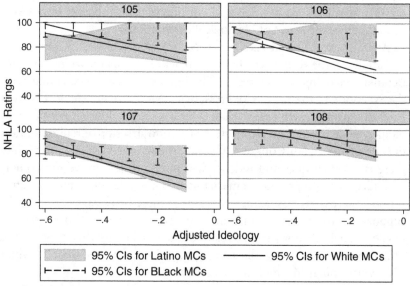

FIGURE 6.2. Estimated Marginal Effect of Ideology on NAACP and NHLA Ratings for White, Latino, and Black Members of Congress (MCs), by Congress

to gauge the variation in ratings; King, Tomz, and Wittenberg 2000.) The gray areas are the CIs for one's own group, the lines present the CIs for white MCs, and the dashed ranges are the CIs for minority MCs from the "other" group (Latinos for NAACP ratings, and blacks for NHLA ratings). The general relationship is thus a range of estimates for each group such that when the ranges overlap, there is no statistically discernible difference between the groups. First, note that in each of the graphs there is a general pattern indicating that minority MCs show little variation in their support for co-ethnic issues. Black ratings are generally flat across the range of ideology scores for NAACP ratings and the same (non)pattern is reflected in the effect of ideology on Latino MCs NHLA ratings. However, also note that black MCs tend to support NAACP ratings (co-ethnic interests) at higher levels, and the overlap between black MC and white MC ratings occurs only after the adjusted ideology (the white baseline) is about –.3, which represents roughly the top half of white Democrats. Also notable is that the range for Latino MCs is never statistically distinct from that of black MCs for NAACP scores. These findings comport with our previous results and further demonstrate a heightened representation for NAACP support among blacks, and that Latinos, while not different from whites, are also not different from blacks in NAACP ratings across the range of ideological orientations.

A similar pattern emerges in the NHLA scores, but as in our previous analyses, the differences between black, Latino, and white MCs are minimal across most Congresses. The interesting difference is that with the exception of the 108th Congress, black MCs actually support NHLA positions to a greater extent than whites over the lower range of ideologies while there is no clear effect of Latino descriptive representation outside of the 106th Congress. Overall, the graphs highlight that while there is some distinct and independent effect of descriptive representation, ideology also provides a mechanism to mitigate conflict (or enhance support) across groups. And, importantly, while black and Latino MCs' support for their own group's interests are not closely tied to general ideology, such ideology is an substantial factor in why they support the other group's positions at the same rate, and often higher, than do white MCs with similar ideological orientations.

Conclusion

Most scholarship on minority descriptive representation focuses on whether there is an additive effect of descriptive representation, where minority legislators are more supportive of minority concerns or more generally liberal than white legislators. Our analysis in Chapter 5 also addressed this but added substantially to the research by examining how minority representation leads to support for the concerns of the other minority group. To some extent, we found that descriptive representation appeared to spur cross-group support or at least mitigated conflict. Yet considerable theoretical discussion suggests that it is a distinct *outlook* on minority issues that differentiates minority descriptive representation from nonminority representation, not just more often voting for more liberal policies (Minta 2011, 114–5; Mansbridge 1999). In other words, minority descriptive representatives are said to provide a different *kind* of representation from that of white representatives. But the empirical research on minority representation in Congress. including that on roll-call voting, has often ignored *how* minorities practice advocacy (cf. Burden 2007; Minta 2011).

In this chapter we extended and, we think, advanced the literature by examining how decision cues for racial minorities differ from those of the majority and how the role of ideology is conditioned by the consideration of co-ethnic versus other group concerns while also playing a key role in mitigating cross-group conflict. Drawing from data on four Congresses and comparing the two sets of minority group representatives with their white counterparts and with each other, we demonstrated that minority representatives employ different cues when voting on minority group concerns, and go beyond simply being more liberal in their policy stances (Dawson 2001; Canon 1999; Mansbridge 1999). We further demonstrated that black MCs are ideologically unique from white MCs and that their distinctively high liberal orientation influences their voting regarding Latino issues, with the result that black MCs tend to support Latino issues to a greater extent than white (Democratic) MCs. Both minority groups tend to display sustained support for their own groups' interests that are somewhat invariant to (general) ideological orientations. These indicate yet another iteration of the minority group independence identified in previous chapters. However, general ideology links group interests and results in essentially no conflict and instances of support in black-Latino political relations in Congress.

Unlike studies of either black or Latino groups, the inclusion of both black and Latino representatives in our analysis enabled us to show that this racial dimension is group-specific, with black and Latino MCs drawing on the broader ideological cue when considering the other group's issues. Furthermore, by identifying diverging patterns of the advocacy cues across minority groups, we demonstrate the importance of group diversity, and not just minority inclusion, in legislative bodies. In other words, it matters that blacks represent blacks and Latinos represent Latinos since black and Latino representatives rely on differing cues for policy advocacy (Mansbridge 1999). Each group's descriptive representatives bring unique perspectives to the aggregate decision-making process in Congress.

7

Further Explorations of Black-Latino Relations and Policies in National Politics

There is a very limited body of previous scholarship on minority inter-group relations in national politics; it describes just a few issues and examines a limited range of evidence. Furthermore, these works are sel-dom guided by theoretical frameworks attentive to potential differences in how policies and intergroup relations might vary across levels of gov-ernment. As demonstrated in this book thus far, examining the national level systematically and in several ways and different venues reveals virtu-ally no evidence of minority intergroup conflict; this stands in some con-trast to what has often been identified in the urban politics and similar research literatures. In this chapter we supplement our previous analyses in Chapters 3–6 with a broad overview and description of black-Latino relations on several public policy issues and thus further explore whether and how the relations between the two minority groups may vary across policy issues at this level of government. The evidence from the examples we assess here is consistent with what we have found to this point: vir-tually no indication of conflict, but indications that the groups often act independently. These assessments notwithstanding, several prior studies of black-Latino relations at the national level suggested something differ-ent from what we have reported; we begin by noting those other claims.

Vaca's (2004) analysis of the "presumed alliance" between Latinos and blacks identified several instances where the two groups had diverged on major federal legislation in the past. The 1975 law extending the landmark Voting Rights Act of 1965 ultimately addressed "language minority" and Latino concerns in its final version but did so over the initial objections of the NAACP. The NAACP felt the addition of language provisions (and inclusion of Latinos, and others) would undercut the previous legislation's central focus on blacks and the effectiveness as intended in the original 1965 law. Similarly, some members of the Leadership Conference on Civil Rights (LCCR), a group closely linked to black interests (especially at the time), succeeded in revising the language assistance provisions of the 1985 voting rights legislation which "directly affected Latinos and other minorities in such a way as to reduce its coverage for language groups." Efforts in Congress in the mid-1980s to make English the "official" language of the United States, while ultimately defeated, were only nominally opposed at the outset by certain civil rights groups, including the LCCR, according to Vaca. During congressional consideration of provisions for employer sanctions under the Immigration Reform and Control Act (IRCA, 1986), Latino groups requested that their (presumed) black allies oppose employer sanctions; but the NAACP and the AFL-CIO opposed that request. Other employment discrimination concerns were identified in the mid-1980s and Latino advocates argued that existing statutes did not provide adequate protection for Latinos; thus they made numerous requests for new enforcement programs, but those requests were not supported by civil rights groups. As depicted by Vaca (2004), then, issues associated with immigration, language policy, and particular forms of discrimination were grounds for conflict in Latino and black coalition building on national policies. (Vaca also cites instances of tensions in the voting behavior of blacks and Latinos in several mayoral elections.)

Tichenor (2002, 233) also says that Hispanic and African American groups "clashed in the 1970s" on issues similar to those noted by Vaca, regarding employer sanctions that were part of immigration legislation, and tensions also "surfaced over coverage of the Voting Rights Act, federal jobs programs, and public education." But, Tichenor adds, over the course of the 1970s, "African American and Hispanic groups averted open conflict by forging new alliances on voting rights, education, anti-poverty programs and other issues. Instrumental in this regard was a Working Committee on the Concerns of Hispanics and Blacks formed in the 1970s by presidents of the National Urban Coalition [NUL] and the NCLR [National Council of La Raza]" with the avowed purpose of encouraging "cooperation and joint action by the two largest U.S. minority groups." The committee "brought together the NAACP, the National Urban Coalition, the NCLR, LULAC [League of United Latin American Citizens], and other groups" (Tichenor 2002, 233). There is thus evidence of earlier black and Latino policy conflict or competition, but later negotiation and some cooperative efforts on national policy issues, as these stories suggest.

An interconnection of the black and Latino political conditions and situations regarding other dimensions of American politics has been raised as well, and one can imagine that these might become a source of interminority group tension. The increasingly large Latino population is "transforming the electorate." The number of Latino voters has the potential to double in size if all adult Latinos currently in the United States gain legal immigration status, become citizens, and register to vote (Pew Hispanic Center 2006). The views and behaviors of new citizens may affect the overall profile of public opinion in the United States. Fraga (2005) argues that a consequence of the growing Latino population will be its implications for national politics, particularly evident in party politics, and the positioning of blacks and Latinos in the larger electoral process.

Immigration, and especially perceptions of Latinos as immigrants has served to enhance the political capital of Latinos to the Republican party. The national competitiveness of the Republican party is grounded in consistent levels of support from states in the traditional south. The support from this region ... has come almost exclusively from white Southern voters. The playing of the race card in the South, in all of its contemporary rhetorical transformations, makes it virtually impossible for the Republican Party to make genuine appeals to African American voters or to seem responsive to the interests of African Americans. By contrast, this is not the case with Latinos. (Fraga 2005, 1–2)

This suggests that Latinos' role in American elections has at least indirect ramifications for the influence of black voters in national politics. On the one hand, Latino immigrants, often including the undocumented, are perceived as seekers of economic opportunity and as "the prototypical examples willing to work hard and sacrifice to achieve the American dream." At times they are compared, if only implicitly, to others, including African Americans, in the society who may not be depicted as equally motivated to work. On the other hand, Latinos may be "vilified targets of American nationalists promoting public policy designed to limit their upward mobility once in the U.S."; and "as an immigrant-derived ethnic group, Latinos both benefit and suffer." Furthermore, when Latinos are characterized by Republicans "as the most recent in a long line of ethnic immigrants seeking a better life and opportunities for their children, they can serve to moderate the Southern-based racially conservative image of the Republican party." Rather like the "racial triangulation' suggested by Kim, in which whites compare blacks unfavorably to Asians in their economic and social attributes and aspirations, Latinos may be in a triangulated national election situation, arising from their comparison to blacks (by whites), and also affecting the policy positioning and appeals of the two major political parties. These impacts are attributable not only to the size and growth of the Latino population but also to Latinos' and blacks' spatial concentration and the Electoral College structure that amplifies those conditions. A possible upshot is that Latinos might (eventually) be played off against blacks in some ways. This is a potential source of inter-group tension that harkens back to disagreements between blacks and Latinos in national politics during earlier periods as described by Vaca, Tichenor, and others.

Beyond these few descriptive studies of black-Latino relations in national politics there has been little other research. However, a study (Brader et al. 2010) of black attitudes about immigration is relevant and consistent with the general arguments we make in this study.

In that study, Brader et al. (2010) found that blacks are consistently more permissive on immigration than whites across a host of different (immigration-related) policies. They claim that blacks' "group attitudes, not material interests drive differences in both black and white opinions about immigration" and conclude that "in general, the pattern of findings strongly supports the notion that immigration opinion is driven by sym-bolic concerns like group identity, and less by class or individual material interests." The conceptualization of Brader et al. regarding "symbolic" politics is very similar to our notion of ideas or ideology (related to gen-eral rights) which they contrast with (material) interests, much as we do. The evidence of Brader et al., using survey data and on a policy that is primarily a national government responsibility, accords with our finding and thesis about intergroup relations.

In Chapters 3 to 6, we used descriptive statistics and quantitative anal-yses to examine various aspects of black-Latino relations at the national level. There was essentially no indication of black-Latino conflict; rather, we see mostly "independence" and concurring or parallel behaviors. Bits of evidence of direct and clear-cut cooperation exist but were not abundant. In this chapter we consider public policies and black-Latino relations in another way – through evidence from public pronouncements by advocacy groups and congressional caucuses, among others.[1] These provide exam-ples and illustrations in some detail about activities not well captured in the other dimensions and forms of evidence used in our study to this point.

Deciding which policies to examine is neither simple nor straightforward for several reasons. Similar to a point we raised when discussing possible

---

[1] We acknowledge and express appreciation to Patrick Flavin and Michael Keane for their work in collecting evidence and helping draft some of the materials used in this chapter.

selection bias in the urban politics and other studies of interminority group relations (see Chapter 2), the examples we choose are likely to influence our broader assessments. We might choose based on evidence from our previous chapters and focus on issues that are salient to both groups and have, at the same time, generated high conflict versus little to no conflict. However, as our data showed, there were very few policies that seemed consistently and highly salient to both black and Latino advocacy groups to begin with; and we were hardly able to detect any conflict to speak of in the various analyses we undertook. In contrast, the urban politics research has examined areas presumed to be highly salient to both minority groups but has also frequently found conflict on the issues selected.

We might examine specific policy areas that are as roughly comparable as possible to those explored in the urban research; however, as we emphasized, because of the very different geographic scope, the particular kind and extent of policy responsibilities, and other differences in the essential character of national and local governments, we believe we can contrast and juxtapose but cannot really undertake comparisons as such. We might nonetheless identify and consider some national level policy issues that are broadly parallel to some studied in research on black-Latino relations at other levels of government. The policies we actually consider in this chapter have one or more of the attributes just noted. We examine some that have been on advocacy group legislative scorecards, suggesting salience, including one that is quite salient to one group: immigration. Another policy has been addressed extensively in local studies, education, though the particular elements of education considered here and those considered in the local school district research are rather different. And another policy considered deals with economic inequality at the national level: welfare.

We discuss five policies, including some that reflect topics appearing in the advocacy group scorecards. These are welfare (particularly the 1996 welfare reform legislation), education (No Child Left Behind), voting rights, immigration, and NAFTA/CAFTA (North American Free Trade Agreement/Central America Free Trade Agreement). These policies address various important issues that have occurred at different points in time. Welfare and the welfare reform legislation in 1996 would probably be expected to have characteristics of both shared interests and shared ideology for blacks and Latinos; that is, since both black and Latino communities have high levels of poverty and presumably would benefit from strong welfare programs, common interests should lead to common positions on this type of reform. Yet common economic disadvantage does not always lead to cooperation. Recall that Gay (2006) claimed that commonality and competition may work in different ways in shaping black attitudes toward Latinos (also see Oliver and Wong 2003). Recognition of shared disadvantage relative to whites might encourage a more positive orientation, and socioeconomic environments influence attitudes by privileging one fact of black-Latino relations over the other (Gay 2006, 995). We suspect the impact of the socioeconomic environment is itself also conditioned by jurisdiction or which government is responsible for policies; broader versus narrower arenas and policy authority may affect perceptions of commonality versus competition. And indeed Latino-black group competition over economic resources, including such resources relevant to economic well-being (government jobs, certain city policies affecting minority businesses, for example) along with certain political resources (election to city government positions, etc.), were sources of tension rather than commonality, according to much of the urban politics and the mass attitudes research (see various research described in Chapter 2).

Education is often considered a linchpin for improving economic mobility and moving toward greater economic equality for racial/minority groups in American society. Yet studies of the implications for minority students of local education policies have found second-generation discrimination. More to the point, some of these studies, from the early 1990s and more recently, also examine issues of interminority group relations in local education and often show an inverse relationship between several indicators of black and Latino outcomes, indicating negative intergroup implications (as we described in Chapter 2). The educational reform of the No Child Left Behind Act (NCLB) seems to foster similar interests and ideas based on concerns for equitable educational outcomes for all minorities and to address shared high levels of need among the constituents of both black and Latino advocacy groups. The ostensibly different expectations and findings merit further inquiry.

Voting rights is an issue that our expectations suggest would facilitate cooperative orientations, with ideology driving advocacy for equal access to the ballot box. However, as Vaca and Tichenor argue (summarized earlier in this chapter), blacks were concerned that including Latinos under voting rights legislation would dilute the substantive and symbolic importance of black voting rights. Most of these differences appear to have been worked out through discussions between minority advocacy groups but further attention is warranted.

Immigration is an issue where black and Latino interests might be expected to diverge, because of (perceived) economic competition, and thus conflict may emerge. Indeed, Tichenor (2002, 37) notes that as far back as the 1860s, Frederick Douglass, the noted black leader, "endorsed immigration limits, lamenting that 'every hour sees the black man elbowed out of employment by some newly arrived immigrant,'" and that labor leaders during the 1920s also expressed concerns about the impact of immigration because it "undercut the wages, working conditions and job security of American workers." And during the 1970s, Tichenor notes that efforts of Mexican American advocates to "mobilize civil rights groups against employer sanctions" in immigration legislation "faced potential opposition from a coalition of African American groups that traditionally viewed illegal aliens as competitive with poor blacks for jobs and public benefits" (Tichenor 2002, 232). Also, recall that 47 percent of blacks supported Proposition 187 in California, which concerned the denial of public services to illegal immigrants (in 1994) but only 23 percent of Hispanics (a twenty-four point difference) did so (see Hajnal et al. 2002). On the other hand, Jesse Jackson had spoken out strongly against this measure (Tichenor 2002, 276), and recent studies (Brader et al. 2010) suggest less black disagreement (compared to whites) about immigration. Our empirical analysis in earlier chapters found no evidence of conflict regarding immigration, perhaps because of the negotiations and agreements reached between black and Latino advocacy groups at the national level during the 1970s–80s. It is thus worth examining this issue in greater detail.

Finally, free trade, specifically the NAFTA and CAFTA, provide an interesting case where an overlap in either interests or ideology between blacks and Latinos is not entirely clear. For some observers these trade treaties raised concerns because they might lead to American jobs being moved to other countries, including countries from which Latinos had immigrated. Whether this would negatively affect American workers, particularly low-skilled black and/or Latino workers, or create more job opportunities because of the purported increase of overall economic activity was debated. Furthermore, some believed that Latino-owned businesses might be especially well positioned to benefit from increased trade because of their niches in and presumed advantages in markets in Mexico and elsewhere in Latin American countries.

On the whole, these policies seem reasonably representative of black-Latino advocacy group and elite officeholders' (here, members of Congress) views and activities in national-level debates regarding some major and visible public policies. The policies provide some degree of variation in terms of interests, broader purposive ideas, and the extent to which those converge or diverge, and ultimately they shed further light on the nature of black-Latino relations to complement our foregoing analyses.

Our evidence comes from a comprehensive examination of the websites of the major black and Latino interest/advocacy groups and the websites of the Congressional Black Caucus (CBC) and the Congressional Hispanic Caucus (CHC), the latter of which gave us views of minority members of Congress. We explored (electronic) links regarding the policy areas of interest and also scanned the websites more generally. Furthermore, we looked for stories and public pronouncements by advocacy group spokespersons and members of Congress through Lexis/Nexis searches seeking the names of the groups and organizations as well as the names of minority members of Congress over an extended time; we emphasized periods when the specific policy was most visible on the public agenda and summarized the most relevant and important points given the purposes of our study. We attempt to present what we found in a consistent, deliberate manner to provide evidence on each policy arena. This analytical approach and the evidence it uncovers are consistent with our previous findings and larger claims.

Welfare Reform

In August of 1996, Congress passed sweeping welfare reform through the Personal Responsibility and Work Opportunity Reconciliation Act (PRWORA), legislation that President Bill Clinton promised would mark "the end of welfare as we know it." Enacted by a Republican-controlled Congress, welfare reform faced opposition from political liberals as well as from advocates representing racial and ethnic minorities. In particular, advocacy organizations representing blacks and Latinos were quite vocal in their opposition to various provisions in the proposed reforms. While their agreement in opposing several specific reforms proposed in PRWORA is clear, the extent to which black and Latino advocacy groups shared the same justifications, expressed similar interests for their positions, and cooperated with one another to pursue similar goals is less clear.

Black Advocacy Organizations

The NAACP, the Urban League, and the Congressional Black Caucus (CBC) all publicly opposed PRWORA, and nearly every member of the CBC voted no on the bill.[2] Myrlie Evers-Williams, at that time the president of the NAACP, publicly denounced the legislation.[3] Hugh Price, then-president of the National Urban League, shared this sentiment: "It's almost as if Washington has decided to end the War on Poverty and begin a war on poor children."[4] At the heart of black advocacy groups' concerns with PRWORA in 1996, and concerns with its reauthorization in 2002, is the disparity between whites and blacks in several well-being indicators. On the National Urban League's website (www.nul.org), their mission statement reads: "The mission of the Urban League movement is to enable African Americans to secure economic self-reliance, *parity*, power and civil rights" (emphasis added). Similarly, websites of both the CBC (www.congressionalblackcaucus.net) and the NAACP (www.naacp.org) place a strong emphasis on reducing inequality between African Americans and their white counterparts.[5]

In pointing out problems with welfare-to-work programs, the National Urban League stated on its website that "generally, minority working mothers on TANF [Temporary Assistance for Needy Families] do not receive the necessary subsidies to transition to work – including child care, transportation assistance, and college degree assistance – at the same rate as white working mothers. More than 70 percent of Hispanic and African American women did not receive any subsidies for work-related activities as compared with 62 percent of white women." Note that Hispanics are mentioned in the comments.

However, it would be incorrect to claim that advocates for blacks were uniformly against all of aspects of PRWORA. Specifically, most differences in preferences came when states were charged with actually implementing the welfare reform legislation. For example, the Maryland state chapter of the NAACP supported Governor William Donald Schaefer's proposed welfare reforms that would "deny additional aid to mothers who bear children while receiving benefits. NAACP leaders said they support

---

[2] David Broder, "Clinton's Welfare Decision Will Divide Democrats in 2000," *South Bend Tribune* (Indiana), August 7, 1996, p. A7.

[3] "NAACP Warns GOP of Consequences; Chairwoman Predicts Cuts Would Invoke Violent Backlash," *Charleston Daily Mail* (West Virginia) May 3, 1995, p. 3A.

[4] Carl T. Rowan, "America Will Rue the Results of Welfare 'Reform,'" *South Bend Tribune* (Indiana), August 5, 1996, p. A6.

[5] The CBC's website reports: "Since the formation of the Congressional Black Caucus (CBC), the core mission of the CBC has been to close (and, ultimately, to eliminate) disparities that exist between African-Americans and white Americans in every aspect of life."

the controversial experiment."[6] Local affiliates of the Urban League also supported various state proposals to implement PRWORA after it was passed. In addition, the *Washington Post* reported that "the National Black Election Study recently completed at Ohio State University found that 64 percent of blacks supported the five-year lifetime cap on welfare benefits contained in federal legislation passed last year – a position at odds with that of the NAACP."[7]

Welfare reform as passed in 1996 was, for the most part, opposed by African American advocacy groups. However, some if not many supported the "spirit" of welfare reform: for example, the NAACP, along with National Black Caucus of State Legislators and the Caucus of National Black Churches, indicated that it "strongly supported meaningful welfare reform."[8] Nonetheless, most groups also believed that PRWORA would deny racial minorities living in poverty the basic resources they needed to survive. In sum, though they supported the sentiment that something had to be done with the way welfare was administered in the United States, African American advocacy organizations overwhelmingly opposed the legislation that was eventually enacted in 1996 and reauthorized in 2002.

Latino Advocacy Organizations

Advocacy organizations representing Latinos also supported the spirit of welfare reform but opposed many specific provisions in PRWORA. For example, the League of United Latin American Citizens (LULAC) posted a statement on their website (www.lulac.org):

LULAC supports fair welfare reform that acts as a safety net for those who need assistance for valid reasons. Reform should encompass providing bilingual job training, funding for child care, an increased minimum wage and job opportunities to meet the needs of urban and rural welfare recipients, with reasonable time limits and individual review, and monitoring to ensure they do not increase poverty. But, like black advocacy groups, Latino advocacy groups convey concern with whether welfare recipients are given adequate resources to make a smooth transition from welfare to work.

---

[6] Graciela Sevilla, "Md. NAACP for Welfare Overhaul; Bid to Tighten Rules Gets Surprise Support," *Washington Post*, March 6, 1994, p. B1.

[7] Michael A. Fletcher, "Low-Profile Year 'Extremely Productive' for NAACP, Mfume Says," *Washington Post*, February 16, 1997, p. A3.

[8] Frank A. Aukofer, "Gwendolynne Moore among the Critics; Groups Hit Welfare Plan Proposed by Governors; Poor Would Be Denied Help, Organizations Say in Letters to Congress," *Milwaukee Journal Sentinel* (Wisconsin), February 14, 1996, p. 3.

Moreover, the NCLR argued that language barriers make transition from welfare to work difficult, citing that Latinos have left the welfare rolls at a slower pace than whites and African Americans. They contended that TANF does not do enough for non-English speakers who are willing and able to work, and as a result, Latinos made up 25 percent of welfare caseloads in 1999 (up from 17 percent in 1990 before welfare reform). To address this problem, the NCLR asks that "states improve access to English language instruction, assess individuals' proficiency in English, and develop strategies for addressing language barriers." Additionally, much of the attention of Latino advocacy groups was directed toward challenging a single provision in PRWORA that affects a considerable number of their constituents: a provision that prohibited states from providing Medicaid, Supplemental Security Income, TANF, and food stamps to most *legal* immigrants until they have resided in the United States for at least five years. The U.S. Commission on Civil Rights (www.usccr.gov) reported that as a result of these restrictions, "many immigrants have left the rolls, and the living conditions of these poor families continue to decline; significantly fewer legal immigrants, although eligible, receive TANF assistance, food stamps, and Medicaid. The changes to eligibility had a significant effect on children of immigrant parents; even the participation of U.S. citizen children who live in immigrant families has declined."

As welfare reform legislation was being crafted, the Congressional Hispanic Caucus (CHC) strongly urged that the Senate strip the House-passed welfare reform bill of this provision that denied benefits to legal immigrants.[9] When the legislation was passed and signed into law, several Latino advocacy groups voiced discontent with President Clinton, even though he promised to restore the cuts later (and it is important to note that SSI and Medicaid benefits to most legal immigrants were in fact restored in 1997). In a notable showing of support for Latino concerns, the Urban League also voiced opposition to restricting benefits to legal immigrants[10] (also see Hero and Preuhs 2007).

When the 1996 welfare reform was up for reauthorization in 2002, this particular provision continued to draw intense scrutiny from Latino advocacy groups as well as from the Catholic Church, often their ally in the welfare reform debate. Cecilia Munoz of NCLR put the debate this

---

[9] Tim Lopes, "Hispanic Caucus Raps Welfare Bill," *Palm Beach Post* (Florida), March 31, 1995, p. 7A.

[10] C. R. McFadden, "Howard Veal: Reform Is Needed, but Children Must Be Protected," *State Journal-Register* (Springfield, Illinois), July 31, 1996, Local, p. 3.

way: "Legal immigrants pay taxes, they register for Selective Service....
We should give them the same access to the safety net.... Immigrants are
not talking about a different set of standards. We're simply talking about
equity."[11] When President George W. Bush tried to limit states' discretion by proposing to continue a ban on welfare assistance for most legal
immigrants, even after announcing that he wanted to restore immigrants'
eligibility for federal nutrition subsidies, Munoz said, "We are hopping
mad."[12]

In sum, Latino advocacy groups opposed PRWORA in 1996 and several aspects of the reauthorization in 2002 for many of the same reasons
voiced by black advocacy groups. However, Latino advocacy groups had
two additional motivations for their opposition: (1) failure to adequately
address language barriers and (2) restrictions on welfare benefits to legal
immigrants. While the concerns they shared with African American advocacy groups were important, these two additional concerns constituted a
majority of the public statements made by Latino advocacy groups, likely
because these particular provisions affected their constituents almost
exclusively.

African American and Latino Relations and Welfare Reform
To evaluate the extent to which African American and Latino advocacy
groups cooperated in their opposition to welfare reform, the websites of
the following organizations were examined: NAACP, Urban League, CBC,
NCLR, LULAC, CHC, and LCCR. The general finding from canvassing
these websites is that each group focuses on its particular constituency
group first, and only secondarily does it address broader issues facing
all racial and ethnic minorities. In other words, African American advocacy groups devoted most of their time to pursuing "African American
issues" while Latino advocacy groups devoted most of their time to pursuing "Latino issues." Sometimes these issues overlap, sometimes they do
not. On the particular issue of welfare reform, both African Americans
and Latinos signified it as an important issue, and both had very similar
policy positions. While each group does seem to take an interest in the
well-being of racial and ethnic minorities generally, there does not appear

[11] Karen Branch-Brioso, "Advocates Seek to Restore Safety Net for Immigrants," *St. Louis
      Post-Dispatch* (Missouri), March 8, 2002, p. A1.
[12] Amy Goldstein, "Welfare Reform Plan Unveiled; Democrats on Hill Question Adequacy
      of Bush Proposal," *Washington Post*, February 27, 2002, p. A4.

to be much formal collaboration between African American and Latino advocacy groups on the issue of welfare reform.

A Lexis-Nexis search for newspaper articles covering welfare reform from 1994 until the summer of 2007 was also undertaken. Most articles that contained the name of one or more advocacy organizations tended to reference an advocacy group leader or spokesperson to articulate their organization's position on the issue. Much like the survey of the advocacy organizations' websites, this search of newspaper articles turned up no significant examples of African American and Latino advocacy groups taking joint action or making joint public statements. Overall, it seems that the relationship between African American and Latino advocacy organizations on the issue of welfare reform was one of shared positions but there is very little, if any, clear evidence of formal collaboration.

Education and No Child Left Behind

Early in his first term of office, President George W. Bush frequently proclaimed that his No Child Left Behind (NCLB) education plan would "end the soft bigotry of low expectations." In December of 2001, Congress passed NCLB with large bipartisan majorities in both chambers.[13] According to the U.S. Department of Education (www.ed.gov/nclb), the legislation was centered on four principles: (1) stronger accountability for results, (2) more freedom for states and communities, (3) utilization of proven education methods, and (4) provision of more choices for parents. Perhaps the most important change instituted by NCLB for blacks and Latinos is stricter accountability standards for individual schools that now must demonstrate adequate yearly progress in student achievement and provide information on the advancement of disadvantaged students and racial and ethnic minorities.

Both African American and Latino advocacy groups hold education as one of their highest policy priorities. In the face of underachieving urban schools that serve most black and Latino students, these advocacy groups strongly supported the spirit of education reform and the promise of NCLB to hold underperforming schools more accountable and to ensure that the achievement gap between whites and racial minorities is narrowed. It is no surprise, then, that members of the Congressional Black Caucus (CBC) and the Congressional Hispanic Caucus (CHC) overwhelmingly supported NCLB. However, this support gave way to

---

[13] The legislation passed 381–41 in the House and 87–10 in the Senate (www. vote-smart org).

concern over funding and questions about the extent to which NCLB is effective in reducing racial disparities in education. Though African American and Latino advocacy groups shared similar concerns about NCLB, we could find only a handful of instances where they formally collaborated with one another to pursue these shared policy goals.

African American Advocacy Organizations

The NAACP, the Urban League, and the CBC were all strong proponents of provisions in NCLB that require schools to provide disaggregated data on the academic progress of racial and ethnic minorities. Indeed, some supporters went so far as to say that NCLB may surpass the Supreme Court's *Brown v. Board of Education* decision in importance for providing equal education to all students regardless of race. In addition, according to the NAACP's website (www.naacp.org), before NCLB was even passed into law the group's National Education Department issued a "Call to Action" which outlined concrete steps that states and districts could take to reduce racial disparities in education by 50 percent over the next five years by focusing on resource equity, teacher quality, class size, special education, suspension and expulsion, and testing.

Though the NCLB promised much, African American advocacy groups argued that the Bush administration had not provided enough funding for states and school districts to meet the accountability requirements. The NAACP posted on its website: "NCLB remains ... severely under-funded, and many states continue to grapple with the need for federal assistance to reach the legislation's equity goal."[14] The CBC reported on its website that the cumulative NCLB funding shortfall was $56.7 billion since it was signed into law in January of 2002. Among the most pressing education concerns the CBC identified are ensuring adequate funding for early childhood education and Head Start, student nutrition, identifying and providing education and assistance appropriate to the needs of each individual student to fulfill the promise of NCLB, dropout prevention, after-school programs, school modernization and infrastructure improvement, and equipment enhancement. In addition, most African American advocacy groups are committed to reducing high school dropout rates among young African Americans and ensuring increased access to federal loans for higher education, such as the Pell Grants.

---

[14] Karla Scoon Reid, "Civil Rights Groups Split over NCLB," *Education Week*, August 31, 2005.

Both the NAACP and the CBC express concern with "high stakes testing," the primary tool with which student achievement is measured. The CBC writes on its website:

In light of recent revelations about the quality of test questions and the integrity of the data processing of the testing companies, the Congressional Black Caucus must reassert its position against the reckless administration of standardized tests.

This concern was not uniformly shared by the Urban League, however, as Seattle Urban League President James Kelly argues that NCLB is all about "high expectations." For those who complain about the high failure rate among African Americans, he has a rejoinder: "The bar has been raised. Get over it."[15]

While concern over funding levels left many African American advocacy groups skeptical about the effectiveness of NCLB, they did not abandon it altogether. James Edward D'Auguste, an attorney representing the NAACP, argued: "The NAACP doesn't necessarily agree with every aspect of the No Child Left Behind law ... but the one thing it does agree with is that there are some excellent provisions within the statute designed to increase opportunity for minority students to get a quality education."[16] In fact, the NAACP submitted legal briefs in support of the federal government and NCLB in Connecticut where the state sued over the legislation. Connecticut argued that with its stringent accountability measures and less than promised funding levels, NCLB amounts to an unfunded mandate that states should not be required to comply with.[17]

In sum, African American advocacy groups maintained a stance on education policy that supported increased accountability. For instance, to ensure that racial disparities in education are identified and addressed, these advocacy groups have been watchdogs on a loophole in NCLB that allows school districts not to report student achievement disaggregated by race if students of a certain race do not make up some minimum number, essentially allowing some schools to "game the system." At the same time, these advocacy groups continued to lobby Congress for more resources to make the promised reforms in NCLB a reality.

[15] Nina.Shapiro, "The Stress Test," *Seattle Weekly* (Washington), November 23, 2005, p. 17.
[16] Matt Apuzzo, "Judge: NAACP Can Argue against No Child Left Behind Lawsuit," *Associated Press State & Local Wire*, April 18, 2006.
[17] Avi Salzman, "N.A.A.C.P. Is Bush Ally in School Suit versus State," *New York Times*, February 1, 2006, p. B3.

Latino Advocacy Organizations
The National Council of La Raza (NCLR), the League of United Latin American Citizens (LULAC), and the CHC also supported NCLB when it was signed into law in early 2002. Like African American advocacy organizations, these groups conveyed strong support for provisions that require schools to report student achievement and progress disaggregated by racial group. Melissa Lazarin, an education reform analyst with the NCLR, said the federal law was helping children struggling to learn English get the attention they need.[18] However, Latino advocacy groups communicated concern with current funding levels for NCLB. On its website, LULAC (www.lulac.org) reported:

> Although LULAC embraces the vision documented by the No Child Left Behind Act, which holds schools, districts and states to high accountability standards for all students, we believe that the result of this Act may increase the negative impact on poor, under-financed, urban public schools. If they fail to meet state standards by at least 50 percent, they risk losing funding. The provision in the Act which provides that students in poor-performing schools may leave, fails to create incentives for school improvement.

Similarly, Raul Gonzalez, legislative director for the NCLR, said he was initially hopeful about the law's potential but has grown "deeply disappointed."[19]

Latino advocacy organizations place a high priority on securing additional funding for educating students with limited-English proficiency and for providing more opportunities for immigrant students to pursue higher education. For example, the NCLR (www.nclr.org) urges passage of the "DREAM Act," which would "provide a path to U.S. citizenship for hardworking and talented immigrant students who have been raised in the U.S. [and is] critical to improving the pipeline from high school to college and providing meaningful employment for Latinos." In addition, LULAC recommends more funding for dropout prevention programs for students for whom English is their second language, noting that Hispanics account for 56 percent of all U.S. immigrants yet they account for 90 percent of all immigrant dropouts. LULAC is also an advocate for many of the same issues that African American advocacy organizations lobby for, such as conveying concern with the emphasis place on high-stakes testing

---

[18] "New Test Monitors Michigan Students' English Proficiency; Evaluation Part of No Child Left Behind Act," *South Bend Tribune* (Indiana), April 6, 2006, p. B2.
[19] Diana Jean Schemo, "States' End Run Dilutes Burden for Special Ed," *New York Times*, June 7, 2004, p. A1.

and the inequality of de facto racial segregation taking place in urban public schools, as well as pushing for increased funding for early childhood education programs like Head Start and Even Start.

MALDEF has asserted the importance of Latino integration (desegregation) as central to achieving better educational outcomes. In response to, and in an effort to pursue, policy goals within the parameters of the 2007 U.S. Supreme Court decision that limited policy options to address school segregation, MALDEF argued for four strategies to encourage desegregation: (1) strategic site selection for new schools; (2) designing attendance zones that maintain diversity and/or avoid racial isolation; (3) recruiting students and faculty in a targeted fashion to "choice schools" to "ensure that minority families know about their options and feel welcome in "choice schools" so that they will apply in time to obtain some of the seats"; and (4) the importance of "keeping racial statistics" on local school district websites, which allows "local community groups, civil rights groups, and ... the general public" to better analyze "developing patterns of re-segregation, of educational equity, and of the educational opportunities and gaps at each school" (MALDEF 2008; www.house.gov/baca/chc/tsk-education.shtml). Finally, we also note the stated priorities of the Congressional Hispanic Caucus (CHC) on education issues (see Appendix 7.1 at the end of the chapter). Those priorities essentially consist of modifying and improving NCLB.

Some Instances of Collaboration, but Mostly Shared Positions with Little Interaction

African American and Latino advocacy organizations share very similar policy positions on education. While they supported No Child Left Behind when it was originally enacted in 2002, both groups became increasingly concerned with the way in which education reform was implemented, particularly with funding levels that do not measure up to their expectations. African American and Latino groups devoted most of their energies to lobbying for funding increases and pushing for stricter monitoring of states and school districts to ensure that the academic achievement and progress of racial and ethnic minorities are accurately reported.

After examining each advocacy organization's website and searching newspaper articles on Lexis-Nexis from 2000 to July 2006, we found that the relationship between African American and Latino groups appears to be one of shared positions with only a few instances of formal collaboration. And African American groups are most likely to collaborate with other African American groups while Latino groups are most likely to collaborate with other Latino groups. This is similar to the pattern found for welfare reform and advocacy for the poor.

However, there are some notable instances of formal cooperation. Perhaps the most important is the partnership between the CBC and the CHC in lobbying for reforms of the NCLB law. To this end, the two caucuses (in partnership with the Democratic Party) published a joint report in 2003 entitled "The Impact of the Bush Budget on Black and Hispanic Families: Leaving Too Many Behind."[20] A significant portion of the document discusses programs that specifically aid African American and Latino students, and advocates increased spending in these areas. In addition, the NAACP, the Urban League, and LULAC (along with many other education advocacy organizations) signed onto a joint statement in fall 2006 calling for substantial changes to NCLB, which was due for renewal by Congress in 2007.[21] The coalition called for reforming the way the federal government assesses school progress and for changes in the sanctions imposed on underperforming schools. It also calls for NCLB to be fully funded at the levels promised when enacted in 2002.

There are also examples of support for another racial group's concerns. Most notably, the NAACP states in its education resolutions: "All states must guarantee the training of English as Second Language (ESL); that teachers at all schools provide adequate education for all students and that appropriate steps be taken to remediate academic deficiencies identified in students who have exited from the Alternate Language Program (ALP)." Since ESL students make up only a fraction of the African American population, this may be an instance of the NAACP showing support for Latino policy concerns.

Overall, African American and Latino advocacy organizations share very similar positions on the education policy issues examined here. However, only a few instances of formal collaboration between these groups were identified.

Voting Rights Act Renewal

The July 2006 renewal of several provisions of the Voting Rights Act of 1965 (VRA) that were set to expire in 2007 are useful for examining

---

[20] The report can be accessed at www.house.gov/clay/BlackHispanicBudgetCommittee.pdf.

[21] The joint statement can be accessed at www.nea.org/presscenter/nclbjointstatement.html.

relations between Latino and African American advocacy groups and political elites in the policy process. Though the VRA's renewal was essentially politically noncontroversial[22] (it passed 390–33 in the House of Representatives and 98–0 in the Senate),[23] both African American and Latino advocacy groups featured the renewal process prominently in print and website literature. The renewal was of particular importance to Latino advocacy groups because a section of the VRA (203) that includes a provision applied frequently to states with large Latino populations was set for expiration in 2007; that section mandated that states with significant minority populations with limited-English proficiency must provide voting materials in the native language of the particular minority population. For African American advocacy groups, in the absence of sustained opposition to the renewal of the VRA, the symbolic nature of the process was paramount. The renewal process offered the opportunity to reaffirm one of the major victories of the civil rights movement for African American advocacy groups and political elites.

During the renewal process there were strong endorsements from the National Urban League, NAACP, MALDEF, LULAC, the Congressional Black Caucus, and the Congressional Hispanic Caucus. However, Latino advocacy groups like MALDEF, LULAC, and the CHC were more likely to stress the renewal of the law's mandate that voting materials must be provided in the native language of significant minority populations, while African American groups focused more broadly on issues of civil rights. However, in a moment of explicit cooperation, the Congressional TriCaucus – made up of members from the CHC, CBC, and the Congressional Asian Pacific American Caucus – issued press releases strongly supporting renewal and then commending the VRA's easy passage through the House and Senate.

African American Advocacy Groups

The NAACP, National Urban League, and Congressional Black Caucus all offered firm and unqualified support for the renewal of the Voting Rights Act. In addition, some of the literature (in print and on the web) of these organizations used the occasion of the VRA's renewal to recall the law's roots in the civil rights movement. Congressman Melvin L. Watt, chairman of the CBC, called the VRA "the most important civil rights

---

[22] After an initial challenge of Section 203 language requirements from conservatives opposition from southern representatives faded.

[23] www.vote-smart.org/issue_keyvote_detail.php?vote_id=3873.

statute ever enacted," which "strengthens the very foundation of our democracy"[24] and that "passage of the bill with such a resounding margin is especially gratifying." A July 25, 2006, press release by the National Urban League quoted President Marc Morial expressing similar sentiments and enthusiasm.[25] NAACP president Bruce Gordon celebrated the renewal of the VRA, but cautioned that "the law is only as good as its enforcement."[26] One of the key provisions of the VRA, Section 5, which requires certain jurisdictions with a history of voter discrimination to pre-clear voting law changes with the Department of Justice, was up for renewal. Gordon cited several concerns that the pre-clearance requirements had been relaxed, including the approval of Voter ID requirements in Georgia and the failure of the state of Louisiana to "accommodate the unique voting requirements of Hurricane Katrina evacuees."

Latino Advocacy Groups

With enthusiasm and language similar to that of African American advocacy groups, several prominent Latino organizations issued strong statements of support for the renewal of the VRA, and applauded its passage through the House and Senate. In addition, these organizations, including LULAC, MALDEF, and the Congressional Hispanic Caucus, focused particularly on the renewal of the Section 203 language provisions. In a July 20, 2006, release, MALDEF interim president John Trasvina observed, "'Today's vote to extend the Voting Rights Act is a historic reaffirmation of our Nation's commitment to democracy. The Voting Rights Act empowers a new generation of Latino, African American, Asian American and Native American citizens to vote, to govern and to lead America forward in the 21st Century."[27] In a release also dated July 20, LULAC observed that it had "joined forces with its allies from the civil rights community in working toward reauthorization of the Voting Rights Act" and applauded the Senate for the easy passage of the renewal.[28] LULAC praises the VRA as the "most effective civil rights legislation ever passed," which has "enabled millions of African American, Latino, Asian American and Native American citizens who were previously denied access to the polls to fully participate in the political process and elect candidates of their choice."

[24] Available at www.congressionalblackcaucus.net/.
[25] Available at www.nul.org/PressReleases/2006/2006pr346.html.
[26] Available at www.naacp.org/news/2006/2006–07–27.html.
[27] Available at www.maldef.org.
[28] Available at www.lulac.org.

The Congressional Hispanic Caucus in particular focused on the language provisions contained in Section 203, which had come under attack from a small number of southern representatives. In a June 23, 2006, letter to House Speaker Dennis Hastert and Majority Leader John Boehner, the CHC leadership noted that "despite the bi-partisan support this bill enjoys, a small fraction of your conference is misinformed about the importance of preserving Section 203 of the VRA." The CHC letter argued that "language assistance protects the ability of citizens to cast informed ballots that reflect their own intent. Vote fraud or vote denial is far more likely to occur when citizens are denied language assistance necessary to understand the ballots they are casting," that "most jurisdictions incur little or no costs for providing language assistance," and that "language assistance unites our Nation by enabling all citizens to participate in our democratic process." While the letter explicitly cites the potential language difficulties encountered by Alaska Natives, American Indians, Filipinos, and Vietnamese, the broadest application of Section 203 has historically been in jurisdictions with large Spanish-speaking populations. Of particular note in the case of the VRA renewal is a joint statement by the Congressional TriCaucus, which includes members of both the CBC and the CHC. The language of the press release is nearly identical to that of the individual releases of each of the organizations, but it is unique in that it demonstrates some level of explicit cooperation rather than the independence otherwise suggested.

In sum, the behavior of African American and Latino political elites on the renewal of the Voting Rights Act has many elements of cooperation. However, Latino advocacy groups like the CHC show some independence in focusing particularly on the language provisions, which were of special importance to Spanish-speaking constituents. At the same time, the joint statement by the Congressional TriCaucus provides evidence of explicit cooperation, albeit on an item relatively noncontroversial, and of mutual benefit to Latinos and African Americans. On the whole, it appears that the most prominent African American and Latino players exhibited a pattern of (tacit) cooperation under the broad compatible interests and ideas of civil rights, with some degree of "independence" to pursue particular interests. Nevertheless, a higher degree of cooperation was displayed in this policy arena in terms of explicit coalitional activity.

Immigration

After passage of H.R. 4437 (The Border Protection, Antiterrorism, and Illegal Immigration Control Act of 2005) on December 16, 2005, immigration became an increasingly visible issue in national policy debates. Immigration has consistently been a policy priority of Latino advocacy organizations like the NCLR, MALDEF, and LULAC. Yet, as the Senate debated an amended version of H.R. 4437 (S. 2611, The Comprehensive Immigration Reform Act) and protests and demonstrations occurred across the United States, a wide variety of interest and advocacy groups crafted press releases regarding immigration law. The heightened publicity surrounding issues of immigration – at that time, and into the present – provides considerable evidence with which to consider the policy positions of Latino and African American advocacy organizations and assess intergroup relations.

African American Advocacy Organizations

The NAACP, Urban League, and Congressional Black Caucus have each adopted carefully worded official positions on immigration that call for comprehensive immigration reform and do not endorse the criminalization or deportation of undocumented immigrants. For example, the NAACP website (www.naacp.org) features a statement from President Bruce S. Gordon, released on March 31, 2006, calling for immigration policy "consistent with humanitarian values and with the need to treat all individuals with respect and dignity." It maintains also that "legislation to address genuine immigration reform should include proposals that would allow people to earn the right of citizenship through hard work, the commitment of several years, and meeting several monetary, security and related requirements." Gordon notes that a single-minded focus on enforcement will not address broader problems related to immigration, including job training, small business programs, and federal education assistance.

The National Urban League (www.nul.org/) did not explicitly outline a policy position in its website literature. However, a May 2006 release by the National Urban League president and the National Urban League Policy Institute director notes that "any efforts to criminalize undocumented immigrants are totally unacceptable"; "any proposal to criminalize or penalize anyone who provides humanitarian assistance to fellow human beings is unacceptable"; and that "comprehensive reform must include an earned path towards citizenship for the 11 to 12 million undocumented immigrants who are currently here in the United States."[29] The Urban League press release echoed the NAACP in noting that "we

---

[29] Available at www.urbanleague.org/docs/morialimmigration5–06.pdf.

must look at the broader economic needs of our nation to insure that all Americans have access to jobs, job training, business programs, and federal education assistance." With this language calling for immigration reform without criminalization or deportation, the Urban League did not contradict previous statements that opposed certain expansions of immigration policy as threatening the job prospects of African Americans.[30]

The Congressional Black Caucus also had little in its web literature on official immigration policy positions. However, in the CBC's weekly "Message to America" of May 5, 2006, Congressman Jesse Jackson Jr. attacked H.R. 4437, arguing that "its draconian 'enforcement-only' provisions turned undocumented workers into illegal felons and made those who gave them humanitarian assistance criminals."[31] In a manner similar to that of the NAACP and Urban League, Jackson promoted "a comprehensive immigration reform bill" and argued that "meaningful immigration reform must protect our security, allow our economy to grow, protect the wages of U.S. workers, honor our value of rewarding hard work, and respect the tradition of the United States as a dynamic country of immigrants." Most notable among the comments of Jackson and the CBC was an explicit call for African Americans to identify with immigrants. Jackson ended his speech with these words: "African Americans came here as slaves, not as immigrants, so why should *we* identify with the immigrant cause? We should identify out of principle, and the principle should be: *human rights for all human beings.* No other human being is an 'illegal alien.' No human being should have his or her human rights violated. No human being should be treated any less than as a full human being and in a humane way." According to Project Vote Smart (www. vote-smart.org), only one member of the CBC, Harold Ford Jr. (D-TN, representing District 9) voted to pass H.R. 4437.

The large majority of the CBC's commentary and Jackson's speech mirror the sentiments of the NAACP and the Urban League. In the pronouncements from all three groups, these African American political elites affirm a need for immigration reform while strenuously opposing

---

[30] For example, see www.nul.org/PressReleases/2000/2000pr54.html in which the Urban League registers opposition to the expansion of the H-1B Visa program, noting in particular that "currently, our estimates are that African Americans make up 11 percent of information technology workers, and that Latinos make up another 7 percent. Those numbers show that, for now, our communities have a share of jobs that positively reflects our share of the work force. We do not want that current track record to be jeopardized by a policy, which lacking adequate study, is poorly thought through."

[31] Available at www.house.gov/list/press/nc12_watt/pr_cbc_050506_jackson.html.

the most divisive elements of H.R. 4437, namely, criminalization and deportation. However, there is some evidence of a disconnect between African American political elites and the black population in general; while African American advocacy groups largely opposed H.R. 4437, among African Americans in the general public there was a stronger current of suspicion that new immigrants take blue-collar jobs from blacks and drive down wages in those same occupations.[32] Some media accounts have speculated that this is the reason African Americans have not played a prominent role in immigration protests in the first half of 2006, though Cleveland NAACP director Stanley Miller argued that this was "an overworked excuse" and that the true reason was "a little bit of apathy"[33] (however, cf. Brader et al., 2010).

Anti-immigration black advocacy groups like Choose Black America have attacked the NAACP for losing touch with the needs and concerns of black citizens; in response, NAACP president Bruce Gordon defended his organization's record and reaffirmed the NAACP's commitment to "look at the demographic shifts and needs of our nation in a larger context."[34] In the days leading up to the NAACP's annual convention in July 2006, media accounts debated whether black advocacy groups – which had joined with Latino political elites in issues like voting rights, health care access, and education funding – would be misrepresenting the views and desires of African Americans in the general population by supporting Latino groups on immigration reform.[35] The different views of black elites and masses, with the former emphasizing the importance of the "larger context" is generally consistent with the broader claims of our analysis, in which we acknowledge possible differences in policy orientations associated with the broader geography of national politics, among other factors.

Latino Advocacy Groups

Latino advocacy groups like MALDEF, NCLR, and LULAC have taken strong, proactive stances against the type of immigration reform

---

[32] Erin Texeira, "Many Blacks Concerned that Legalizing Undocumented Immigrants Would Hurt Low-Wage Workers," *Associated Press*, April 6, 2006.

[33] Robert L. Smith, "Blacks, Asians Largely Absent from Immigrant Protests," *Plain Dealer* (Cleveland), p. B2, May 5, 2006.

[34] Bruce S. Gordon, "The NAACP's Voice on Immigration," *Washington Post*, April 18, 2006, p. A18.

[35] Sean Mussenden, "NAACP Seeks to Join Forces with Hispanics; but Some Say Strategy Hurts Poor Blacks in Battle over Immigration," *Richmond Times Dispatch* (Virginia), July 15, 2006, p. A-4.

contained in H.R. 4437 and similar proposals. In addition, these organizations have acted to organize large numbers of Latino protestors to raise the issue in the national consciousness. For example, LULAC director of Policy and Legislation Gabriela Lemus argued that "given the current state of the U.S. economy, its national security interests and the slow growth of its future work force, it is imperative that Congress take up comprehensive immigration reform."[36] The official LULAC position presented on its website also acknowledges the need for immigration reform but argues that "such reform must include an earned adjustment for immigrants currently working in the United States; create legal channels for the future flow of immigrant workers; and reduce the vast backlogs in family-sponsored immigration."[37] The statement also affirms that "we feel compelled to state clearly and unequivocally that legalization should not be obtained at the cost of future inequities."

LULAC, MALDEF, NCLR, and the National Association of Latino Elected and Appointed Officials (NALEO) also joined together in a December 16, 2006, letter to President George W. Bush stating, "We are shocked and saddened by your Administration's statement of strong support for H.R. 4437," and claiming that "House Republicans have provided this shortsighted and mean-spirited bill which is intended to appear tough on immigration without resolving our nation's immigration problems. Only a comprehensive approach that provides a path to citizenship for current undocumented immigrants, creates new legal channels for future flows of needed immigrants, reduces family immigration backlogs, and protects worker rights will reduce undocumented immigration and bring order to our immigration system."[38]

In sum, the policy environment on immigration (at least as it stood during mid-2006) showed some elements of explicit cooperation between African American and Latino political elites. Organizations like the NAACP, Urban League, and CBC released statements that echo the language of arguments made by MALDEF, LULAC, and NCLR; they acknowledge and support the need for comprehensive immigration reform while strongly condemning the provisions for criminalization and deportation contained in legislation like H.R. 4437. This opinion congruence reaches beyond independence when African American leaders

---

[36] Available at www.lulac.org/advocacy/issues/immigration/comprehensivereform.html.
[37] Available at www.lulac.org/advocacy/issues/immigration/immigrationprinciples.html.
[38] Available at www.nclr.org/files/35766_file_Latino_letter_to_WH_on_SAP.pdf.

like Jesse Jackson and Bruce S. Gordon appear at immigration rallies and speak in terms of political alliances with Latino groups.[39] However, unlike the case of voting rights, there may be some distance between African American political elites and black citizens, who show concerns in public polling about how immigration might affect low-income jobs and wages (again, refer to Brader et al. 2010).

NAFTA and CAFTA

NAFTA
The North American Free Trade Agreement (NAFTA), ratified by Congress in November of 1993, eliminated tariffs on half of the goods traded between the United States, Canada, and Mexico, with remaining tariffs and other trade barriers scheduled for elimination within fourteen years of passage. (Note that NAFTA was voted upon *prior to* the Congresses for which we have the data that were analyzed in Chapters 5–6, on voting in Congress.) President Clinton, who championed the trade agreement as one of the primary objectives of his young presidency, faced strong opposition from many Democrats in Congress, especially those with strong ties to organized labor. In the end, NAFTA passed the House by only a slim margin, with more Republicans than Democrats supporting the trade agreement.[40]

The chief concern among opponents of NAFTA was that it would cost American jobs when companies moved their production facilities to Mexico to take advantage of much lower labor costs. Clinton and NAFTA's supporters, in contrast, argued that the agreement would bring increased trade and stimulate economic activity in all three of the nations involved. With a close vote expected, members of the Congressional Black Caucus (CBC) and the Congressional Hispanic Caucus (CHC) were heavily courted for their votes because neither had a completely unified position on the issue. In addition, African American and Latino advocacy organizations publicly took opposing positions on the issue, each citing different interests and concerns in support of their position.

---

[39] Bruce S. Gordon, "The NAACP's Voice on Immigration." *Washington Post*, April 18, 2006, p. A18.
[40] In the House, the bill was passed 234–200 with 132 Republicans and 102 Democrats voting in favor. NAFTA was ratified by a vote of 61–38 in the Senate.

African American Advocacy Organizations

The NAACP, the Urban League, and the CBC all formally opposed NAFTA. Wade J. Henderson, director of the NAACP's Washington bureau, argued that NAFTA would hurt the African American community. Although the NAACP supported international trade, it said any trade agreement must include a package of "tailored benefits" that would help black communities adversely affected by the pact. Henderson said that even though the legislation included some job-training programs, they were "at best theoretical ... and a long way off."[41] Indeed, the chief justification for the NAACP's opposition to NAFTA came from fears that the relocation of U.S. businesses to Mexico would take jobs away from African American workers.[42] Similarly, John Jacobs, then president of the National Urban League, noted that blacks made up about 28 percent of all textile workers and more than 16 percent of all apparel industry workers. Faced with the reality that these industries were expected to move their operations to Mexico, he concluded: "African-American workers appear to be the most at risk of losing jobs in the rush to the Mexican cheap labor havens. They are concentrated in industries most likely to be flight prone and in communities most vulnerable to the social upheavals that come from higher unemployment."[43] Like the NAACP, Jacobs and the Urban League wanted assurances that workers would be retrained and job placement programs offered if NAFTA was implemented.

While African American advocacy organizations appeared rather unified in their opposition to NAFTA, elected officials and leaders in the African American community had more differentiated preferences. Though the CBC formally opposed NAFTA, eight of its thirty-eight members voted *for* the trade pact.[44] Civil rights leader Jesse Jackson opposed NAFTA, but former general Colin Powell supported it. Representative Kweisi Mfume (D-MD), chairman of the Congressional Black Caucus, was against it, but U.S. Senator Carol Moseley-Braun (D-IL) voted for it.[45]

[41] Dorothy, Gilliam, "Blacks Take a Hard Look at NAFTA," *Washington Post*, November 13, 1993, p. B1.

[42] Marc Sandalow, "NAFTA Push Sways State's Lawmakers; Clinton Wins 9 New Votes from California Members of Congress," *San Francisco Chronicle*, November 13, 1993, p. A1.

[43] Zion Banks, "Trade Pact Concerns Minorities; More Job Losses Feared," *Press Enterprise* (Riverside, CA), October 17, 1993, p. A1.

[44] Thomas J. Brazatis and Tom Diemer, "Clinton Wins NAFTA, Loses Friends," *Plain Dealer* (Cleveland, OH), November 19, 1993, p. 1A.

[45] Carl T. Rowan, "Many See Chance to Benefit from NAFTA; Pact Might Create New Jobs for Many African Americans," *Chicago Sun-Times*, November 17, 1993, p. 49.

Many news commentators and political pundits observed that while many groups were split over NAFTA, African Americans were perhaps the most conflicted group. At the heart of the debate was each side's differing opinion on the effects of NAFTA: supporters promised it would increase economic activity and create new jobs for African American workers while those who opposed it argued that semi-skilled jobs that African American workers tended to fill would be shipped to Mexico in search of cheaper labor. In sum, while African American advocacy groups appeared largely united against the trade pact, there was not the same level of agreement among African American elected officials.

Latino Advocacy Organizations

The National Council of La Raza (NCLR) and the Mexican American Legal Defense and Education Fund (MALDEF) both supported NAFTA and organized a grassroots campaign to build popular support for the trade agreement among Latinos.[46] As one important component of this campaign, these advocacy groups sought to combat the racist stereotypes of Mexican Americans used by some opponents of NAFTA. Cecilia Munoz, senior immigration policy analyst at the NCLR, noted that the immigration controversy within NAFTA mirrored the larger anti-immigrant battle raging across Middle America.[47]

Latino support for NAFTA was largely contingent upon a provision in the legislation that would fund the North American Development Bank (NADBank). The bank would issue bonds and provide long-term capital for border improvements, such as bridges, toxic clean-up, and educational facilities and its money could also be used to target economic development in blighted areas that had lost jobs because of NAFTA.[48] The NCLR, along with MALDEF and the Southwest Voter Research Institute, formed the National Latino Consensus on NAFTA. The group's strategy was to focus on the fifty most heavily Hispanic congressional districts when most tallies had the Clinton White House fifty votes short of winning approval for NAFTA. As one newspaper noted, their campaign was a simple one, "No NADBank, no NAFTA," and "when the development bank was finally approved, votes of Hispanic congressmen began

---

[46] Peter Behr, "$3 Billion Development Bank Backed; Administration Gains Support for NAFTA," *Washington Post*, October 28, 1993, p. B13.
[47] Liz Balmaseda "NAFTA Has Become Launching Pad for a Barrage of Immigrant-Bashing," *Atlanta Journal and Constitution*, September 24, 1993, p. A13.
[48] "Business," *California Journal Weekly*, September 13, 1993.

shifting from against and undecided to pro-NAFTA, seriously eroding the opposition vote count and setting off a bigger erosion of the opposition."[49] The Latino members of Congress at the time were ultimately about evenly divided in their votes on NAFTA.

While Latinos were somewhat divided, though more likely to support NAFTA than African Americans, they soon voiced concern with the manner in which the trade legislation was implemented. One newspaper reported: "Widespread delays in providing displaced workers the job retraining called for under the North American Free Trade Agreement are one reason national Hispanic groups such as the [National] Council of La Raza and the League of United Latin American Citizens have recently softened their support for NAFTA."[50] When President Clinton began trying to expand trade agreements later in his presidency, many congressional Democrats, especially members of the CHC, insisted that any new trade agreement must have strict protections for American workers and the environment, noting that NAFTA safeguards on these issues are "not strong enough to be enforced."[51]

In sum, Latino advocacy groups were largely supportive of NAFTA as long as certain conditions were met. The NADBank played an instrumental role in eliciting the support of Latino legislators, but the Latino members of the House split essentially evenly (8–7) on the final NAFTA vote in that chamber and it was these same elected officials who quickly came to voice concern about worker protections in future trade pacts. Therefore, even though Latino and African American advocacy organizations took different positions on NAFTA, they shared and expressed some common concerns of protecting jobs for racial minorities from exportation to other countries, and there was division within members of Congress from the two minority groups as well.

CAFTA

The Dominican Republic-Central America Free Trade Agreement (DR-CAFTA) was ratified by the United States Congress in July 2005 and began to take effect in Central American countries as early as March

---

[49] Carlos Guerra, "Give Credit Where It's Due on Trade Bank," *Austin American-Statesman* (Austin, TX), April 2, 1994.

[50] Sherri Chunn, "Red Tape Entangles Worker Retraining," *Albuquerque Journal* (New Mexico), September 29, 1997, p. A1.

[51] Wendy Koch, "NAFTA May Mold Clinton Effort to Expand Free Trade," *Plain Dealer* (Cleveland, OH), August 31, 1997, p. 19A.

1, 2006. CAFTA extends the basic provisions of NAFTA to a new set of trading partners, and immediately eliminates 80 percent of tariffs on U.S. goods entering participating countries when it takes effect. Due to many of the same objections that were raised against the passage of NAFTA, CAFTA passed by a slim margin in the Senate (54–45) and came even closer to failing in the House (217–215, with two abstentions).

African American Advocacy Organizations

Members of the Congressional Black Caucus, the NAACP, and the National Urban League all registered opposition to CAFTA. As Congresswoman Barbara Lee of the CBC and NAACP Washington Bureau director Hilary Shelton note in a co-authored article, "members of Congress should not be fooled about this agreement, not when blacks' wages have been basically stagnant in real terms since the 1970s (despite vast gains in productivity that should lead to increased real wages and living standards), and when the ranks of the black middle class are being decimated by long-term displacement. Both problems are linked to the increased competition with lower wage countries that these corporate trade agreements bring."[52] In a criticism reminiscent of the NAFTA debate, Lee and Shelton also saw CAFTA as "a step backward for labor rights." Notably, as well, they cited the potential public health impact on "Afro-Latinos, who make up a third of Latin America's population, but represent 40 percent of Latin America's poor." CBC member Elijah Cummings, in a letter to *The Hill*, also expressed his misgivings about CAFTA, noting that "CAFTA could hurt several domestic farm industries," "result in annual losses to the U.S. textile industry of more than $1 billion," and "not guarantee critical labor protections for Central American workers affected by the agreement."

However, while some members of the Congressional Black Caucus registered vocal opposition to CAFTA, there was not unanimous opposition. Congressmen Gregory Meeks, Edolphus Towns, and William Jefferson voted for CAFTA's passage; Jefferson campaigned actively for its approval.[53]

Latino Advocacy Organizations

In a July 2, 2005, statement, LULAC president Hector Flores called for opposition to CAFTA, arguing that "poor farmers in Central America will

[52] Barbara Lee and Hilary Shelton, "CAFTA Is a Bad Deal for African Americans," *The Hill,* July 21, 2005, p. 18.
[53] Christopher Evans, "Moderate Democrats Make a Pitch for CAFTA," *Human Events,* July 25, 2005.

not be able to compete with U.S. Agribusiness," and "protection of worker rights and environmental protections are very weak."[54] In a separate statement released the same day, Flores argued that "the passage of CAFTA would further encourage the relocation of manufacturing jobs to cheaper labor market depicting U.S. Latinos and Mexicans against citizens of the global south in a race to the bottom." However, some state-level LULAC chapters broke ranks with National LULAC, including the Texas chapter, whose president, Roger Rocha, argued "CAFTA is good for Texas. We have the country's largest inland port in Laredo; we have the large seaports in Houston and in Corpus Christi; and we have El Paso."

The Congressional Hispanic Caucus also officially opposed the passage of CAFTA. In a press release of May 26, 2005, Chairperson Representative Grace Flores Napolitano noted the CHC's "strong opposition" to the trade agreement, a position taken "based on the concerns of our constituents, the impact of the agreement on the United States, and the effect this trade agreement could have on millions of our Latino brothers and sisters in the western hemisphere."[55] Napolitano acknowledged the support that some CHC members offered NAFTA, saying: "A decade after the passage of NAFTA, an agreement that some CHC members supported, it is clear some sectors in the Latino community benefited. As a caucus, however, we are gravely concerned those benefits were lopsided." However, just as some members of LULAC supported CAFTA despite opposition from the national organization, several members of the CHC voted for CAFTA despite the group's official position, including Representatives Henry Cuellar, Solomon Ortiz, and Ruben Hinojosa;[56] note that all three are from Texas, suggesting state/regional differences within the Latino congressional contingent on this issue.

In sum, it is difficult to assess the level of cooperation and/or conflict between African American and Latino political elites on the passage and implementation of CAFTA, since many of these organizations do not express unanimous policy positions with the full support of their members. However, the national-level NAACP and LULAC offices, as well as the leadership of the CBC and CHC, do exhibit a pattern of similar expressed concerns: in each case these political elites register opposition to CAFTA based on reservations about environmental protection, labor rights in Central American countries, and the effect upon American

[54] Available at www.lulac.org/advocacy/resolutions/2005/CA2.htm.
[55] Available at www.citizen.org/documents/CHC%20AGAINST%20CAFTA%205–26–05.pdf.
[56] www.vote-smart.org/issue_keyvote_member.php?vote_id=3585.

industries such as textiles, which employ large numbers of racial and ethnic minorities.

Conclusion

In this chapter, we examined policies at the national level concerning welfare reform, education, civil rights, immigration, and free trade to further consider the black-Latino advocacy group and elite intergroup relations with different types of evidence from that employed in earlier chapters. Selection of the policy issues was informed by several considerations including salience and findings of conflict versus noncompetition as shown in previous studies at the local level and at the national level, as well as in our earlier chapters in this book with regard to broadly parallel policies. The policies ranged somewhat in terms of the ideational and interest basis, the breadth and narrowness of impact on each of the groups, and group support or opposition to the policies, among other things. Our evidentiary base was drawn from an extensive examination of advocacy groups' websites and the Black and the Hispanic Caucus websites, and we also drew on various newspaper (through Lexis/Nexis) information in several instances.

An absence of conflict and some cooperation, whether explicit or based on mutual positions, are the norm in national-level black-Latino advocacy group relations in the policy examples discussed. Also notable is that specific interests were highlighted by different groups even while the overarching policy goals were generally shared. Yet even when there might seem to be a clear divergence in interests (e.g., immigration), ideological framing in terms of fairness and equality apparently led the groups to take similar positions. The most contentious issue was free trade; divergence of opinion on that issue rested on interest-based arguments, but *intra*group agreement on the issue was also not especially strong. On the whole, outright and clear conflict between black and Latino advocacy groups simply did not emerge in any instance. In short, once again we find there is a good degree of independence, which typically led to congruent policy positions, though there are few if any cases of clear-cut cooperation. As such, the narratives in this chapter firmly reinforce, and do little or nothing to undermine, the evidence in Chapters 3 to 6 or the theoretical speculation about the importance of policy geography and type, and also suggest the impact of political party and ideological similarities.

Appendix 7.1

Congressional Hispanic Caucus Statements regarding Education and the Reauthorization of "No Child Left Behind"

A. Reauthorize the No Child Left Behind Act to improve the following:

- Full participation of English Language learners and Hispanics students in the entire curriculum
- Implementation of the Title III state grants for English language acquisition
- Implementation of electronic system of transferring migrant student records within and across states
- Progress on school accountability for Hispanic students, with emphasis on high school completion
- Implementation of the Adequate Yearly Progress (AYP) measures in the No Child Left Behind Act, especially with respect to LEP children
- Valid and reliable assessments of state content standards for LEP students
- High school outcomes and opportunities for Latino students
- Healthy school climate (no bullying, no gangs, mental health support)
- Preparation, training, and number of high quality teachers in schools serving large populations of Hispanic and LEP students
- Parental involvement

B. Efforts to improve technology in the classroom are critical and must:

- Maintain a strong E-rate program, and support and develop efforts to improve the use of technological resources in schools with large minority and low-income student populations.
- Strengthen the education technology programs in the No Child Left Behind Act

Source: Education (from: www.house.gov/baca/chc/tsk-education.shtml).

8

Conclusions

Historically distinct and ongoing social and demographic developments in America, particularly pronounced during the last third of the twentieth and the early twenty-first centuries, are altering the larger polity. While the color line between whites and blacks has been and remains fundamentally significant to the American experience, dimensions of racial/ethnic relations have emerged that bring important additional variation and complication to intergroup relations in American racial politics. A demographic transformation combined with formal equality has emerged from the civil rights era, yet continuing high racial/ethnic economic disparity raises an array of questions and has numerous implications for the political system. One major implication of this social change is that relations between Latinos and blacks – the two largest minorities – have grown in importance and constitute a significant dimension of American politics. Black-Latino relations will play a pivotal role in affecting and being affected by America's racial/ethnic *inter*minority as well as minority/non-minority politics, and interclass politics, more generally.

At the same time, these issues are part of larger arguments about pluralism as a description of and prescription for democracy in the United States in that competition or coalition across numerous groups is an important part of pluralism's analytical emphasis. Assembling and integrating a wide array of evidence, we focused on a significant though largely neglected sphere of black-Latino political relations, the national government arena, which is a distinct part of and access point in the American political system. Our central empirical findings that there is little or no conflict and considerable evidence of independence between blacks and Latinos may be surprising, given what other research (on urban politics and mass attitudes) has found and impressions might lead us to expect. We believe these findings are significant in themselves, and had we done only this, our study would have made a notable contribution as an untold story in black-Latino relations and American politics more generally.

Along with the striking findings, we also posited what we believe is a plausible explanation for why our findings differ from those of other relevant studies on urban politics. The different geography of authority and the types of policy responsibilities (along with the different impacts of political party and/or ideology) in the national realm may well account for some of the differences found between levels of government. A core finding here is that conflictual relations between these groups are not evident at the national level; the frequent finding of black-Latino conflict in urban politics was not replicated in our study (cf. Telles et al. 2011). Scholars and other observers should thus be careful about drawing conclusions regarding these intergroup relations based on findings from only one level of the governmental system. The various levels of American government are different in their essential character because of the federal structure, with attendant variation in geographic reach, types of policy authority, and other differences across levels of government; and these differences appear to play a role in minority intergroup relations that seems less frequently contentious at the national level, at least over the last several decades.

The significance of the social circumstances and activities of socioeconomically disadvantaged groups for American politics has been well recognized and has engendered a considerable body of research over the last twenty to thirty years. As discussed in earlier chapters, that research has examined black and Latino relations at the local government level and as manifested in surveys of mass attitudes and black and Latino politics, separately, at the national as well as local and state government levels. However, because little research has examined black-Latino *inter*group relations at the *national* level, our understanding of minority intergroup politics has been incomplete. This inadequacy in the research and our belief that these issues are an important aspect of recent American political development led us to examine a range of activities with the purpose of more fully explicating the nature of black-Latino relations – conflict, cooperation, or something else – in the national governmental arena.

The preceding chapters of this study provided the first and the most empirically extensive analysis of various aspects of black and Latino intergroup relations at that level of which we are aware. We considered the activities of minority advocacy (interest) group organizations and their efforts to influence policy decisions of the national government (particularly Congress and the Courts) as well as the behaviors of minority representatives in Congress (the House, specifically) from several angles. We found no evidence of interminority conflict to speak of.

Our study and findings are yet more compelling, we think, because in most instances we examined data from a relatively long period of time. The congressional testimony and the amicus brief evidence we drew on each spanned a thirty-year period. This longevity was also evident, albeit to a lesser degree, in the advocacy groups' "scorecard" data – used to examine the groups' selection of issues, the salience and intergroup congruence on these issues, and congressional voting on these issues. This analysis included four (and sometimes five) Congresses, or eight to ten years. In contrast, even several of the leading studies of Congress and racial representation focused on only one session of Congress [1] and, with some important exceptions (e.g., Browning, Marshall, and Tabb 1984), most studies of black-Latino relations have examined brief periods. Some evidence, mostly prior to the mid-1970s, had suggested some tension between the groups at different times in national politics. However, our data (much of it from the mid-1970s to early 2000s) consistently indicated no conflict and identified "independence" as most common, along with instances of concurrence and hints of cooperative relations; but it did not find conflict/competition. This empirical analysis and our findings are substantial standing alone, but they are even more consequential when set in a larger context.

To situate our own empirical analysis in a broader literature on black-Latino relations, we began (in Chapter 2) with a careful review of the previous research most closely relevant to our theoretical concerns. Most directly relevant was the sizable body of work on governance in urban politics and local school district politics. We took that research to be authoritative because of its volume and rather consistent findings (though we also noted possible selection bias and other potential limitations). Another reason for accepting the urban politics findings at face value is that our concerns were prompted more by the incompleteness of the research on black-Latino relations than its accuracy (which we, again, grant or concede). Furthermore, we believe the ultimate differences and incommensurability between the national and local government

---

[1] For example, Canon (1999) examined the 103rd Congress only, and Griffin and Newman (2008) drew on data for the 107th Congress only.

arenas, including distinct types or dimensions of policy authority and responsibility – which underpin the explanatory hypothesis of our findings – make direct comparison rather than contrast and juxtaposition dubious. That said, what lessons were we able to draw from the findings of the urban politics/school district research?

One message of the research on urban politics, the school district, and sometimes mass attitudes is that the type of policy issue at stake makes a difference in black-Latino relations; and public policy researchers make similar claims about the importance of the type of policy more generally (Lowi 1964). Whether policies are more zero sum versus less zero sum or win/lose, versus presenting other, less pointedly divergent outcomes for each of the groups, plays a major role in defining cleavages around a policy and affects the levels of tension between particular groups. Part of the reason conflict/competition is found to the extent it is in studies at the urban level is perhaps because issues there are more frequently zero sum, and thus more likely to incite narrower, material interests; on the other hand, national-level policies more frequently deal with broader ideals and principles for minority groups. For example, when only a limited number of government jobs or city council seats or school board seats are available, one group's success diminishes that of the other group. Perhaps zero-sum decisions are proportionately less frequent at the national level where the breadth and types of policies make compromise, log-rolling, and the like more possible and thus racial/ethnic interminority group conflict less likely, as suggested by Meier et al. (2004). Moreover, the extent and nature of the role of political parties at the local versus national level is very different (Trounstine 2010); for instance, the role of the Democratic Party in bridging black-Latino concerns is more consistent and clearer at the national than the local level.

An apparent assumption regarding the issues most often examined in urban studies of black/Latino relations should be noted: an implicit and entirely understandable assumption of the urban studies research is that the issues examined are highly salient to both groups. The findings of Meier et al. (2004), Gay (2006), and Hajnal et al. (2002), for example, suggest that the nature of the issue or policy matter a great deal for intergroup relations and attitudes. And we agree. We add, however, that the degree of salience and other dimensions of policy are themselves modified by various factors, such as the jurisdictional and geographic setting; this point is too often overlooked, however, when (and if) we think about black-Latino relations in the larger governmental system. Both the geographic and jurisdictional attributes of politics (Madison, *Federalist*

10; Schattschneider 1960; Peterson 1981) and the associated particular nature of policies (Lowi 1964; and Eshbaugh-Soha and Meier, 2008, e.g.) are each well recognized as important to understanding political processes and outcomes; we emphasize this and further stress that we see these two aspects as strongly interrelated. Therefore, we question whether it can appropriately or simply be assumed that policies examined in, say, local and school board research are necessarily salient in the *same way and/or* to the *same degree* to the groups and/or the groups' spokespersons (advocacy groups and MCs) at the national level as they are at the local level. Decision makers have different breadth and/or depth of policy authority and responsibility at the national level. These differences make it unlikely that policy issues pose the same substantive challenges or have the same types and forms of policy resources (legal, financial, administrative, and otherwise) and policy tools for possible solutions at the national as at the local governmental levels.

Newer questions in American politics, such as black-Latino relations, have arisen and they are partly understandable by older insights. Certain claims emanating from ideas of Madison, Schattschneider (1960), and others (e.g., Peterson 1981) about American politics also seem to apply to the case of black-Latino relations in helping us understand the very different national-level findings here (Chapters 3–7) compared to urban-level findings. In a nutshell, the overall gist of our empirical assessment and arguments is as follows. If the geographic arena of decision making itself shapes policy – as is widely argued – and if policy affects the nature of politics – as is also widely agreed upon – it stands to reason that geographic breadth would *also* shape intergroup relations and politics with regard to various issues and policies. And because the types of policy responsibility of the national (versus local and state) government are different to begin with, finding different intergroup relations at this level might not be all that surprising. But this becomes apparent only when we examine and contrast politics and policy between levels; hence, differences in and potential explanations for minority intergroup relations may be more fully understood when such contrasts are undertaken, as we have done here. Synthesizing these points, then, has implications for explaining interminority group relations across levels of government (and maybe even within institutions at the same level, such as Congress and federal courts). Our findings of black-Latino nonconflict and independence at the national level – and our theoretical hunches which we now summarize and revisit – point in this direction.

The Empirical Findings, Revisited

Following an extensive review of previous literature (Chapter 2), our original empirical analysis began with an examination of black and Latino advocacy groups' participation and expressed views on policies in congressional testimony, and in their amicus brief submissions to the Supreme Court (Chapter 3). In both of these venues in the national interest group arena no conflict was found and a large degree of group independence or specialization was indicated in that the policy areas emphasized in testimony and/or brief submissions overlapped some, but not a great deal. When the advocacy groups did address the same policies, their positions were similar; again, there was no evidence whatsoever of differences suggesting conflict. While the tally of the number and topics on which the groups testified before Congress is useful, we cautioned that the data do not necessarily tell us the direction of the groups' positions. Thus, we supplemented that analysis with a sampling of policy positions and comments of minority advocacy groups drawn from the congressional testimony. Latino and black groups' views were in the same direction or on the same side in every instance, though with some slight differences in emphasis. Moreover, each of the groups even mentioned the other, although not consistently, in support of their own positions. The basic evidence on the amicus briefs, which did indicate the direction of views, demonstrated that blacks and Latinos were on the same side of every case in which they both participated. And additional evidence we provided, from a sampling of the legal arguments put forth in a number of those briefs, showed some differences in emphasis but nothing to challenge the resounding evidence of agreement or concurrence on their basic positions on the cases.

Another dimension of our analysis focused on the issues identified on legislative scorecards by the black and Latino advocacy groups (Chapter 4); two points stood out in our findings. First, the frequency with which the two groups identified the same issues on their scorecards, the degree of overlap, is quite limited; that is, common salience was low. Second, in *every one* of the instances in which there was overlap, the groups advocating for both Latinos and blacks agreed on what was deemed the preferred or "correct" vote. This extent of black-Latino congruence contrasts with the divergence found in many of the studies of urban and/or school district politics. Thus, on both counts the national-level evidence looks very different from that of local government: (a) generally, a low shared sense of salience of certain issues, as well as (b) no evidence of conflict at the national level (versus frequent conflict identified at local levels).

Another element of our examination concerned how blacks and Latinos working in the major formal representative institution of the national government, members of Congress (MCs), vote on sets of issues deemed important by the other group (as indicated by the advocacy groups' legislative scorecards; see Chapter 5). More directly, we were interested in how black MCs voted on the Latino scorecard and how Latino MCs voted on the black scorecard, as well as whether the racial composition of MCs' congressional districts affected voting behavior. The latter variable (district racial composition) is where the impact of local and/or mass influences would most likely be manifested. We analyzed the data extensively and in different ways. Overall, there was essentially very little or no evidence of conflict and the very little that was found was associated with district racial composition but not MCs' racial/ethnic background. Indeed, there were instances in which black MCs had voting records on the Latino scorecards that were notably high (particularly compared to white MCs), and one Congress in which Latino members' votes on the black scorecards were significantly high. Moreover, the findings on MCs' racial background hold even after a number of other factors are controlled, including political party, which was clearly the most substantial influence on MCs' voting behavior (as has been found in numerous other studies). But the strong impact of party is in line with our general argument of how broader concerns come into play for minority group relations at the national (versus local) level; and there were instances where the racial background of MCs mattered, even after accounting for party (and other factors), which we found to be notable. In general, then, the evidence in this chapter indicates (a) no conflict, (b) various null findings consistent with "independence," and (c) even black-Latino MCs' cases of concurrence.

In Chapter 6, we considered black and Latino members of Congress with an eye toward assessing whether their roll-call voting patterns and lack of conflict in those patterns was explained by broader ideological orientations or cues that might be described as group-specific. In sum, we analyzed whether (a) minority members differ from nonminority members, and (b) whether the two sets of minority group members (also) differ from each other regarding unique cues on votes in Congress. Concerning the latter, there were differences and uniqueness between the two sets of minority group MCs, suggestive of independence in their approaches to voting, but nothing to suggest intergroup conflict emerging from that uniqueness. Regarding the former, even after accounting for the strong impact of party, ideology, and other factors, black and Latino members do appear to differ slightly from their white counterparts. While the extent of difference may be modest, that *any* difference is found is notable in light of all the other variables also considered (cf. Burden 2007, 40–5). What seems to be occurring is in line with our general argument and previous findings. Minority MCs base advocacy for their own group's interests on something apart from general ideology. Yet similar ideological orientations, as they are so apparent in national policy considerations, formed the basis for cross-group support. The role of ideology that commonly emerges in national politics is different than when the focus is on the types of policies prevalent at the local level. This again, seems to help explain the differences that emerge from our study in contrast to those at the local level.

Finally, we took another approach to considering relations between the two sets of black-Latino political elites – advocacy groups and elected members of Congress – by assessing several illustrative policy issues (in Chapter 7). Rather than numerical data or statistical evidence, we gauged intergroup relations in five policy areas based on a methodical and wide-ranging scan of advocacy groups' pronouncements; our information was drawn from their websites and from a systematic canvassing of newspaper stories, remarks by their spokespersons, and statements from congressional caucuses. The policies chosen varied and were meant to illustrate examples of issues that parallel those examined in some prior studies of national and/or state and local politics, some of which had shown intergroup conflict in different times and/or contexts. Once more, our evaluation of these examples, individually and collectively, suggested an absence of conflict and even some evidence of cooperation.

Implications of the Empirical Findings

The *absence* of black-Latino political conflict at the national level across all the dimensions we studied is very notable, even more so when contrasted to findings at the local level. Yet that absence also seems something like "the dog that didn't bark." This nonexistent or muted bark probably helps explain the dearth of previous studies examining black-Latino relations at the national level. But from our analytical vantage point, that political quiescence is intriguing in itself, and substantively and theoretically meaningful. Why hasn't or doesn't the dog bark very often (if at all) or seemingly as loud in national politics as at the local level? If black-Latino relations were shaped only by the factors most emphasized in a standard pluralist interpretation of politics, such as the levels of group resources and a range of related factors, one would anticipate broadly similar relations at the several levels of the political system. But that is not what we found. An interpretation we advanced is that we need to consider all government levels and recognize that each of these (national, state, local) is different in its "essential character" (Peterson 1981,15), including whether, how often, and how policy issues of certain types arise and do so more or less intensely. A fuller understanding of black-Latino relations calls for recognition of this as well. It makes sense to appreciate that the component parts or the different levels (and institutions within those levels) of government are unique access points with varying opportunity structures, and in turn, to make those systemic attributes part of our thinking. Given that the system has such levels and dimensions and that those are different in their breadth and configuration, it would be surprising if this did *not* have consequences. Much as the arenas, choices, and other contextual aspects of the presidential selection process shape different stages of outcomes, as we noted at the very outset of this book, we suspect broadly similar types of factors affect black-Latino politics.

Attention to systemic factors implies that structures and processes (of the system) create certain logics, and the logic of the situation is importantly affected by geographic breadth and related factors; sometimes these factors seem "hidden in plain sight." Peterson's (1981) influential analysis explained how features woven into the fabric of America's federal structure, specifically the geographic and jurisdictional bounds of governments, placed limits and constraints on cities such that they tend to avoid certain types of policy and favor others. The particular policy orientations this leads to may not necessarily be intended or even desired by government officials in localities (or jurisdictions at other levels, for that matter) but the structure of governance predisposes them in some directions more than others. In a roughly similar fashion, the logic of the situation may help explain interminority group relations in different settings because context makes certain policies more or less prominent and/or contentious (also see Stone 1980). And a stronger, clearer, and more consistent role of shared partisan affiliation and ideology of blacks and Latinos in national politics probably matters, as we have argued.

As emphasized throughout, our findings contrast markedly from research on urban politics. But it is more difficult to say how much they might differ from black-Latino interrelations at the state level, in large part because this arena has been studied so little. The limited evidence there is suggests somewhat varied patterns. On the one hand, black and Latino state legislators have very similar ideological profiles as shown in

NOMINATE-like measures of their voting patterns (Juenke and Preuhs 2012). On the other hand, mass attitudes on policies, at least as indicated by voting on California ballot initiatives, imply that the specific policy helps explain black-Latino agreement or disagreement on issues (Hajnal et al. 2002). In general, these findings are difficult to compare because they assess the opinions of political elites (state legislators) versus mass attitudes and behavior, and the types of data also differ – legislative roll-call voting on a general indicator of ideology versus survey responses on particular policy questions. The scant information suggests that more research is needed at the state level to better understand similarities and differences with national and local level findings on black-Latino relations.

As important and interesting as it is to examine black-Latino relations across levels, we should again note that we cannot do so in an explicitly comparative manner because of numerous points of incommensurability associated with and imbedded in American federalism (Peterson 1981). Nonetheless, we should continue to assess and contrast or juxtapose these, as we have done here, as it is essential for better understanding black-Latino relations on the whole and for ascertaining the implications of their variation across levels. Further, we can and should continue to study issues within levels – comparing cities to cities, school districts to school districts, states to states. And within the national government, scholars should extend the study of various stages and aspects of policy making in Congress and the Courts (as we have done) but also the presidency and bureaucracy, to compare black-Latino relations in those different institutional venues. Analyses over time would also be valuable.

Much of the research on minority intergroup relations primarily emphasizes group characteristics and resources, but the applicability and value of those resources and characteristics are also contingent on the geography, the policies, and related factors which may vary at different levels of the governmental structure. To link these arguments to other relevant research we return to Gay's claim, noted in Chapter 2 that

> just as it is true that Latinos and blacks *compete* for jobs, educational resources and political power, it is also true that the two groups *share* similar objective circumstances relative to whites. Competition and commonality may work at cross-purposes ... : *competition may predispose [the two groups] toward negative attitudes*; recognition of *shared disadvantage relative to whites might encourage a more positive orientation.* Perhaps *social environments influence attitudes by privileging one fact of black-Latino relations over the other.* (Gay 2006, 995, all emphases added)

Our findings suggest that an element of social environments that influences the intergroup relations predispositions which is privileged, or relatively more prevalent, in decision-making processes is, or is at least significantly shaped by, geographic and jurisdictional formal authority and the particular policies more or less frequently dealt with at the several levels of the governmental system. Indeed, this may be why the competition Gay refers to seems more common at the local level yet apparently is not very common at the national level. At the national level, perceptions of "shared [socioeconomic] disadvantage" between blacks and Latinos, relative to whites, are perhaps more prevalent. Similar class or economic inequality (consistent with the idea of two-tiered pluralism) and broadly ideological concerns of blacks and Latinos, abetted by similar party affiliation, seem to outweigh racial differentiation and material interests at the national level more than in local politics.

Thoughts about Theoretical Connections and Concepts in Previous and Future Studies

In the course of our inquiry, several conceptual distinctions were made that informed the analyses; we revisit some of them here and suggest some for future study. Early on, we stressed the importance of ideas or ideals, or general principles and ideology, and their interplay with material interests and how the convergence or agreement on ideas and interests influenced the likelihood of different forms of intergroup relations – conflict, cooperation, and independence or negotiation.[2] That, in turn, led to a discussion of how interminority group relations at the urban versus national level might be shaped by the relative prevalence of ideas versus interests shaping politics at various levels of the system.

A parallel distinction to that of ideas/interests was echoed; indeed we emphasized this in the zero sum versus non-zero sum conception in the previous research on black-Latino relations in urban and government and school districts (e.g., Meier et al. 2004). When the particular issues at stake present a zero sum situation (e.g., government jobs, election to city council, and the like), competition or conflict is to be expected to a greater degree. The limited opportunities in such circumstances suggest a similarity between interests versus ideas or ideals, broader versus narrower arenas and policy concerns, and several other distinctions we

[2] The distinction between "purposive" and "material" incentives and the implications for the formation, sustenance, and policy orientations of groups bear similarity to the ideas/interest distinction, and others.

highlighted. In short, several ideas correspond considerably with concepts stressed in research on other arenas, suggesting some commonality in the thinking about this topic.

Additionally, we noted a number of policy categorizations and/or typologies that have been used in studying policy issues relevant for minorities and politics, which we recast and used in our analysis. In examining black and Latino advocacy groups' congressional testimony, we drew on data and policy categorizations developed by Baumgartner and Jones. As helpful and rich as that evidence is, the topic designations (refer to Table 3.1 in this book for examples) do not explicitly make the sorts of conceptual distinctions that might be more useful for purposes of theory and analysis in the present study or in similar ones. For instance, we cannot necessarily tell from the basic topic labels of the Baumgartner and Jones data whether a policy is more or less zero sum, or if it is "distributive," "redistributive," or "regulatory" (Lowi 1964). And making these distinctions would require a massive review and recategorization of the data (which we have not pursued here). Similarly, the policy categories used in assessing amicus brief participation and positions, drawn from Spaeth, had different topical categories from those of Baumgartner and Jones, as well as differences with various other policy categorizations that are more directly analytical in nature (cf. Lowi 1964). Developing a way to more effectively link the topic area categorizations in these major data bases on congressional testimony (from Baumgartner and Jones) and court briefs (from Spaeth) to policy categories defined by theoretical grounds would be useful in advancing research on black-Latino relations in national politics.

Beyond these data categorized by general topics or broad substantive policy areas, there are several typologies intended to theoretically classify and explain policies and their political implications. Policy typologies employed in studies of racial/ethnic politics directly inform and suggest additional connections and/or ways of thinking about theoretical and empirical issues addressed in the current study. Analyzing the behavior of minority members of Congress, Canon (1999) categorized policy issues as being more or less "racial" in nature – that is, explicitly, implicitly, or nonracial – as well as whether the policy was concerned with, on the one hand, outcomes or, on the other hand, with procedural or equal access and opportunity. Canon argues that more racially explicit and outcome-oriented policies are the most controversial, while those that are nonracial and procedural or access oriented are the least controversial from the standpoint of racial politics in the United States.

As with other previous research discussed, the type of policy – in this case its racial salience and its specific focus (procedural or substantive) – is pivotal. This is, we think, essentially consistent with our arguments about differences in black-Latino relations at different levels of the political system. As controversial as they often are, issues of civil rights, even affirmative action and the like, have substantial procedural qualities; this is especially important when played out at the national (versus local) level. They are about access and opportunity and do not necessarily preordain specific outcomes. When rights and substantive egalitarian policies have been formally secured, the actual implementation in particular circumstances often presents limited and hard choices in localities, like the distribution of city jobs or elected positions where either/or rather than both/and outcomes are frequent. Aside from that, the extent to which policies can be defined as more or less racial in the first place is probably more complicated than is recognized.

To some degree, the level of racial content of policies is not entirely self-defining, of course; issues may be perceived differently – as more or less racial or "racial" versus "implicitly racial" – from different vantage points, including the view of minorities versus nonminorities. For example, federal legislation that penalized the possession of crack cocaine much more heavily than the possession of powdered cocaine was not racial on its face, but the impact of the law on levels of incarceration was much more severe for blacks than whites. The range and number of policies identified in minority advocacy group legislative scorecards on national policies suggest that these groups are more likely to perceive racially/ethnically unique and/or disproportionate consequences of legislation than are their nonminority counterparts. There are likely to be differences in the salience and the perceptions of the intent versus effect, and the manifest versus latent impact of policies as viewed by minority advocacy groups compared to nonminority interest groups. More directly relevant here, whether policies dealing with roughly similar substantive concerns are seen to be more or less racial in nature is affected not only by the specific policy itself but also by its importance at one level of government versus another. We suspect a higher percentage of policy issues are perceived as having directly differential racial dimensions and consequences at the local level than at the national level (recent research [McCarty, Poole, and Rosenthal 2006] is consistent with this as well).

In an analysis of roll-call behaviors, Whitby and Krause (2001) assessed whether differences between African American members of Congress (MCs) and white MCs resulted from whether the policy issues at stake are of primary versus secondary concern (which we take to be essentially "salience") to the MCs. Level of salience is, in turn, directly linked to whether the policy has concentrated or more diffuse effects for MCs' constituents. They found that primary versus secondary concerns, and concentrated versus diffuse benefits indeed differentiated between African American and white legislators. Salience and the concentration versus diffuseness of policies might also differentiate between African American and Latino MCs, and vary across different governmental levels because policies that are concentrated or targeted, and thus, primary, in one arena might be secondary in another. As seen in Chapter 4, we found considerable difference in the degree of salience of various national policies for blacks and Latinos, and substantial agreement on policies that seem more focused on minorities than whites. We think this affected the nature of minority intergroup relations at the national level.

The policy concerns of minorities may differ from those of whites, and from each other, in that they may be distinct or unique and/or have a disproportionate impact on one group versus another. If a racial minority group is, for example, disproportionately poor, compared to whites and/or to other racial minority groups, then policies that more directly address concerns of the poor are also disproportionately important, whether they address the issues in a direct (racially) targeted way or even if not racially targeted. In any case, our analysis provides a sense of how the concepts identified by Whitby and Krause may be relevant to black-Latino relations (and not just black-white relations) in Congress and other arenas of politics as well.

Along with interest group politics and MCs' decision making, our analysis briefly considered here and there the role of political parties. Much is often made about the importance of political parties as mediating institutions in the American political system, and understandably so. Parties are often discussed as having several elements: the party in government, organization, and in the electorate. Probably part of the reason for different black-Latino relations at the national versus local level is the role of the party as an umbrella or brokering or integrating device. The extent and nature of the impact of parties, and their several components, is different at different levels of the political system. Thus, the way and extent to which parties mediate politics varies considerably across and even within the levels of the political system (Trounstine 2010). For example, many local elections are (formally) nonpartisan and the nature and strength of party systems in the states vary a great deal.

This variation in the role and impact of parties also likely affects relations between minority groups.

The questions we considered were partly framed by a standard pluralist framework, particularly ideas such as (multiple) access points and the like; yet the vantage point of two-tiered pluralism is as (or more) germane. Whether groups in general compete or form coalitions is a central question in pluralism. On the other hand, part of the reason questions of black-Latino relations have drawn a great deal of attention in the first place (in the urban and mass attitudes research) is that both groups have low socioeconomic status, which itself challenges some basic assumptions of standard pluralism but are directly acknowledged in two-tiered pluralism. In a sense, both minority groups are striving toward fully entering and being able to succeed within standard pluralist politics. They are seeking equal opportunity, access, and representation for different interests, which are concerns that essentially seek to remove impediments to political and social equality. Whether groups are, in fact, in conflict or if they cooperate has been at the center of the black-Latino relations literature; however, cooperation in these circumstances would be expected by standard pluralist interpretations. But the groups' shared disadvantage implicitly assumes a situation of two-tiered pluralism, with both groups primarily in the second tier. We would think about and study these issues quite differently if socioeconomic inequality was randomly distributed across racial/ethnic groups in American society rather than found disproportionately among blacks and Latinos. Our study suggests that two-tiered pluralism works differently at different levels of the political system, as do most other political processes.

Stated otherwise or more generally, our study not only acknowledges but highlights that structural attributes of liberal democratic governments – formal institutions and the distribution of authority delineated both vertically and horizontally – are influential in conditioning the role of group interests and outlooks and, in turn, influence whether pluralist politics, including interminority group relations, are more or less contentious or coalitional. As such, the study provides unique and further understanding of diversity and American democracy.

Our study may also speak to the comparative welfare state and multiculturalism and welfare literatures (Banting and Kymlicka 2006), though we gave only limited attention to these in the foregoing chapters. For example, Alesina and Glaeser (2004) have emphasized the importance of racial heterogeneity *and* institutions, including federalism, as major factors explaining the size and nature of the welfare state in Western democracies, including the United States compared to other countries. Our analysis focused heavily, of course, on a specific dimension of American racial heterogeneity, interminority group relations, and has suggested that those relations may be conditioned by levels of government (growing out of federalism). Whether there is more or less conflict or coalition (or something else) between minority groups, and, in turn, whether the nature of interminority group relations influences their ability to affect a larger liberal coalition in behalf of welfare policies, and whether interminority relations vary at different levels of the political system, would seem to have at least indirect consequences for the overall American welfare state. That is, racial/ethnic relations may affect policies addressing economic inequality that are themselves technically not racial, or maybe only implicitly or partly racial. And such questions are further echoed in studies of whether multiculturalism, itself related to racial/ethnic diversity, affects – specifically, whether it erodes support for – welfare policies in Europe and America (Banting and Kymlicka 2006; Hero and Preuhs 2007). In short, we think our study of black-Latino relations, which seem to be conditioned by the institution of American federalism, might have implications beyond those we have examined and emphasized here.

The findings and theoretical framing of our study suggest several research questions for further study. Among these are additional analysis like that presented here, extending the time-frame forward into the future and perhaps backward, and across an array of issues and institutions. Another approach would be historical/institutional studies of a number of especially salient and/or unique policy issues relevant to black-Latino relations. The criteria for and actual selection of cases are not simple, of course. One intriguing possibility would be to assess policies where, say, a black advocacy group's national office has a view or perspective on an issue that is consistent with the view of Latino advocacy groups but one or more of the group's local chapters or affiliates express a different, conflicting view. Our discussion in Chapter 7 indicated instances where the national NAACP took a position which dovetailed with that of national Latino groups but a local chapter took another position. An analysis of such circumstances would appear interesting on its own and would help us test the thesis that geography or sphere of politics and policy might be an important explanatory variable.

It would also be useful to take into account other factors that may affect the activities, positions, and behaviors of national minority advocacy groups and members of Congress. For example, which political party is in the majority or minority at a certain point in time could affect the very agenda of Congress. Which policies are (extensively) considered and come to the floor votes would be affected. And related to this is whether the legislation has more or less zero-sum qualities for blacks and Latinos or whether the provisions are such that Latinos and blacks are likely to be on the same side, but on a different side from other racial/ethnic groups. Similarly, whether class or race dimensions and implications are more prominent in legislation would presumably affect black-Latino positions. More generally, the nature of the times – the general social, economic, and political tenor of the period, past and present – deserves more attention than we have been able to give it here.

In any case, the last two to three decades have witnessed dramatic growth in the Latino population, which occurred after the (largely) black-inspired civil rights movement in the United States. These legal, legislative, and social changes have been profound and have in turn raised profound questions about the evolution of American democracy, including how it has been affected by the increase in the magnitude and nature of diversity. At the same time, these developments have occurred within a political system with certain enduring structural features, including federalism.

This study has, first and foremost, carefully and systematically examined black-Latino relations at the national level, and we arrived at a strong and consistent set of findings of nonconflict between the groups and frequent independence; these contrast with a narrative of competition/conflict identified in urban governance. We also suggested a possible explanation for the findings, one which is rooted in the nature of American governmental institutions. We hope these endeavors have brought forth important evidence, useful insights, and an advanced understanding of America's increasingly multiracial democracy.

Bibliography

Alesina, Alberto and Edward L. Glaeser. 2004. *Fighting Poverty in the US and Europe: A World of Difference.* New York: Oxford University Press.

Baker, Andy and Corey Cook. 2005. "Representing Black Interests and Promoting Black Culture: The Importance of African American Descriptive Representation in the U.S. House." *Du Bois Review* 2 (2): 1–20.

Banting, Keith and Will Kymlicka, editors. 2006. *Multiculturalism and the Welfare State: Recognition and Redistribution in Contemporary Democracies.* New York: Oxford University Press.

Barreto, Matt A. 2007. "¡Si Se Puede! Latino Candidates and the Mobilization of Latino Voters." *American Political Science Review* 101 (3): 425–441.

Barrilleaux, Charles, Thomas Holbrook, and Laura Langer. 2002. "Electoral Competition, Legislative Balance, and American State Welfare Policy." *American Journal of Political Science* 46 (2): 415–427.

Bartels, Larry M. 2008. *Unequal Democracy: The Political Economy of the New Gilded Age.* Princeton, NJ: Princeton University Press.

Baumgartner, Frank R. and Bryan D. Jones. (n.d.). *Policy Agendas* data set. NSF#SBR 9320322. www.policyagendas.org (accessed October 2005).

Beck, Nathaniel and Jonathan N. Katz. 1996. "Nuisance vs. Substance: Specifying and Estimating Time-Series-Cross-Section Models." *Political Analysis* 6:1–36.

1995. What to Do (and Not to Do) with Time-Series Cross-Section Data." *American Political Science Review* 89(3):634–647.

Blalock, Hubert M. Jr. 1967. *Toward a Theory of Minority-Group Relations.* New York: John Wiley.

Bowler, Shaun and Gary M. Segura. 2012. *The Future Is Ours: Minority Politics, Political Behavior and the Multiracial Era of American Politics.* Los Angeles: Sage/CQ Press.

Brader, Ted, Nicholas A. Valentino, Ashley E. Jardina, and Timothy J. Ryan. 2010. "The Racial Divide on Immigration Opinion: Why Blacks Are Less

Threatened by Immigrants." Paper presented at the annual meeting of the American Political Science Association, Washington, DC, September 2–5.

Brambor, Thomas, William Roberts Clark, and Matt Golder. 2006. "Understanding Interaction Models: Improving Empirical Analyses." *Political Analysis* 14 (1): 63–82.

Branton, Regina P. 2007. "Latino Attitudes toward Various Areas of Public Policy: The Importance of Acculturation." *Political Research Quarterly* (Forthcoming).

Bratton, Kathleen A. and Kerry L. Haynie. 1999. "Agenda Setting and Legislative Success in State Legislatures: The Effects of Gender and Race." *Journal of Politics* 61 (3): 658–679.

Brown, Robert D. 1997. "Party Cleavages and Welfare Effort in the American States." *American Political Science Review* 89 (1): 23–33.

Browne, William P. 1990. "Organized Interests and Their Issue Niches: A Search for Pluralism in a Policy Domain." *Journal of Politics* 52: 477–509.

Browning, Rufus P., Dale Rogers Marshall, and David H. Tabb. 1984. *Protest Is not Enough: The Struggle of Blacks and Hispanics for Equality in Urban Politics.* Berkeley: University of California Press.

Browning, Rufus P., Dale Rogers Marshall, and David H. Tabb, editors. 2003. *Racial Politics in American Cities.* 3rd ed. New York: Longman.

Bullock, Charles S. I. 1992. "Minorities in State Legislatures." In Gary F. Moncrief and Joel A. Thompson, editors, *Changing Patterns in State Legislative Careers*, 39–58. Ann Arbor: University of Michigan Press.

Burden, Barry C. 2007. *Personal Roots of Representation.* Princeton, NJ: Princeton University Press.

Cameron, Charles, David Epstein, and Sharyn O'Halloran. 1996. "Do Majority-Minority Districts Maximize Substantive Black Representation in Congress?" *American Political Science Review* 90 (4): 794–812.

Canon, David T. 1999. *Race, Redistricting, and Representation.* Chicago: University of Chicago Press.

2005. "The Representation of Racial Interests in the U.S. Congress." In Rodney E. Hero and Christina Wolbrecht, editors, *The Politics of Democratic Inclusion*, 281–313. Philadelphia, PA: Temple University Press.

Carmichael, Stokely and Charles Hamilton. 1967. *Black Power.* New York: Vintage.

Casellas, Jason. 2007. "Latino Representation in Congress: To What Extent Are Latinos Substantively Represented?" In Rodolfo Espino, David L. Leal, and Kenneth J. Meier, editors, *Latino Politics: Identity, Mobilization and Representation*, 219–231. Charlottesville: University of Virginia Press.

Chavez, Cesar. 1990. "Lessons of Dr. Martin Luther King, Jr." January 12, 1990. http://www.aztlan.net/cesarMLK.htm (accessed July 2008).

Chavez, Linda. 1991. *Out of the Barrio.* New York: Basic Books.

Chong, Dennis and Dukhong Kim. 2006. "The Experiences and Effects of Economic Status among Racial and Ethnic Minorities." *American Political Science Review* 100: 335–351.

Clarke, Susan E., Rodney E. Hero, Mara S. Sidney, Luis R. Fraga, and Bari A. Erlichson. 2006. *Multiethnic Moments: The Politics of Urban Education Reform.* Philadelphia, PA: Temple University Press.

Crespin, Michael H. and David W. Rohde. 2007. "Dimensions, Issues, and Bills: Appropriations Voting on the House Floor." Paper presented at the annual meeting of the Midwest Political Science Association, Chicago, IL.

Dahl, Robert A. 1961. *Who Governs?* New Haven, CT: Yale University Press.

Davidson, Chandler and George Korbel. 1981. "At-Large Elections and Minority-Group Representation: A Re-examination of Historical and Contemporary Evidence." *Journal of Politics* 43 (4): 982–1005.

Dawson, Michael C. 1994. *Behind the Mule: Race, Class and African American Politics.* Princeton, NJ: Princeton University Press.

2001. *Black Visions: The Roots of Contemporary African-American Political Ideologies.* Chicago: University of Chicago Press.

Deering, Christopher J. and Steven S. Smith. 1990. *Committees in Congress.* 2nd ed. Washington, DC: Congressional Quarterly Press.

De Leon, Richard E. 2003. "San Francisco: The Politics of Race, Land Use and Ideology." In Rufus P. Browning, Dale Rogers Marshall, and David H. Tabb, editors, *Racial Politics in American Cities*, ch. 6, 3rd ed. New York: Longman.

Dovi, Suzanne. 2002. "Preferable Descriptive Representatives: Will Just Any Woman, Black or Latino Do?" *American Political Science Review* 94 (4): 745–754.

Engstrom, Richard and Michael McDonald. 1981. "The Election of Blacks to City Councils: Clarifying the Impact of Electoral Arrangements on the Seats/Population Relationship." *American Political Science Review* 75 (2): 344–354.

1986. "The Effect of At-Large versus District Elections on Racial Representation in U.S. Municipalities." In Bernard Grofman and Arend Lijphart, editors, *Electoral Laws and Their Political Consequences.* New York: Agathon Press.

1987. "The Election of Blacks to Southern City Councils: The Dominant Impact of Electoral Arrangements." In Laurence Moreland, Robert Steed, and Tod Baker, editors, *Blacks in Southern Politics*, 245–258. New York: Praeger.

Erikson, Robert S., Gerald C. Wright, and John P. McIver. 1993. *Statehouse Democracy: Public Opinion and Policy in the American States.* Cambridge: Cambridge University Press.

Eshbaugh-Soha, Matthew and Kenneth J. Meier. 2008. "Regulation." In Virginia Gray and Russell Hanson, editors, *Politics in the American States*, 381–414, 9th ed. Washington: CQ Press.

Espino, Rodolfo 2007. "Is There a Latino Dimension to Voting in Congress?" In Rodolfo Espino, David L. Leal, and Kenneth J. Meier, editors, *Latino Politics: Identity, Mobilization and Representation*, 197–218. Charlottesville: University of Virginia Press.

Fellowes, Matthew C. and Gretchen Rowe. 2004. "Politics and the New American Welfare States." *American Journal of Political Science* 48 (2): 362–373.

Fleisher, Richard. 1993. "Explaining the Change in Roll-Call Voting Behavior of Southern Democrats." *Journal of Politics* 55: 327–41.

Fording, Richard. 1997. "The Conditional Effect of Violence as a Political Tactic: Mass Insurgency, Electoral Context and Welfare Generosity." *American Journal of Political Science* 41 (1): 1–29.

Fox, Cybelle. 2004. "The Changing Color of Welfare? How Whites' Attitudes toward Latinos Influence Support for Welfare." *American Journal of Sociology* 110(3): 580–625.

Fraga, Luis R. 1992. "Latino Political Incorporation and the Voting Rights Act."In Bernard Grofman and Chandler Davidson, editors, *Controversies in Minority Voting: The Voting Rights Act in Perspective,* 278–292. Washington, DC: Brookings Institution.

2005. "Latinos in National Politics." (unpublished manuscript).

Fraga, Luis R., John A. Garcia, Rodney E. Hero, Michael Jones-Correa, Valerie Martinez-Ebers, and Gary M. Segura. 2006. *Latino National Survey.* http://dx.doi.org/10.3886/ICPSR20862.v5.

Fraga, Luis R., Kenneth J. Meier, and Robert E. England. 1986. "Hispanic Americans and Educational Policy: Limits to Equal Access." *Journal of Politics* 48 (4): 850–876.

Francis, Wayne L. 1989. *The Legislative Committee Game: A Comparative Analysis of the Fifty States.* Columbus: Ohio State University Press.

Friedrich, Robert J. 1982. "In Defense of Multiplicative Terms in Multiple Regression Equations." *American Journal of Political Science* 26 (4): 797–833.

Frymer, Paul. 1999. *Uneasy Alliances: Race and Party Competition in America.* Princeton, NJ: Princeton University Press.

Gay, Claudine 2006. "Seeing Difference: The Effect of Economic Disparity on Black Attitudes toward Latinos." *American Journal of Political Science* 50 (4): 982–997.

Gilens, Martin. 1999. *Why Americans Hate Welfare: Race, Media and the Politics of Antipoverty Policy.* Chicago: University of Chicago Press.

Giles, Michael W., and Arthur Evans. 1986. "The Power Approach to Intergroup Hostility." *Journal of Conflict Resolution* 30 (3): 469–486.

Gray, Virginia and David Lowery. 1996. *The Population Ecology of Interest Representation: Lobbying Communities in the American States.* Ann Arbor: University of Michigan Press.

Griffin, John D. and Brian Newman. 2008. *Minority Report: Evaluating Equality in America* Chicago: University of Chicago Press.

2007. "The Unequal Representation of Latinos and Whites." *Journal of Politics* 69 (4): 1032–1046.

Grofman, Bernard, Lisa Handley, and Richard Niemi. 1992. *Minority Representation and the Quest for Voting Equality.* New York: Cambridge University Press.

Grofman, Bernard and Lisa Handley. 1989. "Black Representation: Making Sense of Electoral Geography at Different Levels of Government." *Legislative Studies Quarterly* 14 (2): 265–279.

Grose, Christian 2005. "Disentangling Constituency and Legislator Effects in Legislative Representation." *Social Science Quarterly* 86 (2): 427–443.

Guiner, Lani. 1992. "Voting Rights and Democratic Theory – Where Do We Go From Here?" In Bernard Grofman and Candler Davidson, editors, *Controversies in Minority Voting: The Voting Rights Act in Perspective,* 283–291. Washington, DC: Brookings Institution.

Gutman, Amy and Dennis Thompson. 1996. *Democracy and Disagreement.* Cambridge, MA: Belknap Press of Harvard University Press.

Haider-Markel, Donald P., Alana Querze, and Kara Lindaman. 2007. "Lose, Win or Draw? A Reexamination of Direct Democracy and Minority Rights." *Political Research Quarterly* 60: 304–314.

Hajnal, Zoltan L., Elisabeth Gerber, and Hugh Louch. 2002. "Minorities and Direct Legislation: Evidence from California Ballot Proposition Elections." *Journal of Politics.* 64(1): 154–177.

Hajnal, Zoltan L. and Taeku Lee. 2011. *Why Americans Don't Join the Party: Race, Immigration, and the Failure (of Political Parties) to Engage the Electorate.* Princeton, NJ: Princeton University Press.

Hawkesworth, Mary. 2003. "Congressional Enactments of Race-Gender: Toward a Theory of Race-Gendered Institutions." *American Political Science Review* 97 (4): 529–550.

Haynie, Kerry L. 2001. *African American Legislators in the American States.* New York: Columbia University Press.

Hedge, David, James Button, and Mary Spear. 1996. "Accounting for the Quality of Black Legislative Life: The View from the States." *American Journal of Political Science* 40 (1): 82–98.

Hero, Rodney E. 1989. "Multiracial Coalitions in City Elections Involving Minority Candidates: Some Evidence from Denver." *Urban Affairs Quarterly* 25 (2): 342–351.

Hero, Rodney E. 1992. *Latinos and the U.S. Political System: Two-tiered Pluralism.* Philadelphia: Temple University Press.

 1998. *Faces of Inequality: Social Diversity in American Politics.* New York: Oxford University Press.

 2005. "Crossroads of Equality: Race/Ethnicity and Cities in American Democracy." *Urban Affairs Review* 40 (6): 695–705.

Hero, Rodney E. and Robert R. Preuhs. 2007. "Immigration and the Evolving American Welfare State: Examining Policies in the U.S. States." *American Journal of Political Science,* 51(July): 498–517.

Hero, Rodney E. and Caroline J. Tolbert. 1995. "Latinos and Substantive Representation in the U.S. House of Representatives: Direct, Indirect or Nonexistent?" *American Journal of Political Science* 39 (3): 640–652.

Hero, Rodney E. and Susan E. Clarke. 2003. "Latinos, Blacks, and Multiethnic Politics in Denver: Realigning Power and Influence in the Struggle for Equality," In Rufus P. Browning, David H. Tabb, and Dale Rogers Marshall, Editors, *Racial Politics in American Cities,* 3rd Edition: 309–330.

Hicklin, Alisa and Kenneth J. Meier. 2008. "Race, Structure, and State Governments: The Politics of Higher Education Diversity." *Journal of Politics* 70(3): 851–860.

Hochschild, Jennifer L. 1995. *Facing Up to the American Dream: Race, Class and the Soul of the Nation.* Princeton, NJ: Princeton University Press.

Hochschild, Jennifer L., and Reuel Rogers. 2000. "Race Relations in a Diversifying Nation." In James Jackson, editor, *New Directions: African Americans in a Diversifying Nation.* National Planning Association, 2000: 45–85.

Hochschild, Jennifer L. and Reuel R. Rogers. 2010. "Race Relations in a Diversifying Nation." In James S. Jackson, editor, *New Directions: African Americans in a Diversifying Nation*. Washington, DC: National Policy Association.

Hojnacki, Marie. 1997. "Interest Groups' Decisions to Join Alliances or Work Alone." *American Journal of Political Science* 41: 61–87.

Holbrook, Thomas A. and Emily Van Dunk. 1993. "Electoral Competition in the American States." *American Political Science Review* 87 (4): 955–962.

Hood III, M. V. and Irvin L. Morris. 1998. "Boll Weevils and Roll-Call Voting: A Study in Time and Space." *Legislative Studies Quarterly* 23: 245–269.

Hula, Kevin W. 1999. *Lobbying Together: Interest Group Coalitions in Legislative Politics*. Washington, DC: Georgetown University Press.

Hulse, Carl and David M. Herzenhorn. September 30, 2008. "House Rejects Bailout Package, 228–205; Stocks Plunge." *The New York Times*, online edition. http://www.nytimes.com/2008/09/30/business/30bailout. html?pagewanted=print. (accessed September 2012).

Huntington, Samuel P. 2004. *Who Are We: The Challenges to America's National Identity*. New York: Simon and Schuster.

Hutchings, Vincent. 1998. "Issue Salience and Support for Civil Rights Legislation among Southern Democrats." *Legislative Studies Quarterly* 23: 521–544.

Jenkins-Smith, Hank C., Gilbert K. St. Clair, and Brian Woods. "Explaining Change in Policy Subsystems: Analysis of Coalition Stability and Defection over Time." *American Journal of Political Science* 43(4): 851–880.

Jewell, Malcolm E. and Marcia L. Whicker. 1994. *Legislative Leadership in the American States*. Ann Arbor: University of Michigan Press.

Joint Center for Political and Economic Studies. 2004. "Table 2: Black Elected Officials 1999." http://jointcenter.org/DB/table/graphs/heo_99.pdf (accessed October 25, 2004).

Jones-Correa, Michael. 2011. "Commonalities, Competition and Linked Fate." In Edward Telles, Mark Q. Sawyer, and Gaspar Rivera-Salgado, editors, *Just Neighbors? Research on African American and Latino Relations in the United States*, 63–95. New York: Russell Sage.

Juenke, Eric Gonzalez and Robert R. Preuhs. 2009. "Trustees or Delegates? Black and Latino Representation at the State Legislative Level." Paper presented at the annual meeting of the Western Political Science Association, Vancouver, Canada, March.

2012. "Irreplaceable Legislators? Rethinking Minority Representatives in the New Century." *American Journal of Political Science*. 56: 705–715.

Kaiser Family Foundation. 2008. "Eliminating Racial/Ethnic Disparities in Health Care: What are the Options?" *Health Care and the 2008 Elections*. Menlo Park, CA: Kaiser Family Foundation.

Karnig, Albert K. and Susan Welch. 1982. "Electoral Structure and Black Representation on City Councils." *Social Science Quarterly* 63 (1): 99–114.

Katznelson, Ira. 2005. *When Affirmative Action Was White: An Untold History of Racial Inequality in Twentieth Century America*. New York: W.W. Norton.

Kaufmann, Karen M. (2003a). "Cracks in the Rainbow: Group Commonality as a Basis for Latino and African-American Political Coalitions." *Political Research Quarterly* 56 (2): 199–210.

(2003b). "Black and Latino Voters in Denver: Responses to Each Other's Political Leadership." *Political Science Quarterly* 118 (1): 107–126.

2007. "Immigration and the Future of Black Power in U.S. Cities." *Du Bois Review* 4 (1): 79–96.

Keele, Luke and Nathan J. Kelly. 2005. "Dynamic Models for Dynamic Theories: The Ins and Outs of Lagged Dependent Variables." June 21. http://polmeth.wustl.edu/workingpapers.php?year=2005 (accessed July 6, 2005).

Key, V. O. 1949. *Southern Politics in State and Nation*. New York: Knopf.

Kim, Claire Jean. 2000. *Bitter Fruit: The Politics of Black-Korean Conflict in New York*. New Haven, CT: Yale University Press.

1999. "The Racial Triangulation of Asian Americans." *Politics and Society* 27 (1): 105–138.

Kinder, Donald R. and Lynn M. Sanders. 1996. *Divided by Color: Racial Politics and Democratic Ideals*. Chicago: University of Chicago Press.

King, Desmond and Rogers M. Smith. 2005. "Racial Orders in American Political Development." *American Political Science Review* 99 (1): 75–92.

Klinkner, Philip A. and Rogers M. Smith. 1999. *The Unsteady March: The Rise and Decline of Racial Equality in America*. Chicago: University of Chicago Press.

Kymlicka, William. 1995. *Multicultural Citizenship*. New York: Oxford University Press.

Lavariega Monforti, Jessica. 2005. "Conclusion: The Myths and Realities of Black and Latino/a Politics." In William E. Nelson Jr. and Jessica Lavariega Monforti, editors, *Black and Latino/a Politics: Issues in Political Development in the United States*, 249–253. Miami, FL: Barnhardt and Ashe.

Leal, David L., Valerie Martinez-Ebers, and Kenneth J. Meier. 2004. "The Politics of Latino Education: The Biases of At-large Elections." *Journal of Politics* 66 (4): 1224–1244.

Lower-Basch, Elizabeth. 2000. "TANF 'Leavers,' Applicants, and Caseload Studies: Preliminary Analysis of Racial Differences in Caseload Trends and Leaver Outcomes." Washington, DC: U.S. Department of Health and Human Services. http://aspe.hhs.gov/hsp/leavers99/race.htm (accessed July 6, 2006).

Lowi, Theodore J. (1964). "American Business, Public Policy, Case-Studies, and Political Theory." *World Politics* 16 (4): 677–715.

Lublin, David. 1997. *The Paradox of Representation: Racial Gerrymandering and Minority Interests in Congress*. Princeton, NJ: Princeton University Press.

Mansbridge, Jane. 1999. "Should Blacks Represent Blacks and Women Represent Women? A Contingent 'Yes.'" *Journal of Politics* 61 (3): 628–657.

Marschall, Melissa and Anirudh Ruhil. 2007. "Substantive Symbols: The Attitudinal Dimension of Black Political Incorporation in Local Government." *American Journal of Political Science* 51 (1): 17–33.

Marquez, Benjamin. 1993. *LULAC: The Evolution of a Mexican American Political Organization*. Austin: University of Texas Press.

Mayhew, David R. 1974. *Congress: The Electoral Connection*. New Haven: Yale University Press.

McCarty, Nolan, Keith Poole, and Howard Rosenthal. 2006. *Polarized America: The Dance of Ideology and Unequal Riches*. Cambridge, MA: MIT Press.

McClain, Paula D. 1993. "The Changing Dynamics of Urban Politics: Black and Hispanic Municipal Employment – Is There Competition?" *Journal of Politics* 55: 399–414.

2006. "Racial Intergroup Relations in a Set of Cities: A Twenty-Year Perspective." *Journal of Politics* 68 (4): 757–770.

McClain, Paula D., Niambi M. Carter, Victoria M. DeFrancesco Soto, Monique L. Lyle, Jeffrey D. Grynaviski, C.Shayla Nunnally, Thomas J. Scotto, J. Alan Kendrick, Gerald F. Lackey, and Kendra Davenport Cotton. 2006. "Racial Distancing in a Southern City: Latino Immigrants' Views of Black Americans." *Journal of Politics*, 68 (3): 571–584.

McClain, Paula D. and Albert K. Karnig. 1990. "Black and Hispanic Socioeconomic and Political Competition." *American Political Science Review* 84 (2): 535–545.

Meier, Kenneth, Paula D. McClain, J. L.Polinard, and Robert D. Wrinkle. (2004). "Divided or Together? Conflict and Cooperation between African Americans and Latinos." *Political Research Quarterly* 57 (3): 399–409.

Meier, Kenneth J., Eric Gonzalez Juenke, Robert Wrinkle, and J. L. Polinard. 2005. "Structural Choices and Representational Biases: The Post-Election Color of Representation." *American Journal of Political Science* 49 (4): 758–768.

Meier, Kenneth J. and Joseph Stewart Jr. 1991. *The Politics of Hispanic Education.* Albany: State University of New York Press.

Miller, Lisa. 2007. "The Representational Biases of Federalism: Scope and Bias in the Political Process Revisited." *Perspectives on Politics* 5 (2): 305–321.

Mindiola, Tatcho Jr. and Armando Gutierrez. 1988. "Chicanos and the Legislative Process: Reality and Illusion in the Politics of Change." In F. C. Garcia, editor, *Latinos and the Political System*, 349–362. Notre Dame, IN: University of Notre Dame Press.

Minta, Michael D. 2009. "Legislative Oversight and the Substantive Representation of Black and Latino Interests in Congress." *Legislative Studies Quarterly* 34 (2): 193–218.

2011. *Oversight: Representing the Interests of Blacks and Latinos in Congress.* Princeton, NJ: Princeton University Press.

Mollenkopf, John. 2003. "New York: Still the Great Anomaly." In Rufus P. Browning, Dale Rogers Marshall, and David H. Tabb, editors, *Racial Politics in American Cities*, 115–142, 3rd ed. New York: Longman.

2005. "Immigration and the Changing Dynamic of Racial Politics in New York and Los Angeles." Paper presented at Immigrant Political Incorporation Conference, Radcliffe Institute, Harvard University, April 22–23.

National Association for Latino Elected and Appointed Officials (NALEO). 1984. *1984 National Roster of Hispanic Elected Officials.* Washington, DC: NALEO Education Fund.

NCES. 2008. *Digest of Education Statistics, 2007.* Institute of Education Sciences, National Center for Education Statistics. http://nces.ed.gov/pubsearch/pubsinfo.asp?pubid=2008022 (accessed June 2010).

Nelson, Albert J. 1991. *Emerging Influentials in State Legislatures.* New York: Praeger.

Nelson, William E. Jr. and Jessica Lavariega Monforti, editors. 2005. *Black and Latino/a Politics: Issues in Political Development in the United States.* Miami, FL: Barnhardt and Ashe.

Oliver, J. Eric and Janelle Wong. 2003 "Intergroup Prejudice in Multiethnic Settings." *American Journal of Political Science* 47 (4): 567–582.

Overby, L. Marvin and Kenneth M. Cosgrove. 1996. "Unintended Consequences? Racial Redistricting and the Representation of Minority Interests." *Journal of Politics* 58: 540–550.

Owens, Chris T. 2005. "Black Substantive Representation in State Legislatures from 1971–1999." *Social Science Quarterly* 84(5): 779–791.

Pachon, Harry and Louis DeSipio. 1992. "Latino Elected Officials in the 1990s." *PS: Political Science and Politics* 25 (2): 212–217.

Peterson, Paul. 1981. *City Limits.* Chicago: University of Chicago Press.

Pew Hispanic Center. 2006. *Hispanics and the 2006 Election.* Washington, D.C.: Pew Hispanic Center.

Pitkin, Hanna. 1967. *The Concept of Representation.* Berkeley: University of California Press.

Pinderhughes, Dianne. 1987. *Race and Ethnicity in Chicago Politics: A Re-examination of Pluralist Theory.* Urbana: University of Illinois Press.

1995. "Black Interest Groups and the 1982 Extension of the Voting Rights Act." In Huey L. Perry and Wayne Parent, editors, *Blacks and the American Political System*, 203–224. Gainesville: University Press of Florida.

2003. "Urban Racial and Ethnic Politics," In John P. Pelissero, editor, *Cities, Politics and Policy: A Comparative Analysis*: 97–125. Washington, DC: Congressional Quarterly Press.

Poole, Keith and Howard Rosenthal. 1997. *Congress: A Political-Economic History of Roll Call Voting.* New York: Oxford University Press.

Preuhs, Robert R. 2000. "Beyond the Black Belt: The Minority Power Hypothesis." Presented at the annual meeting of the Western Political Science Association, San Jose, CA.

2005. "Descriptive Representation, Legislative Leadership, and Direct Democracy: Latino Influence on English Only Laws in the States, 1984–2002." *State Politics and Policy Quarterly* 5 (Fall): 203–224.

2006. "The Conditional Effects of Minority Descriptive Representation: Black Legislators and Policy Influence in the American States." *Journal of Politics* 63 (3): 585–599.

2007. "Descriptive Representations as a Mechanism to Mitigate Policy Backlash: Latino Incorporation and Welfare Policy in the American States." *Political Research Quarterly* 60 (2): 277–292.

Preuhs, Robert R. and Eric Gonzales Juenke. 2011. "Latino U.S. State Legislators in the 1990's: Majority-Minority Districts, Minority Incorporation, and Institutional Position." *State Politics and Policy Quarterly* 11(1): 48–75.

Putnam, Robert D. 2000. *Bowling Alone: The Collapse and Revival of American Community* New York: Simon and Schuster.

Radcliff, Benjamin and Martin Saiz. 1995. "Race, Turnout, and Public Policy in the American States." *Political Research Quarterly* 48 (4): 775–794.

Rocha, Rene R. 2007a. "Cooperation and Conflict in Multiracial School Districts."
    In Rodolfo Espino, David L. Leal, and Kenneth J. Meier, editors, *Latino
    Politics: Identity, Mobilization and Representation*, 161–176. Charlottesville:
    University of Virginia Press:
    2007b. "Black-Brown Coalitions in Local School Board Elections." *Political
    Research Quarterly* 60 (2): 315–327.
Rodrigues, Helena Alva and Gary M. Segura. 2007. "A Place at the Lunch
    Counter: Latinos, African Americans and the Dynamics of American Race
    Politics." In Rodolfo Espino, David L. Leal, and Kenneth J. Meier, edi-
    tors, *Latino Politics: Identity, Mobilization, and Representation*, 142–160.
    Charlottesville: University of Virginia Press:
Santoro, Wayne A. 1999. "Conventional Politics Takes Center Stage: The Latino
    Struggle against English-Only Laws." *Social Forces* 77 (3): 887–909.
Schattschneider, E. E. 1960. *The Semi-sovereign People*. Hinsdale, IL: Dryden
    Press.
Schmidt, Ronald Sr., Yvette Alex-Assensoh, Andy L. Aoki, and Rodney E. Hero.
    2010. *Newcomers, Outsiders, and Insiders: Immigrants and American
    Racial Politics in the Early Twenty-first Century*. Ann Arbor: University of
    Michigan Press.
Schneider, Anne and Helen Ingram. 1993. "The Social Construction of Target
    Populations." *American Political Science Review* 87 (2): 334–346.
Segura, Gary M., and Helena A. Rodrigues. 2005. "Latino Political Participation."
    Encyclopedia of Latinos and Latinos in the United States. Oxford University
    Press.
Segura, Gary M. and Luis R. Fraga. 2008. "Race and the Recall: Racial and
    Ethnic Polarization in the California Recall Election." *American Journal of
    Political Science* 52 (2): 421–435.
Sharpe, Christine LeVeaux, and James C.Gerand. 2001. "Race, Roll Calls, and
    Redistricting: The Impact of Race-Based Redistricting on Congressional Roll
    Call." *Political Research Quarterly* 54: 31–51.
Skrentny, John D. 2002. *The Minority Rights Revolution*. Cambridge, MA:
    Belknap Press of Harvard University Press.
Skocpol, Theda. 2003. *Diminished Democracy: From Membership to Management
    in American Civic Life*. Norman: University of Oklahoma Press.
Skocpol, Theda. 2004. *Diminished Democracy: From Membership to Management
    in American Civic Life*. Norman: University of Oklahoma Press.
Sonenshein, Raphael J. 1993. *Politics in Black and White: Race and Power in Los
    Angeles*. Princeton, NJ: Princeton University Press.
    2003a. "Post-incorporation Politics in Los Angeles." In Rufus P. Browning, Dale
    Rogers Marshall, and David H. Tabb, editors, *Racial Politics in American
    Cities*, 51–76, 3rd ed. New York: Longman.
    2003b. "The Prospects for Multicultural Coalitions: Lessons from America's
    Three Largest Cities." In Rufus P. Browning, Dale Rogers Marshall, and
    David H. Tabb, editors, *Racial Politics in American Cities*, 333–356, 3rd ed.
    New York: Longman.
Soss, Joe, Sanford F. Schram, Thomas P. Vartanian, and Erin O'Brien. 2001.
    "Setting the Terms of Relief: Explaining State Policy Choices in the Devolution
    Revolution." *American Journal of Political Science* 45 (2): 378–395.

Spaeth, Harold. 2005. "The Original U.S. Supreme Court Judicial Database." www.as.uky.edu/polisci/ulmerproject/sctdata.htm (accessed October 2005).

Stone, Clarence N. 1980. "Systemic Power in Community Decision Making: A Restatement of Stratification Theory." *American Political Science Review* 74 (4): 978–990.

Strolovitch, Dara Z. 2007. *Affirmative Advocacy: Race, Class and Gender in Interest Group Politics.* Chicago: University of Chicago Press.

Swain, Carol M. 1995. *Black Faces, Black Interests: The Representation of African Americans in Congress.* Cambridge, MA: Harvard University Press.

Tatalovich, Raymond. 1995. *Nativism Reborn? The Official English Language Movement and the American States.* Lexington: University of Kentucky Press.

Tate, Katherine. 2001. "African Americans and Their Representation in Congress: Does Race Matter?" *Legislative Studies Quarterly* 26: 623–638.

Telles, Edward, Mark Q. Sawyer, and Gaspar Rivera-Salgado, editors. 2011. *Just Neighbors? Research on African American and Latino Relations in the United States.* New York: Russell Sage.

Tichenor, Daniel J. 2002. *Dividing Lines: The Politics of Immigration Control in America* Princeton, NJ: Princeton University Press.

Trounstine, Jessica L., and Melody Ellis Valdini. 2008. "The Context Matters: The Effects of Single Member vs. At-Large Districts on City Council Diversity," *American Journal of Political Science* 52 (3): 554–569.

Trounstine, Jessica. 2010. "Representation and Accountability in Cities." In Margaret Levi, Simon Jackman, and Nancy Rosenblum, editors, *Annual Review of Political Science* 13: 407–424. Palo Alto, CA: Annual Reviews.

U.S. Census. 2008a. "2008 National Population Projections." Washington, D.C. http://www.census.gov/population/www/projections/2008projections.html (accessed June 2011).

U.S. Census Bureau. 2004a. "Voting and Registration in the Election of November 2000." February 24. www.cenus.gov/population/www/socdemo/voting/p20–542.html (accessed October 26, 2004).

    2004b. "Voting and Registration in the Election of November 1984." July 22. www.cenus.gov/population/www/socdemo/voting/p20–405.html (accessed October 26, 2004).

U.S. Census Bureau. 2008b. "Table 571 – Civilian Population – Employment Status by Sex, Race, and Ethnicity: 1970 to 2006." The 2008 Statistical Abstract. http://www.census.gov/compendia/statab/2008/cats/labor_force_employment_earnings.html (accessed June 2010).

U.S. Census Bureau. 2008c. "Table 689 – People Below Poverty Level and Below 125 Percent Of Poverty Level by Race and Hispanic Origin: 1980 to 2005." The 2008 Statistical Abstract. http://www.census.gov/compendia/statab/2008/cats/income_expenditures_poverty_wealth/poverty.html (accessed June 2010).

Vaca, Nicolas C. 2004. *The Presumed Alliance: The Unspoken Conflict between Latinos and Blacks and What It Means for America.* New York: Rayo.

Wallsten, Kevin and Tatishe M. Nteta. 2011. "Elite Messages and Perceptions of Commonality." In Edward Telles, Mark Q. Sawyer, and Gaspar Rivera-Salgado, editors. *Just Neighbors? Research on African American and Latino Relations in the United States*, 125–151. New York: Russell Sage.

Welch, Susan and John R. Hibbing. 1984. "Hispanic Representation in the U.S. Congress." *Social Science Quarterly* 65: 328–335.

Whitby, Kenny J. 1997. *The Color of Representation*. Ann Arbor: University of Michigan Press.

Whitby, Kenny J. and George A. Krause. 2001. "Race, Issue Heterogeneity and Public Policy: The Republican Revolution in the 104th U.S. Congress and the Representation of African-American Policy Interests." *British Journal of Political Science* 31: 555–572.

White, Ismail. 2007. "When Race Matters and When It Doesn't: Racial Group Differences in Response to Racial Cues." *American Political Science Review* 101 (1): 339–354.

Wilson, Walter. 2009. *When Latinos Speak: Latino Representation in Floor Speeches to Congress*. Paper presented at the annual meeting of the Southwest Political Science Association, Denver, CO, April 8–11, 2009.

Wildavsky, Aaron. 1988. *The New Politics of the Budgetary Process*. Glenview, IL: Scott, Foresman.

Wright, Gerald C. 2004. Zip file of the CBS/New York Times national polls, ideology party identification, 1976–2003 [Stata 7.0 format]. http://mypage. iu.edu/~wright1/ (accessed June 30, 2006).

Zogby, John and Rebecca Wittman. 2004. *Hispanic Perspectives*. Prepared for the National Council of La Raza, June 2004. www.nclr.org (accessed October 25, 2004).

Index